MW01226032

This book belongs to:

FINDING
JOY
IN YOUR
JOB

Published by Advantage, Charleston, South Carolina.
Member of Advantage Media Group.

ADVANTAGE is a registered trademark and the
Advantage colophon is a trademark of Advantage Media Group, Inc.
Printed in the United States of America

ISBN: 978-1-59932-044-1
Cover design by Bret Healey
Layout design by Oriana Green

Most Advantage Media Group titles are available at special quantity discounts for bulk purchases for sales promotions, premiums, fundraising, and educational use. Special versions or book excerpts can also be created to fit specific needs.

For more information, please write: Special Markets, Advantage Media Group, P.O. Box 272, Charleston, SC 29402 or call 1.866.775.1696.

A WOMAN'S GUIDE TO

FINDING
JOY
IN YOUR
JOB

PATHWAYS TO YOUR GARDEN OF POSSIBILITIES

PAT HEALEY

Advantage

"There came a time when the risk to remain tight in the bud
was more painful than the risk to blossom."

~Anais Nin

For my three entrepreneurial
children, **Bret, Ryan** and **Arianne,**
who never cease to amaze me with
their talent, love and compassion.

TABLE OF CONTENTS

"Growth itself
contains the germ
of happiness."

~Pearl Buck

A BOUQUET OF POSSIBILITIES FOR YOU

I wrote this book for you. How is that possible, you wonder? If you're one of the many women who dread going to work some of the time, then this book is for you. If you've grown bored by your job, and your passion for it has faded, then this book is for you. If you feel stuck in a situation without new challenges or room to grow, then this book is for you. If you're between jobs and you'd like to find a better one next time, then this book will guide you toward that. If you once had a dream of doing fulfilling work but you've lost sight of it, then this book will show you how to find it again. If your job is just a means to a paycheck, then this book can help you discover better reasons to go to work.

Not only that, as far as I can tell, **it's the very first book ever written just for you**. It's not about climbing corporate ladders, crafting resumes or acing interviews. It's not for your boss (though it wouldn't hurt her—or him—to read it). It's not for management types. It's for the millions of women who do the real work that keeps companies alive.

It's for the millions of women who do the real work that keeps companies alive.

Of course, I recognize that plenty of men could also benefit from this, so if you're a guy reading this, then welcome to you too.

Ultimately, I wrote this book to help you find joy and fulfillment where you already work—to help you

bloom where you're planted.

"It is not easy to find happiness in ourselves, but it is not possible to find it elsewhere."
~Agnes Repplier

That's right. Even though nearly half the American workforce is miserable enough to be thinking of changing jobs, I believe it's possible to find true enjoyment in your current job. How? By discovering your unique abilities, by figuring out what would add more meaning to your work and by eliminating the obstacles to your dreams, you can re-imagine your current position and learn how to make it a reality. I believe it, because I've done it myself and shown countless others how to do it too.

Claire had several small ideas that brought big results

Take Claire, for example. After eight years as a customer service representative at her local cable TV company, she was no longer excited by her job. At first, it seemed like a fun business to be involved with, but over time, Claire felt she'd become nothing more than a punching bag. "Most days, I had a headache brewing before my first coffee break," she confides. "It felt like my job description had become: *Get yelled at all day by angry customers who I'm unable to help.* Yikes! Out of desperation I devised a better way to do my job, and asked my boss to let me try my approach for a week. To his surprise—but not mine— more than half my complaint calls were transformed into happy customers, who in turn became our extended, unpaid sales force. I got promoted to Customer Service Manager, and I haven't had a headache in months," she says, her smile audible in her voice.

What was Claire's big idea? Actually it was several small ideas with big results. First, she asked to be empowered to *solve* many of her callers' problems by applying credits to their accounts. In addition, regardless of their complaint, every caller was given a free month's upgrade to premium cable or a free month of pay-per-view events. Claire also mailed them coupons for free popcorn that were just gathering dust in the back room. The net cost? Zip. The result? Some of those unhappy callers enjoyed their upgraded service so much they kept it. Was it more fun for Claire to soothe disgruntled customers with free gifts? You bet. Did satisfied customers say nice things about the cable company to their friends? Absolutely. Did her boss smile all the way to the bank? You guessed it.

Implementing these simple ideas immediately reduced Claire's stress and brought more joy to her job. Instead of transmitting tension to her callers, she had time to make them smile and even laugh. She became *Claire*, the nice woman who was solving their problems, rather than the *roadblock* parked between callers and their satisfaction.

I've redesigned my job, too, but it's been a rocky road. **I'm a recovering Alpha Boss**—the kind who drove my team nuts— all the way to the top of my profession. Yet I'd never been more miserable, and none of my team was getting any joy out of work.

I got clear
about my
own
purpose

Stress was our daily diet. As business owners, we tend to think we have all the answers, and I sure believed I knew how to manage people—hadn't I pushed us to the top of our mountain? So why was everyone so miserable?

To find the answers took years of study on my part—with Dan Sullivan, Kathy Kolbe, Tim O'Brien and Marcia Wieder, to name just a few of my expert mentors. After all that input, I got clear about my own purpose: **To inspire women to create jobs they enjoy and business owners to create work environments that attract and retain the best employees**. Over time, I learned how to be more effective, how to run a business more productively and how to find more balance in my life. Once I believed I'd uncovered some real keys to creating a happy working environment—for myself as well as my staff—I started to share what I had learned by facilitating Team Dreamers Workshops™ for other business owners and their staffs. After years of refining those workshops and getting great feedback from participants, I decided to write this book. It also grew out of my experiences as an employer, owning and operating a State Farm Insurance and Financial Services business for the past 29 years—and my rebirth as a Better Boss.

But enough about me . . . maybe you're one of those people who is sick and tired of trying to succeed in a position where your very best efforts go unnoticed. Perhaps you feel stifled and pressured by a boss who keeps demanding you do more with less time and fewer resources. I'm here to tell you that you're not alone, you're not crazy and you're not a bad employee. How do I know that? Because bad employees don't bother to read books like this—they're too busy bemoaning their crummy jobs. Wouldn't you rather spend time creating your dream job, designing a position that will add meaning to your life? I thought so. Read on, and I'll show you how to do it, step-by-step.

What you can expect to gain from this book

Loving and enjoying your job should not be a rarity. You work hard, you want to do a good job and you absolutely deserve to thrive. All you need is a better understanding of your real

You absolutely deserve to thrive

purpose and a plan to weave that purpose into the fabric of your job. I promise you, that's a prescription for success and fulfillment. Regardless of your age, your level of education or how many years you've been doing the same job, you can indeed create a better position for yourself. Imagine looking forward to each and every day with the confidence that you can manage your fears and doubts and create a life of significance. Imagine heading home after a rewarding day, smiling, even humming a few bars of *Walking On Sunshine*. Imagine arriving home relaxed and cheerful, knowing you made a difference that day.

"All through the long winter, I dream of my garden. On the first day of spring, I dig my fingers deep into the soft earth. I can feel its energy, and my spirits soar."
~Helen Hayes

By following the process outlined in this book, you'll learn:

· How easy it can be to get everything you always wanted out of your career, including success, a sense of pride in your work and great friendships

· How to access your inner dreamer to help you create your ideal job where you already work

· How to improve communication with your boss so you *both* get what you want

· How to find your underlying purpose and activate that passion, which in turn will bring you joy, motivation and fulfillment—no matter where you choose to work

· How to have more fun at work. Really!

· How you are instinctively wired, and how to use that knowledge to improve communication with friends, family and co-workers

· How to really appreciate the different work styles of others, including your boss and associates

· How to enlist support from others for your ideas and how to silence your naysayers

· How to create incredible Mondays

· How to use all kinds of new skills to improve your life as well as your job

· How you can contribute to making your workplace somewhere co-workers and newcomers alike will treasure

This is going to be a fun journey of self-exploration

This book includes a number of exercises designed to reveal your strengths and show you how to put them to their best use. It's also arranged as a journal you can write in, with questions to spark deeper personal assessment and help you apply the concepts to your own situation. Though I arranged my ideas in what I feel is a logical order, if you need to skip around to read what applies to your current situation, that's fine. I even cross-referenced chapters and exercises throughout the book to make it easy for you to find what you need.

As we work through the process, I'll show you how to invent your ideal job and how to identify—and remove—blocks that have stopped you from attaining your past dreams. Then we'll examine strategies for making your new dream job a reality. I'll even offer some advice for dealing with difficult bosses—hey, I do remember what I used to be like! Next, I'll give you a system for evaluating your situation and then moving on, if there seems to be no alternative. Finally, I'll share what I've learned about living a life with more meaning.

As I'm sure you've noticed by now, I want to have a conversation with you, which is why I've written this book as if we were chatting over grande soy lattes—or whatever your beverage of choice is—I'm not picky. I also hope you'll let me know your reactions to these ideas, because **I really am on a mission to show every woman in America how to find more joy in her job.** Hey, there's nothing wrong with dreaming big! (You'll find my contact information at the end of the book.)

The subtitle of this book is **Pathways To Your Garden of Possibilities**. What on earth is a garden of possibilities? I'm glad you asked. For me, it's a metaphor for the vast interior landscape in each of us, our unlimited potential to reshape our lives at any given moment. The garden holds your dreams, your secret desires, your ambitions. The garden is a safe place where you can think about your future and reinvent yourself if you like. Your garden of possibilities is a perfect reflection of you, because you are the one who designs it.

> "May your heart's garden of awakening bloom with hundreds of flowers."
> ~Thich Nhat Hanh

I titled this introduction **A Bouquet of Possibilities for You**, so here it is—but there's one catch—you have to pick the bouquet yourself. *Gee, Pat, that's just like a guy...how do I do that?* You pick your future just as you might a bouquet of wildflowers in a meadow. You survey the vast landscape and choose the shapes and colors that delight you. This book offers you an opportunity to harvest more joy at work by creating a job that excites you, expresses you, rewards you and yes, delights you. I hope you'll join me on this path to a more rewarding life. Ahhh . . . can you smell the wild roses?

"To forget how to
dig the earth and
to tend the soil is
to forget ourselves."

~Mohandas K. Gandhi

Chapter One
PREPARING THE SOIL
IN YOUR GARDEN OF POSSIBILITIES

Chapter One At A Glance

- What you can do about stress
- Benefits to completing this process
- Look at where you are right now
- A tale of two moms who reinvented their lives
- Following the P.R.I.D.E. Formula
- How Donna designed TWO dream jobs
- How satisfying are your days?
- What's your current job landscape?
- Small changes can equal big results
- Adding up your advantages
- Can you commit to yourself?
- A tasty recipe for change
- You earned a reward!

Most of us spend half our waking hours working, so why not get the most out of it?

This first chapter is all about you making a conscious choice to bring more joy to your working life, a life where you no longer let circumstances control you. Instead, you control how you *react* to circumstances—both good and bad. If you think of your ideal job as a garden you get to design, plant and nurture, then the work of this chapter is preparing the soil. I believe I've made this process fun, energizing and simple. You are going to collect a set of tools that can serve you well for the rest of your life. I'll even stick my neck out here, and say that I believe this process can revolutionize your working life—then the rest of your life, as well. In fact, it can even help eliminate the stress that zaps your creative energy.

Stress kills—it's so bad in Japan that they even have a word for sudden death from overwork: *karoushi*. Stress is the underlying cause of much of the heart disease in our country, which is the number one cause of death. More people die on Mondays between 9 and 11 a.m. than at any other time. Those folks aren't having their heart attacks lounging on a beach somewhere—they're just showing up for work. Having day after lousy day at work is needlessly killing people—and it <u>is</u> needless. **There is no reason in these United and Prosperous States of America why anyone should have to endure a job that's killing them!**

Life can be divided into two basic categories: love and work. Since most of us spend a great deal more time at work than on love, true happiness comes when we combine the two by loving what we do at work. When you're happy at work, you're much more likely to be happy at home, and in general, to love life. No matter where your head and heart are at this moment with regard to your current job, there is every reason to believe you can create your ideal job right where you already work—one that absolutely will not kill you!

Think about it—imagine being glad it's Monday! Imagine connecting your job to your personal values and to a larger purpose. Imagine having a job that gives you something way

imagine being glad it's Monday!

beyond a paycheck—it pays you in true satisfaction. Well read on, and I'll show you exactly how to have that job of your dreams.

Benefits to completing this process

· You're going to have a better understanding of yourself, including your strengths, unique abilities and your instinctive ways of making choices and solving problems.

· You're going to have a clear roadmap and a plan for creating your dream position, where you already work.

· By determining your date of significance, the <u>no matter what</u> date you will begin your ideal job, you will have set the process in motion and made your goal concrete.

· You're going to define your own success. You'll have the freedom to be yourself.

Journal exercise

"Ordinary people believe only in the possible. Extraordinary people visualize not what is possible or probable, but rather what is impossible. And by visualizing the impossible, they begin to see it as possible."
~Cherie Carter-Scott

Where are you now?

Journaling is a free and fun method of learning more about yourself and uncovering the underlying reasons why you do what you do. Think of it as peeling an onion—the deeper you go, the better the substance—and yes, there could be tears, but the good kind. The kind that signify you are getting at some core truths. Throughout this book you'll find lots of suggestions for journaling topics, all designed to help you dig down to your true feelings about yourself, your job, what will motivate you to change and so on. I guarantee it will be a fascinating journey!

To start, get out your shovel and break ground for your new garden of possibilities by examining your current mindset. In answering the following questions, please be as honest with yourself as possible. Wherever you are in your working life right now is where I suggest you begin. As much as I'd like to tell you to snap your fingers three times and skip ahead to a more thrilling part of this process, you do need to start right where you are. **You need to acknowledge anything that you think is making you unhappy in your current job.** (We'll get to the positive aspects in a minute.) This is not meant to be a wallow in negativity, but rather a constructive evaluation of your starting point. I suggest you do this away from the office, and please don't just jot down your usual rants and gripes. If you prefer to write your answers in a separate journal, that's fine. Ask yourself these questions:

· **Why did you take the job you now have?**

_____

_____

_____

_____

· **What did you hope to gain from your job in addition to a paycheck?**

_____

_____

_____

_____

· **How big is the gap between what you hoped you'd be doing and feeling at work, and what you're actually experiencing?**

_____

_____

_____

_____

· **Name some aspects about your job you'd like to change.**

_____

_____

_____

_____

_____

"There is no security in what is no longer meaningful. There is more security in the adventurous and exciting, for in movement there is life, and in change there is power."
~Alan Cohen

· **Now consider what role(s) you may have played in creating your current reality.**

_____

_____

_____

_____

_____

table your negativity

This exercise may well have stirred up strong emotions, which is okay. That just means you're invested in this process. What I'd like to urge you to do for the duration of our work together, is table your negativity. Bundle it up, stuff it in a manila envelope and file it under **L for later**. After you've approached this new way of thinking about your job with an open mind, you can always open that file drawer again. But I truly believe that if you commit to taking the steps outlined in this book, you'll be ready to toss that old envelope of regrets, blame and pain right into the circular file where it really belongs.

A tale of two moms, five kids and one great boss

Let me tell you about Lisa, who has experienced this process already and has a lot of joy to show for it. When she first started at a large insurance company, she knew she'd landed a job with a lot of promise. There were some fun perks for working there, including a gym membership. During her first few years, Lisa progressed to a position of moderate responsibility and found a lot of satisfaction as part of a team. "I enjoyed knowing I was doing well and could be relied on," she recalls, "and I knew I was contributing something of value to my company."

Then Lisa had her two children, and her life no longer seemed her own. She never found time to enjoy the gym, her boss continued to heap new projects on her, she felt guilty about not spending more time with her children, her prized vegetable garden went to seed, old friends faded from her life and her husband had become something of a stranger. She'd never really recovered her body from her last pregnancy, and her energy level was at an all-time low. "It was all I could do to show up at work on Monday morning with my hair washed, hoping I could hide the yogurt stain on my blouse with a scarf."

Sound familiar?

Lucky for Lisa, she got a chance to pause the mommy-go-round, step back and redesign her life. Now she does job sharing with another working mom, and they're a great team. "I still work about 35 hours a week—enough to keep my benefits—but some of it I can do from home by telecommuting. Now I have time to take my daughter to the dentist (or even myself, imagine that!)."

By enlisting help from Ellen, a similarly stressed out co-worker with three kids, Lisa was able to present a plan to their boss that provided full coverage for their department phones and administrative needs, as well as more time and energy for larger projects. As a result, their supervisor could be more productive, which made him look good, too. "Getting to be more deeply involved in substantive work renewed my passion for my job," Lisa confides. Sure, it takes real organizational skill to keep the plan working smoothly, but Lisa is so much happier now, that small stresses no longer affect her.

This is just one example of reinventing a job—and a life. There are as many ways to do that as there are jobs.

All you need to do for now is be open to the possibility that the job you currently have can be made much more rewarding.

It helps to take pride in your work

  You have a choice to say "Yes!" to your passion, purpose and dreams. Many people say they want their dreams to come true, but very few really commit to doing what it takes to bring them to life. Agreeing to the following five simple principles will help you attain maximum benefits from this process and is a good way to begin.

  I call it my **P.R.I.D.E. Formula**, because following it will make you feel better about yourself and the new job you create for yourself.

Possibility   Pledge to become a possibility gardener. Learn to say "Yes" instead of "No" to your dreams.

Responsibility   Take 100 percent responsibility for your current state of affairs and for realizing your dreams.

Inspiration   Commit to goals that inspire you, and create experiences that add significance to your life.

Design   Develop and design a strategy to achieve your goals, then take action. Hope is not a strategy!

Engineer   To ensure you reach your goal, engineer it for success: enlist support, do your own research, improve your skills—whatever effort it takes to get there.

The impossible isn't—if Donna can do it, you can do it

  Sometimes, discovering what you're really passionate about leads you in a new direction. I'd like you to meet Donna. She was really stuck in what she was sure was a dead-end job. She was embarrassed by her job and had almost no pride in her work, plus she was experiencing symptoms of depression and overall declining health. An aspiring writer, Donna had taken what she thought of as a subsistence job, as a night manager at a motel in a tourist area of California. "I worked from 3 to 11 p.m.,

"Success is the freedom to be yourself."
~Kathy Kolbe

and I did appreciate that I had some free time in the evenings at the motel to read and work on my own writing projects," she explains. "However, by the time I got home from my job and unwound, I rarely fell asleep before 2 a.m., which meant I wasn't up and ready to begin writing until late morning. Once I finally got rolling and into some kind of flow, it was time to get ready for work, which made me resent my job all the more."

Then a shift began to happen. As time went by, Donna was surprised to discover she enjoyed many of her interactions with motel guests. "They were often alone, traveling for business and they seemed to welcome my advice on restaurants and local services. For tourists, I suggested unusual side trips and attractions that were off the beaten path."

Fairly new to the area herself, Donna had become an expert on it, and she loved sharing her passion for the region. When they checked out, happy guests told Donna's employer how helpful she'd been. "This led to a discussion with my boss, in which I suggested I could be more useful doing marketing for the motel. He agreed to create a new part-time position for me, so now I get to do something I'm wildly enthusiastic about," she says, her excitement bubbling over.

In fact, her enthusiasm brought her to the attention of the local chamber of commerce, and she landed a *second* dream job writing promotional copy and planning special events for the city she adored. What about her health problems? They disappeared on the outgoing tide. This was all because she was willing to infuse her "day job" with authentic passion and a desire to be helpful to others.

> Donna went from one dreary day job to two cheery dream jobs!

It's time to grow up

Up the scale at least. Unless you track your progress toward a dream, it's difficult to know how you're doing, and that makes it easy to quit before you reach it. So I've come up with a method of appraising each day and measuring progress toward your goals. It's your **G.R.O.W. Chart** (on Page 27). As you evaluate your days, think about these sorts of measurements to help you determine your final score for each day.

> "Growth itself contains the germ of happiness."
> ~Pearl Buck

Grin What made you happy?
Reach Did you reach for your goals?
Optimism How was your mindset?
Win What were your wins today?

"The true way to render ourselves happy is to love our work and find in it our pleasures."
~Francoise Demotte Bille

If you can learn to think of each day as another chance to tend your garden of possibilities, another fresh chance to do it better, to find more significance in your life, then I think you'll discover much more pleasure as you work in the garden that is your life.

As you read through the examples on the next page that explain the **G.R.O.W. Chart**, think about how you would define each level. Try aiming for days that are at least in the 5 to 7 range. You can aim for higher levels, but don't beat yourself up if you don't hit it every day—that may not be a realistic goal for you. The good news is, only you get to decide what that looks like for you. In my experience, living at level 5 on a regular basis means you can be proud of what you do, which will make you feel good about your job and yourself, and that in turn colors the rest of your life. Thriving at a high level affects your overall mood and energy level, because you're living a life of satisfaction and meaning.

You can use the **G.R.O.W. Chart** on Page 27 to measure the significance of all aspects of your life. In order to create a life of meaning and significance, I recommend you aim for a level 7. It may take some time to reach it, but it will be very sweet when you do.

How did your dream G.R.O.W. today?

1. *Wilting.* You barely made it through another day at work. You're mentally and physically exhausted.

2. *Sprouting.* Still a fairly blah work day, but when it's over, you still have a bit of energy left and maybe even a glimmer of an idea how to make things better.

3. *Seedling.* By this point, you've noticed some hints of change, some small signs of improvement from implementing an idea or two.

4. *Shooting.* More progress—now others are starting to notice, too.

5. *Leafing.* This is where you really know you're on to something—your boss starts to compliment you on your new measures, and you catch yourself humming and laughing more at work.

6. *Budding.* You notice you're actually looking forward to going to work—you're excited to see what else you can do to improve things around the office, because you now know it's possible. You have confidence in your ideas. This was a wonderful day!

7. *Opening.* Even clients notice something's different, and you're getting along better with your team. Your boss recommends you for a raise. You start brainstorming even more enhancements. Awesome describes this day!

8. *Blooming.* You really see the big picture at work now—how you can enrich your own life—and others—simply by shifting your attitudes, reactions and input. You have greater empathy for your boss, and she responds by giving you more responsibility and rewards. You feel like your old self—your younger self who had more enthusiasm for life. You realize you love your job now.

9. *Branching.* Just when you thought it couldn't get any better, your family notices you seem happier, more relaxed, more fun to be around. They love how you rearranged your schedule to have more time for them, and they no longer feel like annoyances. You cherish being able to watch your daughter play softball, and you relish having energy left over at the end of your day for your spouse—and yourself! This is the life you didn't know you could lead.

10. *Flourishing.* Finally, days at this level are nearly off the charts. These are the kind of days when you feel you could change the world. You have fabulous ideas and aren't afraid to share them. Fruits from past implementations are abundant. You are well compensated and applauded for all that you do in your job and community. These are blue ribbon days you'll never forget.

G.R.O.W.CHART

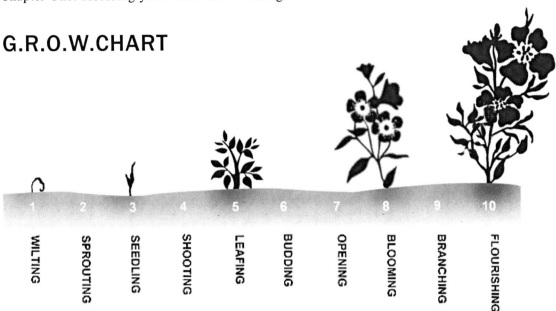

WILTING · SPROUTING · SEEDLING · SHOOTING · LEAFING · BUDDING · OPENING · BLOOMING · BRANCHING · FLOURISHING

Using your own definitions of success, let's apply the **G.R.O.W. Chart** to your current job. Think back over the last few weeks and see how you've been doing. How many level 5 days have you had? Any 6s or 7s? Over the next two weeks, rate each day then total them up. If you aren't hitting close to 25 for a weekly (or five-day) total, that just means you have room to grow—and your working life is going to get a whole lot better. If you are close to that mark, then you might want to consider setting your sights even higher. Only you know where on the **G.R.O.W. Chart** you'll find job satisfaction.

WORK WEEK ONE	WORK WEEK TWO
Day 1 _____	Day 1 _____
Day 2 _____	Day 2 _____
Day 3 _____	Day 3 _____
Day 4 _____	Day 4 _____
Day 5 _____	Day 5 _____
TOTAL _____	TOTAL _____

Now, just for comparison, do the same for your personal life. Take into consideration activities with friends and family, time for other pursuits, such as hobbies, organizations, clubs and so on. Then factor in whether or not you had time to nurture yourself—did you get out and have some fun? Get your hair cut? Go to the gym? Read a juicy novel? If you work full time and have a family, then you probably aren't having high-ranking personal days during your work week. But how about your weekends? Are those rating some good numbers? Rank each day of the next two weeks according to your interpretation of the **G.R.O.W. Chart.**

PERSONAL WEEK ONE	PERSONAL WEEK TWO
Day 1 _____	Day 1 _____
Day 2 _____	Day 2 _____
Day 3 _____	Day 3 _____
Day 4 _____	Day 4 _____
Day 5 _____	Day 5 _____
Day 6 _____	Day 6 _____
Day 7 _____	Day 7 _____

If you're like a lot of women, you probably have a mixture of days off—some are just catch-up days for laundry and other chores. These don't climb very high on the satisfaction meter. (Though crossing things off your Gotta Do List counts for something!) Once in awhile you manage a big bloomer of a day—a 6 or 7 or an 8, and those are the days you treasure and record in your scrapbooks.

"And there in lies the secret to life. No matter what happens in your life, the meaning of what has happened is yours."
~Unknown

The really cool thing about this process you're embarking on, is that by reducing your stress at work, you free up all kinds of emotional and physical energy for the rest of your life—which will lead directly to a lot more high number days—on and off your dream job.

Journal exercise

I urge you to track your days with this tool for at least a few weeks—it has the power to keep you in touch with your reality, and inspire you to seek even better days. If your weekly totals are depressingly low, use that awareness to fuel action toward change.

What's your job landscape?

Here's a chance to apply the **G.R.O.W. Chart** to your current position. If you think of your current job as a garden, is it lush and vibrant, or do you need to plant a few more rose bushes? Is there a lot of dead wood to be pruned away? Or does it need a major redesign with lots of fresh plants?

In the blank space before each question, rate your satisfaction level using the G.R.O.W. Chart for each relevant item, then journal about the questions below.

___ **1. Do you enjoy positive interactions with colleagues and your boss?**

_____

_____

_____

_____

___ **2. Do you enjoy positive interactions with clients and/or the public?**

_____

_____

_____

_____

___ **3. Do you enjoy technical tasks (website, spreadsheets, billing)?**

_____

_____

_____

__ **4. Do you enjoy recurring duties (mail, data entry, reports)?**

_____

_____

_____

_____

_____

__ **5. Do you enjoy unique tasks (non-recurring special projects)?**

_____

_____

_____

_____

_____

__ **6. Do you enjoy finding creative solutions to problems?**

_____

_____

_____

_____

_____

__ **7. Do you enjoy decision making activities (no matter how small)?**

_____

_____

_____

_____

_____

__ **8. Do you find your duties meaningful and do they fit your skill level?**

_____

_____

_____

_____

_____

Getting in touch with how you experience your current job, as well as looking at its dimensions in a quantifying way, is good groundwork for re-imagining your ideal position where you work right now.

> "Small changes, small wonders—these are the currency of my endurance and ultimately of my life."
> ~Barbara Kingsolver

Start small, but start today

Small changes in attitude, desire and skill sets can easily catapult your life to the next level. This book is about helping you become a **superstar in your life**, under your own terms. It can move you from stagnation to

WOW!

Think about it: just one degree changes water from a liquid into steam. **Even the smallest shift in your thinking can affect your attitude**, which can open your mind to opportunities you otherwise wouldn't have considered. Just ask Alice.

As a secretary at a law firm, Alice had gotten lost in the mechanics of the place. "I only knew a few other women who worked at the company. Everyone was under great pressure to perform, and everyday seemed to bring new crises and tension," she recalls. While there was some room for advancement at her company, Alice didn't think it applied to her. She'd lost sight of her earlier dreams of a rewarding career in the legal field—a dream she'd abandoned when family issues led her to drop out of college. Her job had not turned out like exciting episodes of *Law and Order*. Instead, she found herself typing up dictation from attorneys she'd never even met.

After she started using the **G.R.O.W. Chart** to take a hard look at the quality of her days, Alice noticed subtle changes in the choices she was making. "Instead of pulling into a drive-through on the way home to cheer myself up with a chocolate shake, I took a right turn and headed to the park for a half hour of walking," she remembers. She used that time to unwind from her day and really think about what she could do differently. Soon, it became her after-work ritual to spend quality time planning her next moves. (You can just imagine the other benefits of the extra daily exercise.) "Within a month of starting the program, I had figured out what I really wanted to do at the law firm.

> "Within our dreams and aspirations, we find our opportunities."
> ~Sue Ebaugh

"I overheard two women talking in the lunchroom, and I joined in their conversation. They told me about evening classes I could take at a nearby community college that would help me become a legal secretary and then a paralegal." A year after finishing the courses, Alice's life does sometimes resemble her favorite TV show. **It all started with an active awareness of her situation and a desire to improve it.**

You can create your ideal job, too

Let's face it, most of us need to work. In fact, many people who don't need to work, still want to. An AARP 2006 survey shows that 80 percent of Baby Boomers are pondering some form of work after retirement, because they think they've spotted business opportunities that play to strengths they developed while working for somebody else. Besides, for many people, the work they do contributes to their overall satisfaction with life.

Adding up the pluses

A happy, fulfilling life is just a matter of perspective. How you look at the world around you is a matter of attitude. Sadly, most people lead unexamined lives, and that's a key factor that separates those who just get by and make do from those who take charge of their lives and consciously seek growth and betterment. What I'd like you to do now is **think about the advantages of creating a job you love where you already work**. When you take stock and examine the pluses that may already be in place, it gives you clarity—and clarity can protect you from making rash, unwise decisions.

"I have looked at other gardens, but I think I'll simply bloom where I'm planted."
~Unknown

To help get you started, I've listed some reasons to bloom where you're planted that may apply to you—mark ones that do.

· Your skills are valued by your employer.
· You have ongoing opportunities to continue your training and improve your skills.
· You're already comfortable with your surroundings and the requirements of your job.
· You have a good working relationship with your supervisor(s).
· You have a good reputation, which helps you create leverage within the business.
· You have allies within the company.
· You know how things work within your company and what is required to progress.
· You have established friendships with co-workers.
· Your vacation and benefits remain intact, which is extra nice if you've earned higher levels of vacation time, etc.
· Your loyalty to your company—as demonstrated by your tenure there—can be leveraged as an asset in negotiations. Employers know well the high cost of replacing an employee.
· The grass isn't always greener—you could change jobs only to be worse off than you are now.
· Job hopping isn't good for your resume and can even affect your financial affairs, like your credit rating, loan applications, etc.
· Things are rarely as bad as you think—there may be people within your company who would mentor you or at least advise you on redesigning your job there.
· You feel fairly compensated for your efforts.
· You have opportunities to grow in your responsibilities.
· There are some special perks you really enjoy.

Now add to the list other advantages of creating a dream position where you already work. If you happen to be one of those people who think everything about your job stinks, try approaching this process with an open, creative mind.

Making this list may provide you with a quick start to an improved attitude. In Chapter Three you'll have a chance to really work on redesigning your job. Once you know what motivates you, you can tap into your strengths and focus them in a clear direction.

_____

_____

_____

_____

_____

_____

I hope that making this list will encourage you to continue on with this process. However, if your inventory revealed few advantages of staying where you are, then you may want to skip to Chapter Seven, where I discuss other alternatives. That said, I urge you <u>not</u> to give up just yet, because in the next chapter, you'll get to catalogue your personal strengths—good to know wherever you land—and then in Chapter Three, I'll guide you through the process of redesigning the job you have. Even if you are less than optimistic at this point, please give the process a chance to open your eyes to other realities you may not see right now.

Are you commitment phobic?

Journal exercise

This brings us to the subject of commitment. Studies have shown that when you make a written promise to yourself—and review it often—you are much less apt to break it. With that end goal in mind, **please answer and journal about these questions.**

· If you were convinced you could create the perfect position where you already work, would you commit to taking the steps to get there?

_____

_____

_____

_____

· Are you willing to make this exploration a priority now?

_____

_____

_____

_____

· Will you be willing to ask for help along the way if you need it?

_____

_____

_____

_____

 · How much time each day are you willing to commit to growing your dream career position? What if you just spent 10 minutes a day or 30 minutes twice a week working on goal setting and your action plan? (You'll find lots more on creating your action plan in Chapter Four.) If you don't think you can find the time, you need to commit to _make_ the time, whether from your lunch hour, breaks, before work, after the kids are in bed, or whenever you can steal a chunk of time to really think about this process. If you don't make a promise to yourself to do this, it just won't happen. Weeks will go by and you'll forget you ever read this book. (That was hard on my ego, but it's true!) Can you even remember what you did last Thursday?

_____

_____

_____

_____

_____

_____

My point is, **you have to want to make this shift badly enough to take the action steps needed to see it through.** Once you've recorded your answers to these questions, take some time and really think about what you've just written. Does it reflect how you truly feel or are these just words you think others want to hear? Remember, the journaling you do in this book is just for you; you don't need to share it with anyone unless you want to.

> "There came a time when the risk to remain tight in the bud was more painful than the risk to blossom."
> ~Anais Nin

Hope is not a strategy

If this chapter has opened your eyes to greater opportunities in your life, that alone may motivate you to continue on and create an ideal job for yourself. If you recall the P.R.I.D.E. Formula, one of the steps is to design your strategy— and hope is not a strategy. The people I've worked with who now enjoy lives that rate from 7 to 10 on the G.R.O.W. Chart, **always have a plan and know their next steps to accomplish their newest goals.** This is the secret to creating the life you want and deserve. If you stick with me, I'll show you exactly how to form your strategy.

Most people end up living lives of quiet desperation, because even though they may have occasional glimpses or fantasies of a better life, they fail to follow a recipe that would lead them to accomplish their dreams.

The first ingredient in my recipe is caring.

You need to care enough about yourself to discover and embrace your purpose, passion and dreams. We all know many women are conditioned—*still*—to be caregivers, and are inclined to put their own needs and desires so far down their lists, that those ideals rarely see the light of day. I urge you, right now, today, to give yourself permission to explore this process, to put yourself near the top of your list for a change.

I've already touched on the second ingredient, commitment.

Are you at the point in your life where you're not willing to settle for less then what you can be? Are you so tired of being tired that you're ready to do whatever it takes to make your life better? Are you

> Commit
> to do
> whatever
> it takes

prepared to rethink your assumptions—about yourself, your job and your purpose? If you answered "Yes" then you need to **commit** to the process. You need to commit to a timetable for creating your ideal job. Commit to do whatever it takes to realize your dreams. Commit to never just working for money and power. Commit to be true to yourself and doing work that brings you satisfaction and pleasure. Commit to never letting your limiting beliefs diminish the level of passion you have for living your dream. The power is in this moment—just decide right now to turn your job around. I challenge you to fill out this commitment form, then make copies of it and place them where you'll see them often.

Promise to Myself

I, _____, do promise to care enough about myself to commit to a process of self-exploration and envisioning a better work life for myself. I commit to doing the exercises in this program to help me understand and plan my next moves. I commit to enlisting support along the way and discovering how to add more meaning and a sense of purpose to my job and to my life. I make this promise to myself because I know I deserve to live a full and satisfying life.

Date _____

Signed _____

Applause, applause!

And another bouquet

I won't tell you how few people who acquire books ever actually read them, because as an author, it's just too depressing. But suffice it to say, if you've made it this far, you're in a select minority. Congratulations for caring enough about yourself and about bettering your life to read this far. **In fact, I want you to reward yourself for doing so.** New brain research shows just how challenging it can be to create new habits. One of the things that makes it much easier, is giving yourself some kind of reward each step of the way, so I'm going to encourage you to do that, over and over.

In fact, I want you to go nuts with this. Think of all kinds of things you could do to show yourself appreciation—and no, they don't have to include chocolate! Nor am I condoning maxing out your Visa card or any other self-destructive behavior. This is why I really want you to give this some serious thought. **Make a list right here of things you could do to nurture yourself, to acknowledge you are doing something really important that could change the rest of your life.**

you are doing something really important

_____

_____

_____

_____

_____

_____

_____

_____

_____

_____

This will become even more important as the work progresses, so please spend some time on this. Perhaps you could get a massage or have a girls' night out, take a drive in the country with a friend, or by yourself for some quality time to think. Maybe you need an MP3 player, so you can listen to motivational messages while you work out. Or maybe it's as simple as giving yourself permission to sleep in on Saturday. Only you know what feels like a reward.

Now that you've patted yourself on your head for getting this far, don't stop now—**Chapter Two is all about you!** We'll have a lot of fun poking around in your head and learning what makes you the unique individual that you are and how you can use that information to help design your dream job.

"The most noteworthy thing about gardeners is that they always look forward to doing something better than they have ever done before."

~Vita Sackville-West

Chapter Two
WHAT KIND OF GARDENER ARE YOU?

Chapter Two At A Glance

- You have great value
- Is your job a good match for you?
- When and how are you AWEsome?
- What are your starring roles?
- Something you didn't know about yourself
- How is your boss wired?
- Birds of a feather had better not flock together
- Why now, more than ever, your life needs meaning
- Living your life on purpose
- What do you value most?
- Finding your higher purpose at work
- Is your job making you sick?
- Free health insurance for all

Now we move on to a fascinating topic: you!

It can be easy to forget that you possess more talent than you have ever expressed. Studies show that only 20 percent of employees enjoy jobs that really maximize their strengths. You undoubtedly contain a reservoir of ideas, experience and information that rarely gets tapped. **One of the keys to job satisfaction is knowing you have something of value to contribute and being acknowledged for it.**

That's how Sandy sees it, too. She works in publicity for a small publishing company and loves it. "I don't make as much money as I could working for a larger company," she explains, "but my boss is so spectacularly appreciative of everything I do for her, that I wouldn't dream of changing jobs. I've never had a work experience like this—and I've had a lot of jobs in my 57 years. I always feel like she values me as a person first, then as her trusted colleague. She loves finding out about yet another skill I have that I hadn't mentioned earlier—usually because I'd forgotten about it too. I always go home in an up mood, because I know I did well at work. It took me several months on the job, though, to decide my boss was sincere and not just flattering me."

So that's what we're going to do in this chapter—**remind you of your hidden talents** and help you figure out what **your true strengths** are, especially as they apply to creating **your ideal position.** Then we'll look at how you might **find more meaning** in the work you choose to do. It's absolutely true that **your job can also be your calling**—as in being called to a higher purpose—by understanding your unique abilities and designing a job that puts them to good use. Let's get started. As we did in Chapter One, we'll begin right where you are now.

"Everyone has inside him a piece of good news. The good news is that you don't yet realize how great you can be! How much you can love! What you can accomplish! And what your potential is!"
~Anne Frank

Your Job APTitude Checklist

This exercise will reveal how well-suited you are to your current job, whether you have an aptitude for what you do. **In the space below, list the various types of things you do at work during a typical week,** for example: answering phones, solving customers' problems, sales, scheduling, researching new resources, data entry, website updates, analyze information, department meetings, write reports, plan events, etc. At the end of the week, review your list and label each item with one of these letters:

A for Adept—meaning you are very accomplished at this task, give yourself an A! You're great at it and you enjoy doing it.

P for Proficient—meaning you are competent at this task, it's something you understand and can do well.

T for Troublesome—these are things that cause trouble for you, either because you aren't well trained to do them, you don't like doing them or perhaps you put them off until you get behind. Whatever the cause, these tasks are ones you dread.

___ _____

___ _____

___ _____

___ _____

___ _____

___ _____

___ _____

___ _____

___ _____

___ _____

___ _____

___ _____

___ _____

___ _____

___ _____

___ _____

Adept total ____
Proficient total ____
Troublesome total ____

Now add up the number of As, Ps and Ts. Which one predominates? What does that tell you about how your skills are being used? **This score demonstrates how apt you are to be content with your job as it is now defined.** Don't be too concerned if you don't like your score—the process in this book will help you figure out other ways to envision your job and put your talents to work.

IMPORTANT NOTE: Even if you've decided to write your responses to the journal exercises in a separate book, please record the results to this exercise and the rest of the ones in this chapter right here in this book. Throughout the book, I'll be asking you to refer back to the lists you make in this chapter.

"The secret of joy and work is contained in one word: excellence. To know how to do something well is to enjoy it."
~Pearl S. Buck

When are you AWEsome?

The next step in the process of discovering your unique abilities is filling out the **AWEsome Chart** on the next page, which considers your abilities side by side with your willingness to do certain tasks. A high **A**bility for a task + a high **W**illingness to do it = **E**njoyment, or something you are AWEsome at, as well as something that makes you feel AWEsome when you do it.

· The **upper left corner** of the chart is where you list tasks from your APTitude Checklist that you're excellent at and love doing. Another measuring tool might be the G.R.O.W. Chart you learned to use in Chapter One. Do you rate your performance a 7 or higher when doing these tasks? If not, move them to the appropriate section of the chart.

· In the **upper right corner**, I want you to list all the things you have the necessary skills to accomplish, but that give you little or no enjoyment in doing.

· In the **lower left corner**, write what you enjoy doing, but feel you don't quite have the skills to perform at a level 7 or greater.

· In the **lower right corner**, list those items that you don't have the skills to do and that you don't enjoy doing.

This will probably be an eye-opening exercise, as you see for the first time a graphic representation of your current job, including the good, the bad and the downright ugly. Let's look at your star qualities first. Copy everything in your upper left corner to your **AWEsome List** on Page 46. These are the things you not only love doing and have the skill set to complete, but that you also have enthusiasm for doing. These tasks can add meaning to your life and will help you move closer to your dream job.

AWEsome   Chart

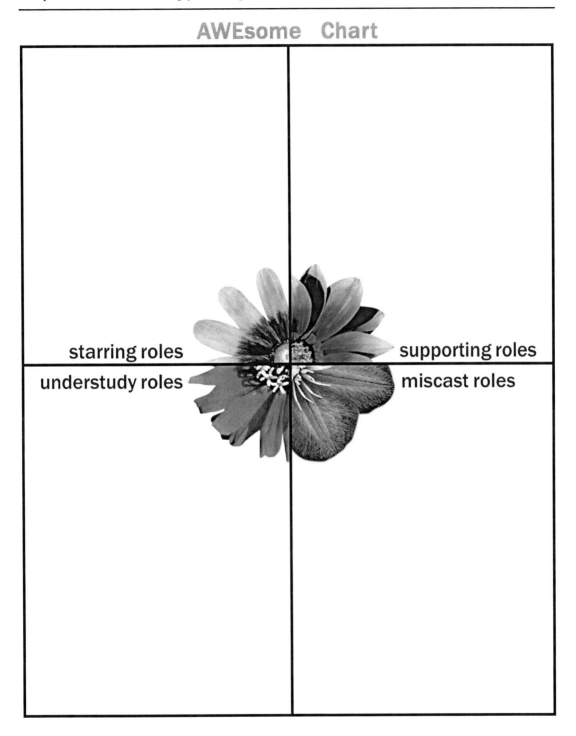

starring roles

supporting roles

understudy roles

miscast roles

So far, you've just written down tasks that derive from your current position. Now I'd like you to add to this list under **Hidden Talents** any other things that belong on this list—whether or not you get a chance to do them in your job as it's now structured. Perhaps you've been trained in sales, and only now that you aren't doing it, do you realize how much you miss it (and how good you are at it). Or maybe you studied writing in college and did well in it, but somehow ended up in a job where you never get a chance to use that talent. These are duties you would rush to work to be able to do. But don't confuse this list with a fantasy job. This isn't *Oh, I'd love to be a TV producer someday*. These are talents you have already developed.

take stock of your portable skills

If you have trouble filling out this list, ask some trusted friends or colleagues who know you well to contribute. Sometimes hidden talents have yet to be expressed in a work situation. Are there hobbies or other activities you pursue that may provide transferable skills? Do you volunteer for organizations? If so, what kinds of things do you enjoy doing? These are all opportunities to develop abilities that you can also take to work. Chandra, for example, offered her photography skills to her team and now enjoys contributing photos to the company newsletter and website.

Sally keeps track of the inventory for her church's thrift shop in her spare time. Geralyn publicizes the quarterly used book sales for her library, and Rhonda does extensive online research in order to make wise purchases for her cut glass collection, but none of these women thought about applying their outside skills to their jobs.

Add your extra abilities to your AWEsome List below.

My AWEsome List

_____

_____

_____

_____

_____

_____
_____
_____
_____
_____
_____
_____
_____
_____
_____

Hidden Talents

_____
_____
_____
_____
_____
_____
_____
_____
_____
_____

"I always wanted to be somebody, but I should have been more specific."
~Lily Tomlin

Now take a good look at your list. These are activities where you play a **starring role** at work, the tasks that others probably know you do well. These abilities will form the core of your new job. When you also factor in things you'd like to do in an ideal job but need training for, then you've just outlined a description of your dream job. One that would allow you to shine as brightly as you possibly can, one that would motivate you to surpass expectations, one that would make you smile—even when the alarm blares on Monday mornings. This is the job you were meant to do. This is the job you deserve to do. This is the job that will add meaning to your life and decrease your stress in the process. This is the job you can create for yourself.

In an ideal world, your job would only consist of tasks on that list. But in the real world, that probably isn't possible. My work with business teams reveals that most people initially are unable to spend more than 50 percent of their time working in their unique talent zone because of how their job was originally constructed. Discovering what you are good at and designing a position that takes advantage of your skills, is the route to upping that percentage.

Now let's examine the upper right corner of your AWEsome Chart (Page 45). The job functions you listed there are those where you can play a **supporting role**. You have superior skills but lack great passion for completing the tasks. However, they are still significant, and the reason for continuing to perform some of these, is that your colleagues probably need your expertise in these areas, and it's important to be valued as part of your team.

never be afraid to ask for training

Moving down to the lower left corner, you'll find the functions where you can meet the minimum standards, but you may have anxiety doing so. These are the tasks you'd like to be able to do better, but you need more training to do so. Here you are an **understudy**, and in an ideal situation, you'd have someone to show you what you need to know. These are important, because training is rarely a barrier. More employers than you may imagine are thrilled when someone takes the initiative and asks to be taught additional skills. Many companies even have funds set aside for outside classes or attending special workshops. Never be afraid to ask—it's a signal to your boss that you're invested in your position and you want to excel at it.

"I believe that when you realize who you really are, you understand that nothing can stop you from becoming that person."
~Christine Lincoln

To be honest, most jobs contain some measure of activities that are less than thrilling to do; that's pretty much unavoidable. But if the lower right corner of your chart is jammed with tasks, then no wonder you aren't the happiest camper at the picnic. In fact, you may be asking: What picnic? The items down here represent failure more than success. Trying to complete these tasks causes you conflict, frustration and stress. These are roles for which you are **miscast**.

Please notice I didn't say roles in which you preformed poorly. We all have our unique areas of expertise, and we all have tastes and desires for different types of work. Knowing which items fit into that corner provides you with a valuable list of what you *don't* want your dream job to entail. You'd be surprised how many people are unhappy at work but never take the time to really figure out why. Well, you just found some important items that may be sucking the joy right out of your job.

In the next chapter, we'll look at strategies for delegating many of your tasks in the last two categories, but for now, concentrate on your AWEsome List. Here's one more note about what's ahead. The deeper we go into this process of designing your ideal job, the more apt you are to encounter feelings of resistance, voices in your head telling you: *What, are you crazy? You'll never have a dream job, you can't make this dramatic change* and so on. For now, try and ignore them. Feeling resistance is a natural part of the process of change. In Chapter Five, we'll explore a whole range of techniques for silencing those voices and overcoming all the obstacles your determined mind can concoct.

Journal exercise

Who is the best you?

I hope you'll take time to study the results of these exercises. This process can be very emotional, as you perhaps admit for the first time what your true strengths and challenges are, so do ponder these questions carefully.

· Can you see a pattern forming as a result of doing these exercises?

_____

_____

_____

_____

· Who are you when you are at your best?

_____

_____

_____

_____

· What qualities distinguish you from others in your profession?

_____

_____

_____

· What are three things you are paid to do?

_____

_____

_____

· If you left the company and came back as a consultant, what would they pay you to do?

_____

_____

_____

· What motivates you, and what does "reward" mean, look and feel like to you?

_____

_____

_____

· Why do you work?

_____

_____

_____

· If you desire change in your job, do you know why you want to make this change?

_____

_____

_____

· How could you utilize your best skills more creatively?

_____

_____

_____

· What kinds of things inspire you?

_____

_____

_____

_____

Document
your best
work...
you'll
thank me
later!

Do this—really, really do this!

I urge you to keep a file of your best accomplishments throughout the year, similar to the way school teachers keep files of each student's best work. You can call it your sunshine file. Make copies of anything you create that you're proud of, from a particularly deft apology email you sent a customer, to reports, press releases, memos—you name it. Include anything and everything that will document the quality of your work, as well as your progress and growth as a team member. Copy files onto CDs, collect printed samples of brochures you wrote, flyers you designed, ads you created. Be sure to include your fan mail—complimentary emails or notes from clients, co-workers and your boss. You might also keep in the folder a running list of projects and their dates in case you need to refer back to them. Why? Because when it comes time for your performance review, you'll have proof of what you've done, should there be any dispute. It will also come in handy as you evaluate what you enjoy about your current job—and what you don't. If you decide to pursue a promotion, this folder will be very useful in demonstrating exactly what your proficiencies are. Also, it's kind of fun to look back over the good things you've done at work—there's nothing wrong with self-appreciation!

Here's something I bet you didn't know about yourself

The next step in cataloging your strengths is understanding how you instinctively initiate solutions and get things done. Instinctively? You don't think that sounds very scientific or quantifiable? Well think again. Research now proves we all have a natural tendency to initiate solutions, prevent problems and respond to changing needs. Human instinct is the power behind our actions. It's the source of our mental energy. Understanding how your instincts combine with your talents and personality will help you optimize your opportunities.

"We don't know
who we are
until we see
what we
can do."
~Martha
Grimes

A brief history of where I'm taking you

More than 40 years ago, an intelligence test was developed by E.F. Wonderlic, which was for many years considered a standard in hiring new employees. The test measured not only how smart the applicants were, but also how quickly they could complete a task with the fewest number of errors. His team figured that with this data, an employer would not only hire the best and the brightest, but employee turnover would decline as a result. As it turned out, while the test provided valuable information to employers, turnover rates did not change.

Then along came Dr. Wonderlic's oh-so-smart daughter, Kathy Kolbe, who shared his passion for understanding how we are wired. After years of research, Kathy developed a simple, effective tool to help people determine their right fit within a company, based on how they instinctively initiate solutions and get things done. If you're like so many people who have ended up in jobs where they felt like square pegs in round holes, having your Kolbe A Index done, in combination with your AWEsome Chart, could prevent that from happening again. For the first time in your life, you'll have valuable, scientific data that explains how you function best in the world and what you really enjoy doing.

For that reason, I suggest you invest in your future and take the index at www.kolbe.com . (You can do it in about 20 minutes, and you'll get your results immediately.) The cost of the Kolbe A Index and a complete online explanation of the results is $49.95 at the time of this writing. (By the way, I have no financial investment in her company, nor do I profit from your ordering your index.) What I can say, is that reading my index results changed my life and has truly given me the freedom to be myself. If you want to ensure you're in the right career, improve job satisfaction and enhance your competitive advantage by capitalizing on your strengths, please consider getting your Kolbe A Index and integrating that data into this process of creating your ideal position. There are other valuable profiles on the market today including, Now Discover Your Strengths and the Caliper Assessment tool, that you may want to explore in the future. For my time and money though, the Kolbe A Index was the easiest to transfer to both my business and personal life.

"When one is a stranger to oneself, then one is estranged from others too."
~Ann Morrow Lindbergh

How are you wired?

I realize not all of you reading this book will take that extra step, so I'll explain the basic principles here to give you a taste of what you could learn about yourself from the Kolbe index.

Kathy Kolbe discovered that people instinctively learn and behave in the world through four action modes. Of course, we are all mixtures of these four action modes. This is a considerable simplification of her system, but understanding these four basic styles will still be useful to you.

Quick Start

You fit into this category if you don't need copious directions, and will readily attempt to prepare a complex dish without an exact recipe. Perhaps someone at work told you about a wonderful, exotic entree she had in a restaurant the night before. After asking a few questions about ingredients, you stop at the store on the way home, and that night fix your version of the dish for dinner. It probably isn't exactly like the meal your friend had, but who cares? You were inspired, took action and had fun trying something new. Tomorrow it'll be something entirely different, because you are an innovator.

Fact Finder

You can claim this label if you also heard your co-worker talking about her delicious restaurant meal and decided you might like to try cooking it yourself. However, your first step would be to call and make a reservation at the restaurant, then order the same dish, so you could see for yourself whether or not you liked it. Then if you did, you might ask the chef if he'd share his recipe. If he would not, then you'd make your own notes about what you thought was in it, then pore over cookbooks and recipes online until you found the one that sounded most likely to work. Next, you'd set aside time on a weekend to try the recipe. You prefer not to be rushed, because you want time to attend to all the details.

Implementor

You are in this booth, if hearing the same call to culinary adventure, you also tried the dish at the restaurant, but saved much of it to take home as a sample. You would then spend some time examining the food in good light and tasting each morsel separately, trying to deconstruct the recipe. Then you'd shop for the ingredients, buying all the variables you could imagine might be in the dish. Finally, you'd experiment again and again until you found the combination that matched—or surpassed—your experience at the restaurant. In the end, you'd feel very satisfied that you had mastered a new recipe and that you'd done it despite the lack of support from the chef. You thrive on building things from scratch.

Follow Thru

Since the dish was served at a Thai restaurant, your approach would be to find out the exact name of the dish, then call all over town until you found a qualified chef who gave lessons in Thai cooking. You'd take the class, learn how to make the dish, practice it, then invite your co-workers over to sample it and be dazzled. Then, you'd probably apply techniques you learned in your classes to other kinds of cooking, which might even inspire you to study all sorts of ethnic cooking styles. For sure, you have some terrific system for organizing your recipes where they are easy to locate. No gravy stained scraps of paper for you!

"We cannot teach people anything; we can only help them discover it within themselves."
~Galileo

The key point here is: **everyone was able to go home and successfully cook some version of the dish.** They all turned out differently, and that's great. No one method of learning and doing is better than another. Figuring out which style you instinctively use will be of enormous value to you in almost every area of your life. Imagine being able to finally figure out what makes your teenager tick or your spouse smile! I've had my entire family take the tests, and what I learned about my kids has been amazing. Of course, the application of this information we're concerned about here, is how it relates to your activities at work. Since I learned about the Kolbe system, I rely on it to help me make good hiring decisions and to develop optimum working relationships with my team.

If you want to grow passionflowers, you need a hot sunny exposure; if you prefer violets, they'll thrive in deep shade. One isn't a better flower, they're just different, but knowing what they need to flourish determines whether they bloom or wither. You can grow passionflowers in partial shade, but they won't be prolific bloomers. We can all learn to adapt by trying to function in a different style, but it will never feel quite right. A Fact Finder who is rushed into delivering a presentation without her usual preparation will feel insecure and stressed, afraid she won't be able to perform up to her usual high standards. Meanwhile, a Quick Start who is asked to design a series of courses before she ever leads one seminar, will go bonkers. She'd rather just jot down a few notes, wing the first seminar and be confident she'll get better each time she does one. Without physical models of what she's trying to understand, an Implementor may well panic when asked to explain over the phone how to fix your laptop. A Follow Thru person will feel very unsatisfied if pushed to create a series of press releases, then move on to a different task without knowing whether or not they were effective.

It's all about doing what is instinctively natural for you.

Journal exercise

Wiring diagrams

I bet your mind is buzzing right about now, trying to figure out where you and your boss and everyone you know fits into this puzzle of life, so take a moment to make some notes while the ideas are still fresh in your mind.

My style of action is _____

My boss is probably a _____

My co-workers are probably _____

Now go back and look at the APTitude Checklist on Page 43 and see how many of the tasks you are currently being asked to do are a good fit for your instinctive style. Is there a correlation between the things you identified you love to do and what you've just learned about your instinctive way of problem solving? Based on what you now understand about yourself, **think of other activities you might like to try**, because you are probably wired in a way that would make learning and performing them easy and fun. **Add these to your AWEsome List on Page 46.**

_____

_____

_____

_____

_____

_____

> "Our deepest wishes are whispers of our authentic selves. We must learn to respect them. We must learn to listen."
> ~Sarah Ban Breathnach

Birds of *different* feathers make a better flock

By now, I think you can see how advantageous it would be to know how all your fellow team members are wired, too. Here's the cool part—**the more variety you have on your team, the better it can function.** Why? Because each work style index is valuable—none more than another—and your weaknesses are someone else's strengths.

- If you're a Quick Start and hate crunching numbers, you need a Fact Finder on your side. She'll gladly turn out spreadsheets all day.
- If you're a Follow Thru who panics when you need a new trade show display, put an Implementor on your team. You'll have a spiffy new sales presentation booth in no time.
- If you're an Implementor, but you can't figure out how to represent the company's entire product line in one flashy slideshow, you may need the organizational vision of a Follow Thru person.
- If you're a Fact Finder who's been asked to come up with three new marketing strategies for a product launch, who 'ya gonna call? A Quick Start, of course.

Don't wear a job that doesn't fit

While you may prefer hanging out in the lunchroom with co-workers of similar persuasion, **do not make the mistake of creating project teams solely with people who think and work alike.** Just as a sound eating plan features all the food groups, your team needs all four basic approaches to problem solving. Besides, when you have them all, everyone gets to do what they instinctively do best, without being forced into ill-fitting shoes. Who wants blisters?

Another useful thing about applying the Kolbe system to groups, is that it works equally well outside of work. Whether you're organizing a church rummage sale, planning a school fundraiser or choosing board members for your homeowners association, the same principles apply. Thinking back, can you recall some committee you've been on that didn't function very well, because everyone wanted to do certain tasks and no one wanted to do others? Now you know why.

Finding meaning in your work

Now that you've identified what you're great at, what you'd rather not do and how you intuitively solve problems, let's go even deeper into the process of finding more joy in your job. At the beginning of this book, I promised we'd look at discovering your underlying purpose and activating that passion, which in turn will guarantee you joy, motivation and fulfillment—no matter where you choose to work. I hope this section gives you some "Aha!" moments, because it may be the single most important part of what I have to share with you.

"No condition is more pervasive in the workplace than stress and no condition has such debilitating consequences."
~Kathy Kolbe

Stress levels in the workplace have never been higher for business owners and their valued employees. Having the time and energy to love and enjoy your life, your career, your family and the people around you, has become more of a fantasy than a reality for most people in the business world. Gallup surveys reveal that in the history of our country, there have never been more people willing to jump ship and leave their current employers. The *Wall Street Journal* reported recently that "Many employees are poised to jump. They're frazzled, searching for more serene and rewarding jobs." One out of every two people is searching for something better, in spite of the fact that salaries are up, and as a country, we have never enjoyed more affluence. In fact, fatter paychecks have done little to elevate our happiness levels.

What's really going on? You may be comforted to learn you're not alone in your feelings of emptiness. In a recent issue, the influential business magazine, *Forbes*, noted that as a country, we are moving into **a new age of meaning** caused by four recent occurrences:

1. 9/11 and our realization as a society that life offers no guarantees.
2. People are examining the fallibility of our leaders. Whether presidents, congressmen or business leaders—can we trust them?
3. Changes in the global economy and shifts in how we work, such as outsourcing and automation.
4. Our aging population, Baby Boomers in particular, are yearning for more meaning in their lives.

So what can you do?

You can choose to live a life of meaning and purpose.

That's right. It's your *choice*. If you were nodding your head at that list, then I think you'll really get excited about this next step in the process.

Living your life on purpose

Let's talk about purpose. In the largest sense, purpose is what gets you excited, what gets you up in the morning. It's who you are at your very core. It's your soul speaking to you. Your life's purpose may be family-centered, about providing a good home and education for your children, about being a partner to your spouse, or perhaps you are simply trying to evolve as a human being. Your life's purpose is probably what fuels your desire to work—you're paying your mortgage or saving money so your kids can go to college. At this point, you may just see your job as a means to those kinds of ends, but I'm suggesting there may also be greater meaning to what you actually do at your job. Uncovering what that is, may well revolutionize how you think about working. Here are some great examples.

your purpose is your soul speaking to you

Anna is a floral designer. She loves flowers and enjoys working with color, form and texture. She's a very good designer, but if you ask what her purpose is as a floral designer, she says, "Helping people with their most important life transitions." You see, she realized that people come into a flower shop most often at key junctures in their lives: proms, weddings, birth of their children, anniversaries, birthdays and funerals. As a designer, her primary job is to understand how she can help her customer express an emotional need through flowers. Very often, she even helps them write the enclosure cards. Her sensitivity to her customers—who are often in a heightened emotional state when they come in—is what sets her apart. **Knowing that she's making a contribution to people's lives, is what keeps her going through long, tough days that often end in back pain.**

Susan has been the bookkeeper for an insurance company for eight years. She originally took the job simply because she needed to help support her growing family. At first, she didn't give any thought to a higher purpose for her job. It was just some place she had to be 40 hours every week, so doing the exercise below was a revelation for her. She started to see the underlying value in many of her tasks and how she contributed to the overall purpose of the company.

After an earthquake damaged many of the homes belonging to company policy holders, Susan got to see first hand how vital a role her company played in assisting people to rebuild their lives. She volunteered to help field calls from distressed clients and found great satisfaction in being able to answer their concerns. This led to a shift in her duties. Now she's delighted because she works much more directly with clients and spends less time isolated in her office, communing only with her calculator. By delving deeper into what motivates and inspires her, Susan has managed to add much more meaning to a part of her life that had previously had very little. In addition, she has learned that the ultimate pain is a life without meaning.

> "When we don't think things through in an empowering way, when we don't have faith there is a higher meaning, we tend to settle for the lowest meaning we can find."
> ~Tony Robbins

Here's a famous example of finding your real purpose—Martha Stewart. After college she took a job as a stockbroker on Wall Street and excelled at it, but it didn't fulfill any of her personal values. After about six years, she quit and began renovating her new home in Connecticut. It was there in her basement that she started her catering company that eventually grew into Martha Stewart Living Omnimedia. Though she's now a media magnate, Martha Stewart has never wavered from her purpose of educating and inspiring others with her passion for gracious living.

Some people get purpose confused with what they *do* at work. Take me, for example. I own an insurance and financial services business, so selling insurance to new and current policyholders is my job—but my purpose is assisting and inspiring clients to make good decisions about how to protect their families from unexpected losses. Though offering team development workshops is another one of my passions, my purpose is to inspire others to discover their hidden talents on their way to creating a life and career of their dreams. If you ask salespeople what their purpose in life is, they might say it was to sell. But for some, their real purpose is to inspire or to help people to make good decisions about products or services that will enhance their lives in some way.

Your purpose is what expands you and takes you beyond yourself. Your purpose is where you connect with the world and your unique place in it. It might be to raise compassionate, open-minded children; it might be to find outlets for your creativity; it might be to crusade for spaying and neutering pets; it might be to raise awareness about diabetes.

> "I long to accomplish great and noble tasks, but it is my chief duty to accomplish humble tasks as though they were great and noble. The world is moving along not only by the mighty shoves of its heroes, but, also, by the aggregate of the tiny pushes of each honest worker."
> ~Helen Keller

While your purpose may be lofty, how you fulfill it doesn't need to be. Maybe you're on a mission to save the planet—working for a disposal company, encouraging one person to use one recycling bin at a time. Maybe you have a strong desire to end hunger, and you do that by rounding up donations for a food bank, one can of tomato soup at a time. The beauty of all this is, only you can decide what the value of your work is.

My office manager, Linda, makes sure everyone who walks in our door has a satisfying experience dealing with her. It's her goal to be sure that everyone she has contact with during the day goes away better off because of their interaction. She knows that what she does for our customers is helping them and could make a significant difference in their lives, if the day comes when they need to rely on their insurance policies. **How you spend your time—literally the currency of your life—determines the depth of your life.**

Let me give you some other examples. My friend Debbie works as an office manager at Shriners Hospitals for Children. If you ask what her purpose is, she doesn't say she's an office manager responsible for keeping things running smoothly in the department, she replies, "My purpose is to be of service to the families, even if it's something as simple as giving directions to the cafeteria". She loves trying to make just a few minutes of what can be very long days a little brighter for parents and their children. It's Debbie's mission to offer empathetic care to parents and children alike.

My savvy daughter, Arianne, entrepreneurial son, Ryan, and visionary son-in-law, Jason, work together purchasing homes, rehabilitating them and reselling them. If you were to ask them what their purpose is, they wouldn't tell you it's to buy and sell homes. They would say their purpose is to heal distressed houses and use their vision and innovative skills to create dream homes for families who don't know how to do it themselves.

the paths you walk create the meaning in your life

I'm sure you've heard the expression *It's about the journey, not the destination*. The reason that's important, is because the path to achieving your goal is actually what is creating meaning in your life. The people you meet along the way, the emotions you feel, the insights you gain on the journey, are what really enhance your life. Most of us have found that chasing goals just for the sake of chasing the carrot provides no lasting satisfaction.

Journal exercise

What do you value?

The first step in finding more purpose in your work, is recognizing what qualities and experiences you value most. Often, we go through life adopting values from our parents and society without giving them much scrutiny—until they are challenged—which can create stress at work if you don't realize what's really going on. I invite you to **start by making a list of traits you respect and admire in yourself and others**, such as: integrity, generosity, authenticity, curiosity, creativity, independence, kindness, ecologically-conscious, and so on. **Next, add qualities you value in a job**, such as: security, diversity, challenge, power, justice or service. **Then consider the questions that follow.**

_____

_____

_____

_____

_____

_____

_____

_____

_____

_____

_____

_____

_____

_____

_____

· As you look back on your life, what were your peak experiences? What do those experiences have in common?

_____

_____

_____

_____

_____

_____

_____

_____

· When you turn 85 years old, what will you want your grandchildren to say about your life?

_____

_____

_____

_____

_____

_____

_____

· What is it you have done that's most important to you?

_____

_____

_____

_____

_____

_____

· What do you need to say "No" to? What do you need to say
"Yes" to, so that your life is satisfying?

_____

_____

_____

_____

_____

_____

· When are you able to be your most authentic self?

_____

_____

_____

_____

_____

_____

How else could you think about your current job? How
could you apply more of your personal life values to what you do at
work—appropriately, of course? If you think about your position at
work alongside your list of values, how would it rate? How many of
your values are supported by what you do at your job? What are the
values of the company where you work, and are they in line with your
own? Are there other positions within your company that might better
satisfy your need for a more purpose-driven job?

Journal exercise

What's your purpose?

Without an understanding of your purpose, it will be difficult to find joy and enthusiasm in your working life. As expert dream coach Marcia Wieder says, "Passion is what drives your purpose." Perhaps it will help if you think about things you're passionate about. What topics get you excited and energize you to action? This doesn't have to be complicated. Looking over the values list you began on Page 61, take a few moments now and in the space below, **write out what might be an underlying purpose for the work you do now**—or the work you'd like to be doing. This doesn't have to be some grand statement. It's an expression of who you are, it's what gets you jazzed about work. It's what opens your heart. It can be as simple as:

· I like helping other people have a better day.
· I show people how they can have the house of their dreams.
· I help make a better working environment for my co-workers.
· I make the best possible widgets I can, because I know how much others rely on them.
· I make sure our guests have fewer problems and more fun.
· I express myself through creativity.

I'm sure some of you are thinking: *This all fine and dandy for some people, but I can't find any higher purpose to my job.* Some of you may be concluding that your current position is just plain dull and you hate it. Well, this book is for people who decide they want to make positive changes, not those who are happy to remain stuck. So if you are committed to change—you did sign your promise to yourself on Page 37 didn't you?—then try and come up with a purpose you'd *like to have* at work. In the next chapter we'll explore how to design your ideal job. For now, just imagine that you already have it.

Here's a secret about all this purpose stuff. What really matters is how focusing on your purpose changes you as a person, how you grow and flourish as your life is enriched with greater meaning.

The true value of any goal is how aiming for it shapes you.

Don't let your job make you sick

As one last way to assess your values, look back at what you wrote in the lower right corner of your AWEsome Chart on Page 45. These are the tasks you have neither the desire nor the skill to do. Compare them to your values list (Page 61) and see if there are any conflicts. Have you been asked to do things that challenge your personal integrity or that contradict in any way some of your core values? If so, then **circle those, as duties you NEVER want to perform.** Doing so is a prescription for illness, on-the-job injuries and all sorts of maladies that would derive from doing things you are philosophically not suited to do. A friend's father actually suffered a heart attack not long after his boss insisted he falsify the company's tax return. Someone who didn't have integrity on their values list might be able to do such a thing, but for someone who saw himself as an honest person, such a request would cause great distress.

Another example comes from Tomika, who as a Kolbe Follow

Thru person, loves to take pride in doing a thorough job and doing it well. You can imagine her dismay when a new manager suddenly asked her to spend half as much time on her reports as she had been spending. In order to meet his demands and still meet her own standards for quality, Tomika was forced to start bringing work home most nights. That made a big dent in the quality of her personal life, angered her husband and reduced the amount of sleep she got, which in turn made her cranky and less productive at work. Worst of all, she couldn't even get bonus points for taking work home, because she was afraid to tell her new manager she couldn't meet his requirements in the time allotted. This is a classic case of personal values clashing head on with a job description. Luckily for Tomika, she was able to confide in her human resources staff and seek a better fit within the company—a position as a quality control officer, where her values were needed and honored.

Write your own free health insurance policy

You had to suspect an insurance guy would get around to this sooner or later! But it's not what you think. I hope you really put some effort into the exercises in this chapter, because I believe that the better you know yourself—your strengths as well as your weaknesses—the easier it will be to create the perfect job for yourself. I'll make one last pitch for getting your Kolbe A Index, because this tool will really help you refine your focus and design your ideal job. Besides, doing what you love gives you unlimited energy and satisfaction. **Knowing you're working in a position that supports your values and creates extra meaning in your life, is one surefire health insurance policy.**

There are numerous studies indicating that most disease is caused or exacerbated by stress, and as we learned in Chapter One, stress kills. Of the people in Massachusetts who die of heart attacks before the age of 50, the number one cause was determined to be job stress. The point is: you don't have to become part of those statistics! You can choose to become someone who loves her job, who looks forward to Mondays—and Tuesdays through Fridays, too. You can choose to spend half your waking hours doing something that nourishes your soul and enhances your self-esteem.

"Life is not easy for any of us. But what of that? We must have perseverance and above all confidence in ourselves. We must believe we are gifted for something."
~Marie Curie

You are not your circumstances, but you are your possibilities!

Applause, applause!

Time for another bouquet

Remember how I urged you to reward yourself at the end of Chapter One? Don't stop now! **You are doing vital work here.** Examining your life and committing to changing it for the better, are things only a small percentage of people ever do. Celebrate that you have the wisdom to pursue this. If you're enjoying writing journal entries, perhaps you'd appreciate having a beautiful, blank hardbound book to track your thoughts, or maybe you'd like to start a scrapbook all about what you value in life. Most importantly, this chapter's reward—just like its subject—is all about you. **Find some creative ways to pamper yourself—you DO deserve it!**

I hope this chapter has revealed to you many things you didn't realize about yourself. I also hope it has proven how unique you are and why your special talents will have value to your team—as long as you make a good match between you and your job. **Now let's get busy and apply all your new self-knowledge to designing the job of your dreams.**

"It isn't a calamity to die with dreams unfulfilled, but it is a calamity not to dream."

~Benjamin Mays

Chapter Three
DESIGNING YOUR
GARDEN OF POSSIBILITIES

Chapter Three At A Glance

- What dreams have you let fade?
- Someday is here, and not a minute too soon
- How big a change do you need to make?
- Get out of your ruts!
- Checking in at the last resort
- Dream your perfect day
- Follow that with a reality check
- Are you really willing to change?
- What are your limiting beliefs?
- Recast the movie of your life
- What's possible for you?
- Beware of bosses bearing gifts
- How to get the most from this process

A friend of mine describes the way we envision our future this way: Dreams are the ropes we use to pull ourselves up out of the ordinary. Dreams have the power to do just that, don't they? Neurologists say that dreaming while we sleep is a vital, biological function, and I believe that dreaming while we're awake is equally essential.

The last chapter was about discovering and acknowledging what a fascinating and talented person you are. This chapter is all about exploring your possibilities. **What do you dream about your tomorrows?** When you think about your future at work, do you feel excitement over upcoming projects, or do you shudder in dread? If negative thoughts have already crept into your head, I urge you to approach this part of the process with an open mind. A really wide open mind. **I want you to suspend belief in any limitations you may have adopted for yourself.** That's right—limitations are overwhelmingly self-imposed. We'll deal with them further on in this chapter, but for now I need you to dwell in the realm of what's possible, without concern for how you might make your visions real. If you find yourself falling into resistance, then you may need to skip ahead to Chapter Five to blast some of those obstacles out of your head. Just be sure you come back and do the work of this chapter—this is the really fun part!

"Your reality can be much bigger than your current capacity for dreaming about it." ~Marcia Wieder

As someone who was trained by Marcia Wieder to be a Dream Coach, I'll be quoting her a lot in this chapter. I especially like her explanation: "I define dreams as the aspirations, desires, goals and hopes that you most want for yourself. These are the dreams you have while you are wide awake." **In this chapter you're going to get excited again by your dreams—and perhaps uncomfortable when you think about making them come true.** Change is rarely easy, but that doesn't mean you can't do it. Take comfort in knowing that creating and having your ideal job is doable. If you're the kind of person who typically responds to opportunities with: *can't, but, what if,* I want to encourage you to give yourself permission to think in terms of *wow, intend, can.* As Dream Coach Marcia Wieder says, **"Start spending more energy and time on your possibilities to ensure that your job will no longer be just a job."**

Dreams = pain is the wrong equation

Sadly, for most adults, the ability to really imagine big dreams for themselves died somewhere along the way. But it can be—and needs to be—revived. Here's my own story of loss.

Picture a beautiful, early fall day in Seattle, Washington. I was about 7 years old, and my sister and I were playing outside, without a care in the world. Everything seemed possible that day. We picked dandelions and blew tiny seeds into the air, certain that whatever we wished for would eventually come true. My sister dreamed of being a famous ballerina, while I dreamed of becoming a fireman. I could see myself sitting on the back of the beautiful red, hook and ladder fire truck, rescuing kids from burning buildings. I could hardly wait to live my dream.

you can revive your dreams

By Christmas morning, I had worked myself into an extreme state of anticipation, because I'd made it clear to Santa how much I wanted the toy fire truck of my dreams. Our Christmas presents were always displayed under the tree in the downstairs recreation room. As I rounded the corner, I immediately noticed the absence of any presents large enough to be my beloved fire truck. I was crushed beyond words. I waited uneasily as the gifts were handed out to me and my sisters, but as the gift opening celebration slowly wound down, I realized the emptiness in my stomach was not going away. I wanted to throw-up. I had done everything to get that truck. I prayed and dreamed and wished upon a star and wrote to Santa.

My parents always made Christmas a memorable event, even though they didn't have much money left over at the end of the month. I learned many years later how my dad would get the broken display toys from the department store where he worked, bring them home Christmas Eve and repair them for us until the wee hours. Even though I did get a lot of nice gifts, my wish just didn't come true that year. I was devastated.

As the morning wore on, my Dad, who had always been a jokester, casually got up from his chair and said, "Pat, what's behind the tree over there in the corner? It looks like a present with your name on it." As I leaned down and looked into the dark corner, I saw the hidden box with my fire truck. But I have to tell you, as much as I loved my Dad, and as well-intentioned as he was, the thrill was gone.

Unintentionally stolen from me forever. Even though I always enjoyed my fire truck, it became a constant reminder of the potential pain associated with unrealized dreams. I learned two lessons that Christmas. **The very worst dreams were those with an outcome out of my control and the biggest unfulfilled dreams often hurt the most**. These were my first lessons in dream pain, and sadly, it taught me to avoid dreams for much of my life.

Since then, I've found that I'm not alone in my experience of dream pain. Many of us have felt the severe hurt of having big dreams that didn't come true. As I look back on my life, dreaming big dreams was replaced by living a life filled with practical goals. Imagining a fun, unencumbered, exceptional life had slowly drifted from my thoughts. **Unconsciously, I had allowed the pain associated with dreams to limit my possibilities and potential.**

> "When you hold back on life, life holds back on you."
> ~Mary Manin Morrissey

Journal exercise

What dreams have you let fade?

Your dreams miss you! If you close your eyes and **think back to your own childhood**, can you remember dandelion parachutes floating off on a breeze with your wishes attached? Do you remember how free you were to dream? Try and recreate whatever that experience was for you when you imagined your adult life.

· Can you remember some of your favorite visions of your future?
· What did you want to be when you grew up?
· As a child, who did you admire?
· Can you remember a defining moment in your life when the pain and fear associated with unrealized dreams caused you to stop dreaming? What was that experience?

_____

_____

_____

_____

_____

_____

_____

Looking back on your childhood, perhaps you had a passion for playing sports, being on the debate team, learning how to be a great baker or writing a wonderful novel. Maybe a lack of encouragement caused your passion to evaporate. For some, this developed into a pattern of feeling unsupported. Perhaps you didn't know how to turn your passion into a career—or even realize that was possible. **Over time, you may have learned how NOT to live your dream.**

Obviously, not every little boy who's enamored with fire trucks is destined to be a firefighter, nor were your own childish visions of your future probably very realistic. But what I hope you can recapture is the naïve openness to all possibilities. That state of believing in everything.

So now move ahead in time to your **late teen or young adult years**, and see if you can recall what you were thinking at that time.

> "Adults are always asking little kids what they want to be when they grow up because they're looking for ideas."
> ~Paula Poundstone

- How do you want your life to look?

_____

_____

_____

- How do you want to spend your days?

_____

_____

_____

- How successful do you hope to be?

_____

_____

_____

- How do you define success?

_____

_____

_____

· What matters most to you?

_____

_____

_____

_____

· Are you excited about your future?

_____

_____

_____

_____

Someday has arrived!

Why do you suppose so many dreams and ideals die on the vine? Why do so many women slowly allow their youthful visions of what their lives could be disappear into over-scheduled reality? Can you still see the faint outline of ambitions and desires that once excited you? Do you remember the thrill of your first job? What happened? Life happened. Perhaps you compromised for the sake of your family. You made adjustments to create stability in your life. Increasingly, you took the safer routes. Eventually, you may have allowed greater meaning to leach out of your life, like nutrients washed away from the soil with rain after hard rain.

But it's not too late. This process of self-discovery and realization will guide you to revise your work situation and help you add back the meaning you may fear your job has lost. **It's almost always possible to create a job you love where you currently work.**

"I don't want to get to the end of my life and find that I lived just the length of it. I want to have lived the width of it as well."
~Diane Ackerman

Do you see any nuggets of desire that may still lie unfulfilled in your heart? Do you get a glimpse of a different you, one who may seem happier than you are now? Is it painful to confront dreams you may have let die? Your answers from that era of your life may already reflect an absence of possibility thinking. It all depends on what kind of life you've had and what encouragement and support you received.

Here's the good news: none of that matters now. **As adults we make our own opportunities, and we are all given exactly the same number of hours in every day to shape our lives.**

If you didn't get the kind of education you wanted, take some night classes or get your degree online. If no one cheered you on or applauded your dreams, start a mastermind group of like-minded people who will support each other's plans. Wonder how you ended up working at your county health department, when what you really wanted was a career in the media? Why not find out if your skills are transferable to a job at a local radio station or newspaper?

It's rarely too late to bring at least some part of an old dream to life.

Really!

Sure, no matter how many pliées you practice, the ballerina boat has sailed—but you could still work at a ballet school helping young girls reach for their dreams and find a measure of fulfillment that way. Was medical school a goal of yours? Figure out what aspect of being a doctor appealed to you, then search for another job in the healthcare field that offers the same rewards. For example, when her father died, Judy dropped out of college to help support her younger siblings. "Without a degree, I drifted from one unsatisfying job to another," she says, still obviously saddened by the wasted years. Confiding her old goals to a friend one day reignited her passion for medicine. "I realized it was helping patients recover—not the blood and guts of medicine—that attracted me." Eventually Judy became a patient advocate, someone who goes with elderly patients to all their medical appointments, takes notes, gets their prescriptions, researches their treatment options, and so on. In short, she gets the satisfaction from medicine that she had dreamed of many years earlier. **Is there some remnant of an old career dream you could revive and explore?**

Sprout some ideas and let them germinate

Has your experience of life taught you to dismiss all or most of your ideas as soon as they poke their heads above ground? Do you rip them out of your planting beds before you even have a chance to see if they're weeds or if they're volunteer flowers arrived on the wind from a neighbor's garden? If that sounds like you, try being more gentle with yourself and allowing more possibility in your life. You don't need to know how to bring an idea sprout to bloom just yet—but it sure won't have a chance if you stomp all over it right from the get-go. Start by allowing a few new ideas to germinate in your mind—let them simply live in a *maybe* category for now.

"The essential conditions of everything we do must be: choice, love, passion."
~Nadia Boulanger

How big of a change do you need to make?

I see workplace unhappiness as a continuum. On the low end of the scale, your current position may not be all that bad, perhaps just a bit dull or lacking in challenges. Maybe you've just slipped into some ruts (more on those later). Moving along the scale, you may feel a deeper level of dissatisfaction, because you now realize how few of your true talents are getting used. Toward the higher end of the scale, your energy starts to wane, then finally there is so much distress in your workplace that you can barely imagine a resolution. Where do you suppose you and your current job fit along this line? The good news is, wherever you are, there are solutions.

wherever you are, there are solutions

For some people, it's as simple as moving from the front office where there's lots of interaction with customers, to the back office, where they can work uninterrupted by customer complaints and requests. Maybe you now realize you're just not cut out for interacting with the public. There's nothing wrong with that; companies need both kinds of employees. **Just get clear on which type you are, and you're halfway to figuring out your ideal job.**

To better understand this continuum, let's start with Angela, someone at the first level of unhappiness. Angela works in a low-level administrative job at a huge publishing company in New York. She shares her small apartment with three other young women and has to change subways twice to get to work each day. Still, she's working in Manhattan, a lifelong dream. "My actual job bored me to tears," she remembers. It wasn't that she aspired to a glamorous editorial job, but she just wasn't doing anything that she felt made a significant contribution. In fact, Angela suspected she could stay home for a week and no one would even know it. "That's how anonymous I felt."

She was convinced her ideal job existed in that large company—it was just up to her to find it. She began by sitting down with different people every day in the company cafeteria and quizzing them about their departments and their jobs. "I think I kind of drove some people crazy, but I didn't care." She took notes. She ate at different times so she'd be sure to meet new people. After a few months of this routine, Angela decided what she really wanted to do was work in the production department. As someone who enjoyed implementing ideas, she rightly figured that being involved with the actual preparation of the magazines would give her something tangible to point to at the end of the day. She could take a magazine from the newsstand, open it up and say to her friends: "Look, I put those pages together."

To get her ideal job, all she had to do was visit her Human

Resources Department and show them how resourceful she'd been in determining a better placement for herself. They were impressed with her ingenuity and found an opening for her right away.

Could your perfect job be just an elevator ride away? If you work at a large company, you may benefit from discussing your options with someone in your HR department—that's *their job* after all, to find the best people for every position. Don't dump on them all your grievances, just explore what other opportunities might be open to you. If you're on record as wanting a new challenge, you'll be among the first to hear of new openings.

Climbing out of a rut

The next stop on the unhappiness scale: your rut. It can happen to anyone. You know what I mean—you got tired of running quarterly reports, so now you never even look for a better way to represent the data. You've written the in-house newsletter for many years, and it just seems easy to keep doing it the same way. You know your job so well that you do, indeed, do it while half asleep some days. After one bad experience, you decided long ago that you're not a team player, so you never ask for—or offer—help on anything. As the old saying goes, the only difference between a rut and a grave is the depth. Don't let your dreams of a more joyous job get sucked down into a rut—or a grave.

Sometimes all it takes are a few small changes to effect substantial change. Try some of these ideas on for size.

1. **Challenge yourself every once in awhile.** Don't always take the safe route. Are you a mouse in the corner at staff meetings? Try speaking up and see what happens.
2. **Do something differently.** Shake things up a little; maybe a fresh approach will keep you interested. Take a class. Try new software. Talk to someone from another department at lunch and find out what they do.
3. **Ask for a new task.** Doing exactly the same things week in, week out, would numb any mind. Trade tasks with a co-worker for a day. Drive a truck. Go on a sales call. Order supplies. Anything out of your ordinary.
4. **Offer to help a co-worker who is overwhelmed.** You never

"The habit of turning a trail into a rut must be incessantly fought against if one is to remain alive."
~Edith Wharton

know what may come of it. You may find other duties you're well-suited for; you may build a personal ally; you may get points for being a good team member. Gee, you might even have fun!

5. **Reverse your usual mode**. If you usually work on projects alone, try working with a partner, or vice versa. You may be a born collaborator and not know it. Or you may discover you really prefer to be a lone eagle.

6. **Reconnect with your passion**. Why are you working there? What aspects of your job used to excite you? Can you revive those feelings?

"If you want to draw, you must shut your eyes and sing."
~Pablo Picasso

Laurie was in rut, but she didn't realize how deep it was until she jumped out of it one day. She performed competently as the administrative assistant for the ad sales department of a community newspaper in a large Midwest city. It was reasonably interesting work. The salespeople she served directly were usually out of the office, so she had a lot of autonomy. After several years, Laurie realized there wasn't much left for her to learn about her job and no real challenges to keep her interested in it. Then one day, when she heard the office manager ask for a volunteer to help out with distribution because a driver had called in sick, she leapt at the chance to escape the office for the morning.

"To my surprise, I learned I loved delivering the papers," she says, her voice still full of excitement. Laurie got to get outdoors, she was able to talk with small business owners and gather feedback about the paper and she interacted with readers who were happy to see the latest edition arrive. When she got back to the office, she asked her boss if she could create the position of Distribution Manger of the paper—tasks the office manager had been reluctantly squeezing in to her duties. "My boss about fainted that anyone would want such a thankless job, but I was thrilled she agreed."

Laurie liked recruiting drivers and meeting with them on the loading dock, organizing better routes and getting out in the community to find more outlets to carry the paper. She found a good deal on used sidewalk vending boxes, repainted them herself and made a real believer out of her boss. As a result of her efforts, the circulation of the paper nearly doubled within a year, and Laurie not only earned a hefty bonus, but her grateful boss tied a salary incentive to future circulation increases—all because she volunteered to try something new—something she knew nothing about and could not have conceived of doing if she hadn't dared to climb out of her rut.

Try something different—who knows where it'll lead you! If you can think of some other duties where you work that you'd be willing to at least try, list them here.

_____

_____

_____

_____

_____

_____

"I do not want to die until I have faithfully made the most of my talent and cultivated the seed that was placed in me, until the last small twig has grown."
~Kathe Kollwitz

Are you leaving your fruit on the vine?

Farther along on the job unhappiness scale, Diana was in a transitional period in her life, recovering from a divorce—so she decided to move to Cape Cod and start her life over. She settled in a small town to heal and rebuild her life. "There weren't a lot of jobs to choose from, so I ended up waitressing in the fancy dining room of a large, historic hotel—not exactly my dream job," she confides, able to laugh about it now. It was a different sort of job for her, and the one aspect she loved surprised her. Diana found she was great at chatting up the people who ate there, who were also mostly guests at the hotel, often on extended stays.

She especially bonded with a mother and daughter who were spending Christmas there, far from home. "I decided to surprise them by decorating their hotel room for the holidays, using greens from my own backyard and lights I borrowed from the hotel." The guests were thrilled and touched by Diana's thoughtfulness and naturally expressed their thanks to the hotel management. That good deed was just one of many things that Diana began doing for the hotel guests on her own time. She liked being kind of a secret good fairy and knowing she was making someone's stay extra special.

Before long, the hotel manger realized she had a golden asset in Diana, so they sat down to talk about how they could devise a more suitable job for her. "I told my boss I'd love nothing more than filling all the unusual guest requests that I knew were driving the front desk staff crazy. I like dashing all over the place solving peculiar problems, and I love surprising guests with the unexpected." Since this was the kind of hotel where people came to celebrate anniversaries and was the site of many weddings, Diana proposed that she become the hotel's Guest Services Diva. In a very short time, the hotel became known for its specialized and highly personal service, and Diana went on to relish her job for years to come.

One key to Diana's success, was that though she wasn't thrilled to be waitressing, she didn't complain about it. Instead, she found creative ways to be of service to the hotel's guests, and in so doing, invented a job that hadn't even existed before she thought of it.

Think about your own situation . . . are there unmet client needs that you might want to fill? Perhaps you'll have to pay more attention for awhile to other aspects of how your company works. You could engage your co-workers in some lunchtime talk about gaps they see. Be a detective, do some research. Look at other companies in your industry by visiting their websites. What services do they offer their clients that your company doesn't? I realize this may sound like a lot to do, and your reaction may be: *not my responsibility!* I'm not suggesting you reinvent your company—you're just searching for ways to better utilize your unique abilities in the job you already have—and make a positive impact while you're at it. Write your ideas here.

Diana
found
creative
ways to
be of
service

_____

_____

_____

_____

_____

_____

Here's another example of brilliant innovation. Melissa works in order fulfillment for a large, used book company. The company sells all of its books online, so employees never have a chance for face-to-face contact with customers. It's all very anonymous, so it's been tough to build any kind of customer loyalty. But over the course of her first two years at her job, Melissa had instituted quite a few improvements in their shipping procedures, which added up to speedier delivery for their customers. One day she had her light bulb moment.

"Even if it meant being crazy and out of step with all that seemed holy, I had decided to be me."
~M. Scott Peck

"I told the owner of the company that we could stand out from our competition because we *were* better, but we had to tell our customers how good we were and why," Melissa recalls with great enthusiasm. "I showed him a flyer I had made up that we could insert into every order we shipped. The flyer detailed all the things we do to make sure their books arrive as quickly as possible." She went on to suggest turning the flyer into a coupon for a discount on their next order. Her boss was ecstatic over her initiative and immediately gave the go-ahead.

"That was three years ago. Since then, I've been put in charge of shipping as well as customer relations. I've turned the flyer into a monthly newsletter that contains funny excerpts from the various books that pass under my nose. I hear all the time how much our customers enjoy the newsletter, and repeat sales have really increased." The reason Melissa now finds so much satisfaction in her job, is because her talent for innovation and her creative instincts get used every single month. On top of that, **her job fulfills the purpose she set for herself**: to be excellent at whatever she does and to provide the highest level of service she can envision. All this from a job stuffing old books into padded bags!

Jump ship or bale with a bigger bucket?

Sometimes you have a position you love, but the job itself changes, which can cause extreme levels of unhappiness. No matter what the cause, if you're feeling like there isn't much you can do to salvage your job, first consider reinvention.

Yolanda had enjoyed much of the first 18 years of her career as a nurse on a busy inner city maternity ward. However, over the years, changes in hospital policies meant women no longer stayed more than a day on the ward, and Yolanda had lost all sense of connection to the new mothers and their babies. What had started out as a joyous job helping women adjust to their new roles as mothers, had become a factory situation with way too much paperwork. "The problem I saw was that first-time moms were terrified of being sent home only hours after delivery with very little information or support," she recalls. "It caused me so much anxiety, because here I was with all the answers they so desperately needed, but there was no time for me to share them."

This led her to start an outpatient education course for new moms and dads at her hospital. That went so well that Yolanda convinced the administration to let her expand the first class into a whole series of classes—and into a whole new job for herself. "Now I've come full circle, and I'm back doing what I loved about my old job—helping new mothers learn to care for their babies."

What need could you fill?

For Yolanda, the "aha" moment was realizing that patients still needed her expertise—all she needed to do was figure out a new way to give it to them. It was good for the hospital too, because offering the classes was a big selling point to expectant women choosing a hospital for their births. Yolanda saw a need and filled it. **Have there been changes in your company or industry that have left service gaps?** Can you think of ways to fill them—making both you and your company look good in the process? Write your ideas below.

_____

_____

_____

_____

_____

_____

Checking in at the last resort

Finally, after you've tried everything else, you may come to the conclusion the company you now work for can't offer you the kind of position that will fulfill your purpose and make use of your star qualities. Moving on really is a last resort, and I urge you to at least

first explore repairing your current situation and **investigate the full range of options where you now work**. If you skipped the exercise on Page 33 that examined advantages of staying where you are now, take a look at that again.

In Chapter Seven I'll go into this topic in depth, because there are ways to move on that are far less traumatic than blowing up at your boss one day and storming out of the office. (Even though many people fantasize about doing just that!) If you're already teetering on that brink, step back and go to that chapter now. But I hope you'll eventually complete this process, because it will guide you in creating a *better* position at your next job.

Meet Francie, who successfully navigated the dangerous waters of *several* job changes. Francie is a livewire. She's good at sales and has had considerable success at it—mostly because she has an innate talent for it. Since talking to people, learning what their needs are and solving their problems by pointing them toward the right product, all come instinctively for her, why was she so unhappy at her job selling office equipment? Francie didn't know, so she switched to selling cell phone service. "Big mistake! The high production pressure and the regimented sales scripts combined to make me even more miserable," she reveals.

learning about yourself is the key to a great job that fits you perfectly

After several more switches, Francie finally found her niche: booking meeting rooms for a big resort. When she learned that she was a Kolbe Follow Thru person, she understood why she was always frustrated not knowing how her customers felt about their purchases. "They came in the door, I sold them something, and I never saw them again. It left me feeling empty."

As a solution, she went searching for a sales job that would meet her need for knowing the end of her customer's story. Working in event sales, she gets to have ongoing contact with her clients and help them with details of their functions. She works with them right through their party or meeting, then follows up with them afterward to gather feedback for future improvements. In addition, her creative side, which had lain dormant most of her life, finally blossomed as Francie got more and more involved with her clients' events. She was even offered a promotion to manage the department, but she turned it down, saying: "I've finally found my dream job, and I'm not letting it go!" Francie was in the right profession, just not in the slot best suited to her instinctive work style.

With what you're learning about yourself and the kind of job you really want to have, you can skip the trial and error approach to job selection and move directly to knowing the right job opportunity when you meet it. **Is there a subtle shift you could make that would better suit your preferred way of working?** Brainstorm some ideas here.

_____

_____

_____

_____

_____

_____

I hope all these examples have gotten your mind buzzing with new ideas for your own ideal job. If all these women can find happiness on their jobs, don't you think you can too?

Become a better gardener

After you've allowed a few ideas to sprout and push above ground, learn to accept responsibility for their growth and development—at least until you can determine if they are

weeds or sunflowers.

Nurture them by providing time to research them. Exactly what could make you happier at the job you have? What other responsibilities could you assume? How else could your job be defined? Are your skills being used? What new skills could you develop to up your value as a team member? Do some online research or visit your library—librarians are great resources. Talk to some friends or colleagues who have expertise in the area you're investigating. Request an informational interview with someone who really knows your position. Once you select a seedling of an idea to encourage, learn what it needs to thrive—time, money, education, mentoring, or all of the above. Accept responsibility to keep your young dream alive while you gather information to help it grow. Keep in mind that job satisfaction comes from growing in your job—stagnation isn't good for plants or people.

I very briefly had a staff member who seemed to enjoy online shopping more than doing her job—in an office where performance is required. If that really is what's important to you—having lots of time on the job to attend to personal matters—then you need to acknowledge that and find the sort of undemanding position that will allow that attitude. This woman belonged in a job where she was just needed to answer the phones occasionally. **The goal here is to be honest with yourself.**

Oh wouldn't it be loverly . . .
Now it's time for a pop quiz about your working preferences that may help you define your ideal job. Give yourself permission to enjoy a job that reflects *you*. **Put a check by all aspects that you prefer.**

My Dream Job Checklist

___ desk job (with a great chair, of course)
___ on my feet, moving around
___ inside an office
___ out and about, on the move
___ collaborate closely with a team
___ solo act
___ busy, lively office, lots of stimulation
___ shhhh—people are thinking!
___ large company, with big company benefits
___ small company, more personal relationships
___ handle the general public
___ back office only
___ good with numbers
___ better with words
___ schmooze the clients
___ details are delightful

___ broad strokes, big ideas—let someone else implement

___ deadlines, pressure, adrenaline—bring it on!

___ please don't bug me about anything

___ research, play detective

___ could sell Paris Hilton a room at the Sheraton

___ give me detailed instructions, and I'll comply

___ give me a rough idea what you want, and I'll jump right in

___ gotta have glitz—I live for fashion, glamour, entertainment

___ like knowing I made someone's day better

___ routines make me happy

___ variety is the spice of my life

___ computers are my best tools

___ love talking to groups

___ high tolerance for meetings and planning sessions

___ just send me the minutes

___ want projects that use my creativity

___ want projects that use my powers of reasoning and deduction

___ flex schedule

___ job sharing

___ would love someone to mentor me

___ like structure to my day

___ don't fence me in

___ willing to work late or odd hours

___ a 9 to 5er

___ gotta have feedback, applause, validation

___ respond to incentives, bonuses and contests

___ like knowing other people will be checking my work

___ take full responsibility for my work, no need to double check it

___ want my own office with a door—and hey, why not a window?

___ can function in a cubicle or in a wide open space

"Without leaps of imagination or dreaming, we lose the excitement of possibilities. Dreaming, after all, is a form of planning."
~Gloria Steinem

Let your mind open up to the vast blue sky

Now we've arrived at the heart of this process. Please don't rush through this section—in fact, why not set aside some quality time to do these next few exercises? What I want you to do now is clear your mind of all the stress you may associate with your current job. Put everything that irritates you about it right out of your mind.

Instead, start thinking about these questions:
- What do you really want from your job?
- What kind of work life do you want and how close are you to living it?
- What tasks would you find fulfilling?
- What would make you more productive?
- What kind of rewards do you seek?
- What is the mood or tone of your ideal work environment—professional, casual, free-wheeling, compassionate or what?
- What kind of interactions do you want with others?
- What could management do to support your success?

I keep coming back to gardening, but it really is the perfect metaphor for this process. **Imagining your ideal job is just like designing a garden for the plot of ground where you work.** What kind of garden would you like to plant—a practical one full of edible fruits and vegetables? Or is it all about the beauty of flowers? If you're focused on helping and healing, then a garden full of medicinal plants might be right for you. If you're a creative type, then perhaps you'd enjoy planting an herb garden with 30 different varieties to spice up your recipes. All would be wonderful gardens, but which one inspires you and reflects your interests, personality and values? You, the gardener, get to decide.

What do you need to thrive?

For the next several minutes, close your eyes and let yourself dream about a perfect day at your ideal job. Make this an "anything goes" day, with no fears, no obstacles or limiting beliefs. Focus all your energy on the kind of day you want to have at work. See yourself expressing your unique abilities and talents. Don't worry about whether your vision is possible or probable. Next, write a description of your day in your journal or in the space below.

_____

_____

_____

_____

_____

_____
_____
_____
_____
_____
_____
_____
_____
_____
_____

When you're done, **list the adjectives that best describe your perfect day,** and be sure to refer to your **Dream Job Checklist** you just completed on Page 87.

My Ideal Job is:

_____
_____
_____
_____
_____
_____
_____
_____
_____
_____

Of course the flip side is, what's your day on the job like now? **Give these questions some thought.**
- Are you currently feeling challenged by your job?
- Do you feel valued for your accomplishments?
- What is it about your job that excites you?
- What gets in the way of your productivity?
- What else could management do to support your success?
- What keeps you at your current job?

Next, list all the adjectives that describe how your work day actually is right now. You are the only one who is going to see this, so be honest.

My Current Job is:

_____

_____

_____

_____

_____

_____

_____

_____

_____

_____

Is this a defining moment for you?

How do the two days compare? For most people, this exercise reveals quite a gap and becomes a defining moment that helps them commit to creating a better work life for themselves. Defining moments are when lessons we learn, often from unexpected circumstances, make such an impact on us that they change our lives forever.

When Joanie did this exercise, she quickly realized why she had no energy in the mornings and why she could barely haul herself out of bed most Mondays—because she was mainly doing things she hated at her job. It was important to Joanie to excel at everything she was given to do, but she'd been slowly pushed into doing tasks she was not well-trained for (understudy roles), and that caused her a lot of stress. "I was given responsibilities to do with updating our company website, yet I have no interest in it and no real technical understanding of what I'm doing, so I'm always worried I'll mess up the website beyond repair. When I protested, I was told it was easy and I'd pick it up real fast. Now they keep giving me more and more work to do with the office computers, as though I'm suddenly a tech support person. I hate it! I wish I was back in customer service, where I took pride in my job, because I knew I was good at it."

People
often get
pushed
and pulled
into
unfamiliar
territory
at work

This was, indeed, a defining moment for Joanie, because she took action and discussed her concerns with her supervisor—after she'd taken time to come up with some suggestions for shifting responsibilities in the office. We'll go into those strategies a little later.

Joanie's situation is not uncommon. People often get pushed and pulled into unfamiliar territory at work, especially in small offices where everyone needs to wear a variety of hats. There's a difference between being a team player who pitches in and does her fair share of tasks she may not love—those miscast roles again—and someone who, over time, has seen her job evolve into something totally different from what she was hired to do, into something she doesn't enjoy at all. If most of your work days rate only ones, twos or threes on the **G.R.O.W. Chart**, (Page 25) then you know you need to take action now to save your job—and your sanity.

Take stock of your willingness for change

When you review your two lists, do you have some insights into your situation? If all you see are huge roadblocks separating your current job from your dream job, don't worry—Chapter Five will help you bulldoze them out of the way. For now, **I want you to remain in a mood of possibility as you answer these questions.**

1. In order to enjoy your ideal job, what things are you willing to do differently? For example: learn new skills, take on new responsibilities, let go of some duties you used to perform. Be specific in your list.

_____

_____

_____

_____

2. What new attitude do you need to adopt and why?

_____

_____

_____

_____

3. What do you want to do more of at work?

_____

_____

_____

_____

4. What do you want to do less of at work?

_____

_____

_____

_____

5. If you could create the perfect dream position right now where you currently work, what would you do differently starting tomorrow?

_____

_____

_____

_____

"How does one become a butterfly? You must want to fly so much that you're willing to give up being a caterpillar."
~Trina Paulus

This exercise may have revealed the depth of your desire to change your current situation. It's easy to daydream about a better situation, but once you face taking steps toward making it happen, some people get weak in the knees or lose their desire. Sometimes this is just overwhelm, caused by not knowing what to do next. That's okay to feel. If you stick with me through this whole process, I'll show you how to get from point A to point B. (For some of you, it's more like from point A to point K.)

Can you gain without pain?

The messages are everywhere in our society: No pain, no gain. We are told over and over that we need to hurt in order to succeed, that we have to pay a price for success and happiness. I disagree. Why should you pay a price in order to create your ideal job? Shouldn't you have to pay a price for *not* creating a life—personal and professional—that you really want? Do you think the Williams sisters paid a price to become the best tennis players in the world? No! They love everything associated with tennis, including the long hours of practice, which early on was six hours a day, six days a

Journal exercise

week for four years. When you're fueled by your passions and you're driven by your purpose, pain is not an issue. Just because you've heard "no pain, no gain" a hundred times, doesn't need to make it true for you.

What are your limiting beliefs?

One of the ways we subconsciously sabotage our own dreams is by our limiting beliefs. Often they derive from the deeply embedded voices of our families. You know those voices . . they say things like: *You'll never amount to anything, Where do you get off thinking you can do that?, You don't have the brains of _____* (fill in the blank!). Other limiting beliefs we adopt from the media and society in general. Messages like: *Women can't have a career and a family; good mothers don't work; women don't belong in business.* Some of our negativity stems from our life experiences. **If you get stung often enough, you stay away from bees, but that doesn't mean you avoid the garden all together.** Getting in touch with your limiting beliefs can clear the way for dramatic changes in your life.

What ideas are stuck in your head that may be holding you back and preventing you from realizing your dreams? Look over your life experience and see what lurks beneath your façade.

·   Examine family patterns and history for evidence. How have other women in your family expressed themselves in the workplace?

_____

_____

_____

_____

_____

·   What are the attitudes of the men in your family?

_____

_____

_____

_____

_____

"The only thing that keeps you from achieving your goal is the story you tell yourself about why you can't."
~Tony Robbins

· Are there religious or cultural beliefs you want to examine?

_____

_____

_____

_____

_____

· When you see feminists in the media, what's your reaction?

_____

_____

_____

_____

_____

· Do you have some hidden guilt about working at all? Do you secretly believe you should be home with your kids?

_____

_____

_____

_____

_____

· Do you resent having to work?

_____

_____

_____

_____

_____

· When you see women executives, what's your first reaction?

_____

_____

_____

_____

_____

_____

_____

"Your beliefs are never neutral. They either move your dreams forward or hold you back. But here's the secret—you choose what you believe."
~Marcia Wieder

Any surprises? You may need to let this exercise percolate in the back of your mind . . .more hidden beliefs may surface when you least expect them, so keep watching for them to raise their sneaky little heads above ground like the weeds they are.

Recast the movie of your life

I do hope you're getting to do this work along with your colleagues, because that will make all of this so much easier. If you've found this book on your own, then at some point, I hope you'll make an effort to expose your co-workers to at least some of these ideas, because you're going to need their help. You'd be surprised how many people in an office really have no idea what their co-workers actually enjoy doing.

I met identical twins who worked in the same insurance office for 15 years and didn't really know what the other one preferred to do at work. After doing an exercise similar to the AWEsome Chart, Lana raised her hand and said, "I hate doing claims." Her sister Jana spun around and said, "I never knew that, I absolutely never knew that. I love claims." So the one twin—who adored dealing with claims—took over all the other sister's claim work, and they lived happily ever after in their jobs. They simply traded responsibilities. Lana preferred solving problems rather than listening to people and all their hardships, whereas Jana felt great compassion for people in bad situations and loved feeling she was helping them through rough times.

Now I'd like you to refer back to Page 45 and your **AWEsome Chart**. Look at all the things in your lower right corner, **the tasks for which you are miscast**. Here are some strategies for releasing them from your job experience.

1. Find someone else on your team who loves doing what you hate and trade with them.
2. Technology may be able to help streamline some of these tasks for you or maybe even eliminate them. Talk to your tech person about software options, etc.
3. After completing the process in this book and sharing your results with your manager, there's a chance he or she will hire someone to take these off your back. Once she realizes your commitment to making a substantial contribution to the company by working

Do you know what your team members actually enjoy doing?

primarily in areas that you absolutely love and have the skill set to exceed at, it becomes difficult for her to deny your request.

4. Give up guilt over not wanting to do certain tasks. It's okay to design your ideal job. Sometimes staff members look at giving up some duties as a strike against them, as though they're admitting some kind of failure. That just isn't true. **You only fail *yourself* if you continue to do things you hate, when you could be thriving in a job you love.**

Below, list the items from your miscast section, and next to each one, write something you might do to eliminate that duty from your job description. If you'd also like to let go of some of your understudy duties, (the lower left corner of your chart) include them here as well. Duties that would require more training than is available to you, or tasks that would take too much time to become adept at, are good ones to release for now. You can always add those skills to your repertoire at a later date.

You only fail yourself if you continue to do things you hate, when you could be thriving in a job you love.

_____   _____
_____   _____
_____   _____
_____   _____
_____   _____
_____   _____
_____   _____
_____   _____

Here's a perfect example of how someone who was totally miscast ended up in her right niche. Sandra was hired as a customer service rep for a financial services company, but she really didn't have enough experience to handle the demanding job. "I knew I was in over my head, but I was pregnant and I needed the job," she explains. In fact, when she took maternity leave, she was barely hanging on to her job. Delia, the woman who was hired to fill in while she was gone, was better suited to the position and was doing very well at it. When Sandra returned from her leave, she was told she'd have to work as Delia's assistant. To her supervisor's surprise—and

"It's not trespassing, if the boundaries you cross are your own."
~Allyson Moore

delight—Sandra wasn't upset by the demotion, she was relieved. "I love being an assistant, I enjoy pushing the paper, and I love doing support functions for someone else. I don't miss the pressure." You see, in her former position she was being asked to do too many understudy roles—things she wasn't really trained to do—plus lots of things she simply wasn't good at and didn't enjoy. Being someone else's assistant is an ideal fit and allows her to star in that role. **Would lowering the pressure you are under give your job the quality of life you desire?** If this is a hot button issue for you, make a list of all the triggers that pile the pressure on you. Next to each one, think of creative ways to rid yourself—or at least reduce—the pressure.

_____ _____
_____ _____
_____ _____
_____ _____
_____ _____
_____ _____

Do you think only executives suffer from high job stress? Think again. New research published by Professor Benjamin Amick of the University of Texas, indicates that it's not just people in top jobs who make themselves sick from stress—so do plenty of people in less demanding jobs. In fact, employees who describe their jobs as boring and as ones where they lack much control, are 33-35 percent more apt to die prematurely than those who have more control over their work situation. Furthermore, **people stuck in jobs where they have little or no say over how they spend their workdays have a 50 percent higher risk of premature death**, than do people who have some control over their daily activities.

So what does this mean for you? Well, if that sounds like your job description, then consider it a wake-up call to redesign your job and build more autonomy into it. She who takes what life tosses her without searching for something better, may die young. Don't become a statistic!

"Any human anywhere will blossom in a hundred unexpected talents and capacities, simply by being given the opportunity to do so."
~Doris Lessing

What's possible for you?

Now that you understand what your unique abilities are and you have clarity about your purpose, let's examine your career possibilities where you work now. Even if you doubt there are any, humor me and do this exercise anyway—you just might amaze yourself if you can live in the realm of possibility for a few minutes. For starters, you can't always know what your boss dreams of doing with the business. Perhaps a willingness to expand your skill set would open up additional options for you. (Which is why I had you do an honest assessment on Page 34 of your willingness to make efforts on your own behalf.) The advantage of filling out these charts is, it's going to help you think strategically about your future. This exercise is designed to help you **turn possibilities into viable opportunities.**

Start by returning to your **AWEsome List** on Page 46. These are the skills and talents you already possess which allow you to play starring roles. **I'd like you to pick the five items from the list that you'd most like to use in your ideal job. Write one of them at the top of the chart on Page 100.** Then think of some way to apply that unique skill and write that as your new possibility. (You don't need to know if that's an option in your company at this point.) Below that, add what you'd like to happen as a result of your taking on that new possibility, and then write what reward(s) you imagine gaining from it, whether monetary, emotional or something else.

Give real thought to the added value question, because you're going to have to sell this possibility to your manger or business owner. For example, does your idea save money or time, does it reduce the number of people it takes to do something, does it improve customer service or satisfaction? What problems does it solve? Does it increase production or speed up systems? Continue on, answering the rest of the questions. When you're done, **fill out additional charts for each of your other top five talents.**

For example, Alexandra, who's been suffocating in a dull administrative job at a busy law firm, filled out the chart like this: My unique skill is paying extreme attention to details and a willingness to work odd hours; my new possibility is proofreading legal briefs. My desired result would be to shift to that position in my firm, and my reward would be acknowledgment for doing something I'm really good at and having the option for flex time. The added value for my firm is that I am fast and willing to work from home at strange hours, since the briefs are often not ready for proofing until the middle of the night. This position would absolutely increase my enthusiasm for work, and it aligns with my purpose, which is making a contribution I can measure. Finding errors that might have embarrassed the firm—or worse—would be very satisfying.

Are you pursuing a dream or a fantasy?

I hope this exercise has revved up your excitement level, as you explore how to include your starring roles in your ideal job. If you find this especially challenging, consider brainstorming with a trusted friend or colleague who's familiar with your skills and your company. If this is the moment when your resistance kicks in, then hop ahead to Chapter Five for some motivation to forge ahead. After you're re-energized, come on back to finish this essential exercise.

At this point it's important to understand the difference between dreams and fantasies. **Sometimes when people start developing a picture of their dream job, their result is more a fantasy than a dream.** Planning on winning the lottery to rescue yourself from a stagnant life is a fantasy, because you have no control over the outcome. Ditto: hoping to marry rich or waiting for an inheritance that may never come. If this describes your pattern, do yourself a favor and read my friend Barbara Stanny's excellent book on the subject, *Prince Charming Isn't Coming*.

Dreams, on the other hand, become reality, because you can develop strategies and set goals that move you closer to living your dream—in other words, you control the outcome based on the actions you take.

Possibility Chart

My unique skill

_____
_____

My new possibility

_____
_____
_____
_____

Desired results

_____
_____
_____

Anticipated reward

_____
_____
_____

What added value will this contribute to the company?

_____
_____
_____

Will this change increase enthusiasm for my job?
__Yes __No
Will this change align my work more closely with my purpose?
__Yes __No
Rank this possibility for speed of implementation (from 1 quick to 5 slow) ___

Possibility Chart

My unique skill

_____
_____

My new possibility

_____
_____
_____
_____

Desired results

_____
_____
_____

Anticipated reward

_____
_____
_____

What added value will this contribute to the company?

_____
_____
_____

Will this change increase enthusiasm for my job?
__Yes __No
Will this change align my work more closely with my purpose?
__Yes __No
Rank this possibility for speed of implementation (from 1 quick to 5 slow) ___

Possibility Chart

My unique skill

_____

_____

My new possibility

_____

_____

_____

_____

Desired results

_____

_____

_____

Anticipated reward

_____

_____

_____

What added value will this contribute to the company?

_____

_____

_____

Will this change increase enthusiasm for my job?
__Yes __No
Will this change align my work more closely with my purpose?
__Yes __No
Rank this possibility for speed of implementation (from 1 quick to 5 slow) ___

Possibility Chart

My unique skill

_____

_____

My new possibility

_____

_____

_____

Desired results

_____

_____

_____

Anticipated reward

_____

_____

_____

What added value will this contribute to the company?

_____

_____

_____

Will this change increase enthusiasm for my job?
__Yes __No
Will this change align my work more closely with my purpose?
__Yes __No
Rank this possibility for speed of implementation (from 1 quick to 5 slow) ___

Possibility Chart

My unique skill
_____
_____

My new possibility
_____
_____
_____
_____

Desired results
_____
_____
_____

Anticipated reward
_____
_____
_____

What added value will this contribute to the company?
_____
_____
_____

Will this change increase enthusiasm for my job?
__ Yes __ No
Will this change align my work more closely with my purpose?
__ Yes __ No
Rank this possibility for speed of implementation (from 1 quick to 5 slow) ___

Beware of bosses bearing gifts

Once your supervisor realizes your sincere commitment to this process of making yourself more valuable to the company (and in the process getting the job of your dreams) he may well start to offer you various options and incentives. This is great, because it shows you that management supports your initiative and efforts. **Just be sure that if you accept the opportunities you are shown, they reflect your purpose, your passions and utilize your unique talents.** If not, your boss may be trying to get you to do whatever needs doing that no one else is willing to do. He may mistake your new enthusiasm for a willingness to do anything. If you evaluate all new options against your AWEsome Chart, then you'll be able to tell if it's an opportunity you want to snatch or one to respectfully decline. Nora had to learn this the hard way.

Nora was thrilled with her job at a Los Angeles public relations firm, where she helped authors promote their books. "I love my job . . it has a lot of variety, and I feel like I'm learning something new every day," she confides. All that fit in nicely with her Kolbe Fact Finder work style, and all was well, until the firm's number one client asked her if she'd like to work for her exclusively. "She made me an offer I couldn't—but should have—refused. . . a huge salary increase and a $2,000 bonus for every speech I booked for her."

Nora, who was saving for a down payment on a house, was seduced by the offer and left her wonderful job—even though there were tiny voices in the back of her mind trying to talk her out of it. She should have listened to them. After only six months, Nora was begging for her old job back. So what happened?

"I had a hunch the new job would require me to do things I didn't feel comfortable doing, but I kept hearing advice like 'Do what you fear and the money will follow' and so on. I really wanted to grow, so I decided to challenge myself. In truth, making the cold calls to book the author for speeches literally made me sick to my stomach—every time." Nora hated sales, especially when she didn't know the clients. She just wasn't wired for it, and no matter how much she *wanted* to try it, she was never going to enjoy it or be great at it. **Will alone cannot overcome how you instinctively respond to situations.** That's why the sooner Nora quit that job, the sooner her digestive tract was going to return to normal. As luck would have it, she got her old job back and threw out her antacids.

In my own company, I experienced something similar a few years back when I decided to offer production incentives to my team. I thought the financial bonuses would please them and show them how much I valued their hard work. Instead it backfired on me. What I didn't realize is, my team was already working as hard and as effectively as they could. To them, my offer felt like I was taking a whip to racehorses already running at full speed. In time, they admitted to me that the incentive program was making them crazy and put too much extra pressure on them. They literally felt punished by something I saw as a reward! It was a lesson for all of us.

Never assume you know what your boss—or your team—really wants.

"Be unstoppable. You can have the life you want, the one that works for you. Your possibilities are all waiting for you to let them happen and make your life the magical experience it was meant to be."
~Marcia Wieder

Sadly, studies show that **99 percent of all employees NEVER tell management what they really want**. Believe me, you want to be counted in the one percent who does!

Plant what will give you the most satisfaction

The goal is to create exactly the kind of experience you want for yourself. Do you want to have more dealings with clients? Do you prefer hunkering down in a back office? Are you great on the phone, do people respond to your personality? Would you rather write emails? What do you value—being able to leave by four every day to pick up your kids? Do you like having opportunities to earn extra commissions? Make sure your ideal job reflects exactly what matters most to you. The more significant your dream is, the more passion—and energy—you'll generate to make it real.

I can see clearly now

I trust you've been doing all the exercises in each chapter, and if not, then ask yourself: Why not? Don't you take this process seriously? Just how badly do you want your ideal job, less stress and a higher quality of life? **This is not just a book to read.**

To get the real benefits from it, you have to participate.

In the next chapter, you're going to learn how to bring your plans to life, so there isn't much point in reading that until you have a clear idea what your ideal job would look like at the company where you now work.

For those of you who do have a clear vision, remember the G.R.O.W. Chart from Chapter One? Review that scale again (Page 25), to be sure your ideal job ranks high on your satisfaction meter. Next, **I want you to write your vision on the next page in living color.** Sure, go ahead and get out some colored pens. Maybe some glitter, some gold stars and rubber stamps. **You have a whole page here to record your design for your dream job.** Let today be the day you choose to focus on what's possible. For now, don't worry about obstacles or how you'll make this a reality—so

dream big!

Dream Job Declaration

This is my vision for my ideal job—one that uses the best of my unique abilities, one that I absolutely know I deserve, one that reflects my values and provides me with a sense of satisfaction and contribution. **This dream job is one where I will thrive!**

_____

_____

_____

_____

_____

_____

_____

_____

_____

_____

_____

_____

_____

_____

_____

_____

_____

_____

_____

_____

_____

_____

_____

Applause,
applause!

You bet there's another bouquet!

By now, I bet you're expecting some discussion of reward at the end of a chapter, and I won't disappoint you. At this point, I hope you're feeling your enthusiasm rise like sap in a maple tree. For your reward this time, I'm urging you to do something to further concretize your ideal job, something even more vivid than the description you just wrote out. What I mean by that is this: buy or make something for yourself that is a visual, tangible representation of your dream. Perhaps it illustrates some of your unique abilities. How you do this is your creative choice. It could be something you wear everyday as a reminder of your intentions, such as a ring, bracelet or necklace.

Allison was aiming for a better position at the TV station where she worked—one which would require her to display a lot more self-confidence than she had been showing, so she came up with a fun reward that emphasized the self-empowerment she felt whenever she envisioned her new job. "Being a very visual person, I wanted to honor important benchmarks in my progress with something tangible. I decided to buy a gold chain necklace that I'd wear every day and add small heart charms for every accomplishment. It rests right above my own heart as a constant reminder of my progress."

Cecelia had a great idea for anyone to adapt. "I have a bronze statue of a woman with wings and she's holding a crystal orb. To me it embodies all the promise of my dream, so I took a photo of it in the morning sun and I use that as my desktop image on my computer. Now I'm reminded of my dream all day long."

Another woman made a flipbook out of index cards, listing her unique abilities and all the reasons she was qualified for her ideal job. She reads it everyday to keep herself aligned with her goals. Perhaps you'd enjoy making a treasure map or a dream board—a collage that contains images symbolic of your journey to this ideal job.

Be sure to place whatever object(s) you buy or make where you can see them frequently. **Keeping your vision real, distinct and achievable, not distant and generic, is one of the keys to performing mind over matter changes.**

Do come back though, and continue on to Chapter Four, where we'll map out a grand plan to get your ideal job and talk about enlisting supporters.

"In doing anything,
the first step is the
most difficult."

~Chinese proverb

Chapter Four
BUILDING PATHWAYS TO YOUR GARDEN OF POSSIBILITIES

Chapter Four At A Glance

- What's your level of change?
- Making an internal shift
- What's beneath your pain?
- Change one small thing
- Can you move sideways?
- What color is the grass?
- It's a whole new job
- Ten stepping stones you need for your path
- What will enable your plan?
- Putting up trellises: enlisting support
- Do you know your added value?
- Creating a Job Action Memo
- Be accountable to someone else

There's an old saying that the only job where you start at the top, is digging a hole. That's doubly true today, because it's time to get your hands into the dirt and actually plant your garden of possibilities. You prepared the soil in Chapter One, learned what a great gardener you are in Chapter Two, then you envisioned your garden in the last chapter, so now you're ready to build a pathway to your garden. You Quick Start types out there may prefer to get busy planting seeds, thereby skipping right over this stage. In other words, you may be tempted to just grab your vision of an ideal job, march right up to your boss, lay it out and be settling into it by the end of business today. That's fine. Trying to slow down a Quick Start is like trying to stop an avalanche. If you Quick Starts can stand it, and for everyone else, I suggest you take a more prepared, systematic approach to manifesting your ideal job, though I can reduce the process to this:

think big,

start small, start now.

> "If what's in your dreams wasn't already real inside you, you couldn't even dream it."
> ~Gloria Steinem

What's your level of change?

The way I see it, most job shifts <u>within</u> a company fall into one of these five categories:

1. An **internal change in attitude** toward your job results in changes in your behavior, which in turn create greater satisfaction.
2. **Small adjustments** among co-workers to align duties with instinctive abilities and aptitudes.
3. **Lateral move** to a similar position in another department.
4. Realizing that your ideal job within the company is a **promotion**.
5. Inventing a whole **new position**.

Looking at this list, where does your ideal job fit? Obviously, the larger the degree of change, the more effort it will take on your part to bring it off. This is not meant to dissuade you in the least from aiming high—it's just a little reality check. Let's look at these categories more closely and see how others have implemented better jobs for themselves.

JOB SHIFT LEVEL ONE:

Internal changes

You may be coming to a realization of your own role in your current job situation. Perhaps you weren't surprised when your typical work day rated only a one or two on the G.R.O.W. Chart. Maybe you've been dissatisfied with your job for some time, but you're only now realizing why—and it could have something to do with your attitude. There are a zillion reasons why your attitude may have tanked over time, but the only question now is: **If I can show you a method to improve your approach to going to work, will you try it?** I hope so, because very few job situations are lost causes. I can promise you that making the choice to change your perspective can bring you rewards that are currently unimaginable. Here's the thing about dragging a poor attitude into work every day— it doesn't just stay lodged in your own head. It oozes out and infects your co-workers too, and before you know it, your whole team has the blahs. Of course, if your attitude is that toxic, you're likely to be hauling it home with you where it's also affecting your family—which means you have to break the cycle. (If you'd like to read more right now on assessing and dealing with attitude issues, skip on ahead to Page 183.)

If Jody can improve her attitude, so can you. Jody's career was stalled in middle management at a large telecom company in Georgia, and she saw her enthusiasm for her job evaporating like steam from hot pavement after a rain shower. She maxed out her sick days, came in late, took long lunches, left early and did everything she could get away with to shorten her work days. "I was in a lot of emotional pain," she confides, her voice still colored by the stress she was under. "I was making good money, but as a single woman I needed my job. I had a hefty mortgage, a car payment and two old dalmatians with big vet bills. I had gotten to a place where I couldn't see any value for how I spent my days, which isn't surprising, since I delegated everything I could to my team."

Interestingly, it was a sermon that jolted Jody into a new awareness. "Our pastor asked us one Sunday to contemplate what good we were doing in the world, either through our work or activities away from our jobs. Then he left the pulpit, telling us to sit there for an hour and give that question our undivided attention. This was right after Hurricane Katrina, and helping others was on everyone's mind. I was stunned by his challenge, but I took it seriously and thought deeply about what I did at my job that could possibly be of service to anyone. It took me a whole day of pondering the question, but I finally saw a larger purpose. Instead of just focusing on what my specific job was, I examined the good that the company did and how I contributed to that."

What Jody saw that day, was that **she wasn't in the business of selling cell phone service, rather she was in the business of connecting people to each other, to lifelines for help, to families far away.** She'd observed how many people had used cell phones to stay connected with loved ones from far-flung relocation centers, and how they used camera phones to reassure one another that they were okay. In response, Jody started a drive at her church and then at her company, to provide free cell phones for evacuees who landed in her area, to help them get their lives back in order. Her selflessness in that campaign revived her interest in her job, and she started getting involved with the actual work of her team, looking for even more ways to give back to her community.

"It took a major hurricane to blow the selfishness out of my head and heart, but now I love my job and look forward to taking on each day's new adventures."

Jody found a way to adopt her company's purpose for her own and even expand upon it. Nothing else changed. Her job description and duties remained the same. Only Jody changed. How about you? Can you take some ownership for your current unhappiness?

What's beneath your pain?

Let's start with a purge. List the top ten things you dislike about your current job, then rank them by how much irritation and stress they cause you.

___ 1. _____

Can you take some ownership for your current situation?

Journal exercise

___ 2. _____

___ 3. _____

___ 4. _____

___ 5. _____

___ 6. _____

___ 7. _____

___ 8. _____

___ 9. _____

___ 10. _____

Start with your worst irritant and answer these questions:

· What's the **underlying issue**? For example, it may not be that you are asked to work late, as much as it is the lack of acknowledgment and appreciation when you do put out extra effort.

_____

_____

_____

_____

· What's **your role** in this irritant? Do you have poor boundaries, or weak communication skills that allow this to keep happening?

_____

_____

_____

_____

· What's the **trigger** for repeat occurrences of this irritant? Why does this keep happening?

_____

_____

_____

_____

_____

· What's a **healthier response**? The next time you're asked to work late, could you give an answer that didn't make you feel taken advantage of for the umpteenth time? Perhaps you do rearrange your plans, but you also tell your supervisor that if you do so, you'll need to come in two hours later the next day, in order to do the things you had scheduled that evening. Maybe you could suggest that if several people stayed late, you could finish the project much sooner. Speak up for what will make the request feel more balanced to you.

· What **new habit**(s) could you adopt to change the outcome the next time and every time your boss makes that request? Could you learn to plan ahead more or take more responsibility for seeing that the project doesn't go into overtime again and again? Even if it isn't your responsibility, it seems to end up on your desk, so why not be proactive and rally help *before* it becomes a crisis? Your boss will likely see such actions on your part as taking a burden off his shoulders and reducing *his* stress as well.

· Are there other **team members** who are bothered by the same situation? How could you enlist their help in finding solutions— rather than just griping about it? (Admit it, you do gripe, don't you? Gripe fests always make everyone feel worse, have you noticed?) **Change your intent and you change your outcome.**

   Ask the same questions about the number two most annoying item on your list, and so on down the line. After that, see if there are even more situations you could apply this process to, until there is nothing left about your job that upsets you on a regular basis. The reason it's important to rank your issues and begin with the worst ones, is you may not finish the list. If you don't, at least you'll have knocked out the biggest pieces of gravel in your shoe. As you will see in the next chapter, **some of your obstacles may be caused by your response to external situations**. While it's not your fault that your boss is always late handing you the time-sensitive project to finish, you *can* control how you react and possibly affect the whole process. It starts to change for the better when you decide to stop being upset and do something about it.

Can you think of your job as a gift?

Another way to re-envision your job is to think of it as a gift. Hey, I heard those groans! Admittedly, if you're consumed with negative feelings about your present job, this may be a stretch, but please just open your mind far enough to let this idea inside. I'm not your dad warning you about starving people in China to get you to eat your broccoli—but I do remind you that there are millions of people around the world who would *love* to have a job. Any job. Even your job that you think is so crummy. So try and kindle some gratitude. Jobs give structure to our lives. They give us a place to go to interact with our fellow humans. They give us a chance to share our talents and skills. They give us a way to make a difference in society. They give us a paycheck. The best jobs give us a sense of empowerment, capability and self-esteem, as well as room to grow and evolve as people—and maybe even healthy baked goods in the break room.

Just like Jody and her new attitude toward giving back, see if there are internal changes in awareness you could make to find more joy in your job.

If this is the course you decide to take, the rest of this chapter will not apply directly to you, because it's about preparing to present plans that need management approval. **You don't need anyone's okay to make these internal attitude changes—just do it!**

Small adjustments

Just in case you don't think making **small adjustments** can produce big results, listen to Gloria, who works at a large, New England office equipment company. She's the Assistant to the Sales Manager, though it's purely an administrative position. "I've always loved my job—except for one aspect that I dread every week," she admits. "I hate doing the spreadsheets and charts that track sales. I'm just not a visual person, and whenever I look at a graph of some kind, my brain goes numb and I don't see the errors. I also know that our head bookkeeper is going nuts trying to get the salespeople to be more timely in doing their invoices, so I hatched a plan to trade those two duties."

"Big doesn't necessarily mean better. Sunflowers aren't better than violets."
~Edna Ferber

The bookkeeper, who is of course good with numbers, didn't mind taking over the spreadsheets and charts in exchange for a promise from Gloria that the previous day's invoices would be on her desk when she arrived each day. To further facilitate her plan, Gloria got approval on a trial basis to change her hours, so she could work from noon to 8:30 p.m., which allowed her to be in the office when the salespeople returned from late calls. The sales force was thrilled that Gloria took over the invoicing, because they were sick of being hassled about it and could now spend more time selling. It also made all their lives easier that she was available to them when they were in the office, since communicating primarily by notes had led to many misunderstandings. Gloria also loved that she was trusted to work after hours on her own with minimal supervision.

In addition, the new schedule fit much better with Gloria's lifestyle. A single woman in her twenties, she enjoyed going out with her friends and having late nights. Now she could sleep in and still have time for errands and so on, before she had to be at work by noon. Being in the office after most people had gone home, meant she could be very productive, and it allowed her to deliver the day's invoices to the bookkeeper's desk—as promised—before she left. That in turn meant that the bookkeeper could prepare the sales reports when she got in at 8 a.m. and have them waiting on the owner's desk when he got in each day. This made them <u>all</u> extremely happy and ended all tension around the big issue of the sales reports.

In fact, the owner was so impressed by the new system (and the uptick in sales) that he challenged every department to look for small things to change. Before long, the entire company was functioning much better and became one of those places where people enjoy going to work. In fact, they made a friendly game out of it, with each department vying to make the most positive adjustments.

Phew! That's a lot of results from two people simply trading two tasks. I do believe it's the most cost-effective thing a business owner can do to improve team morale and productivity in the same fell swoop. I call it the **C.O.S.T.-effective system**:

"How wonderful it is that nobody need wait a single moment before starting to improve the world."
~Anne Frank

Change

One

Small

Thing

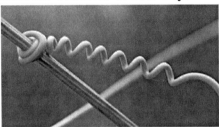

The cost: absolutely nothing! If more business owners empowered their teams to make adjustments to their jobs to reflect their strengths, instinctive work styles and experience, then I believe they'd see amazing results. **When team members are given some control over what they do, attitudes soar and turnover drops.** In fact, study after study reveals that lack of control is one of the greatest stressors on employees, so anything you can do to empower yourself will pay off in job satisfaction.

What one small thing could you change? How could you reinvent your job in a small way? If you work in a small office, and the first change(s) you want to make are minor, then you'll probably be able to implement them without going through most of the steps in the rest of this chapter. You may still want to write a **Job Action Memo** (Page 140) just to clarify your idea and to have something in writing to give your boss, but the detailed path outlined in this chapter will be much more than you need.

Moving sideways, for the right reasons

The third level of job shift is making a lateral move within the company, usually to a similar job in a different department. There is rarely much change in duties or in salary; this is mostly a change in context. Obviously, this solution only works at companies large enough to *have* various departments.

For many years, Erica had been working in the purchasing department of a large textile manufacturing company, and she realized she was just bored with her same old routine. "I jumped at an opening in the accounting department, where I could advance my bookkeeping skills," she explains. "I absolutely love what I call the Zen of numbers—knowing that the accounts I work on are always balanced gives me such a deep feeling of peace, that I can barely explain it. It makes me calm and happy to know everything is in order—and when it isn't, I also enjoy the detective work of figuring out why not. It was a simple move, but it radically changed how I feel about coming to work."

A lateral move may be all you need to revitalize interest in your job. **WARNING!** (Imagine a siren and flashing red lights right about now.) Be very afraid of the **Grass Is Greener Syndrome**, in which you want to move to another department because of personality conflicts within your current department. Sure, sometimes two or more people really are temperamentally ill-suited to work well together. It happens. In those cases, a lateral move may solve the problem. However, if you do make such a move and STILL have similar problems, you'll be forced to look at the one constant in the two situations: *you*. I love this saying:

Wherever you go, there you are.

In truth, almost all personality conflicts can be laid at the feet of *all* participants.

Journal exercise

What's my role in this conflict?

If you are, indeed, having trouble getting along with co-workers, take some time to deconstruct some of the conflicts. Ask, and honestly answer, these questions:

· Did I ever get along with this person? If so, when, and why did that change?

_____

_____

_____

_____

· What's the conflict really about? Did I innocently (or not) tread on someone else's territory? Have I been undermining a co-worker's confidence? Have I shirked tasks that I was supposed to do?

_____

_____

_____

_____

"The grass is not, in fact, always greener on the other side of the fence. Fences have nothing to do with it. The grass is greenest where it is watered. When crossing over fences, carry water with you and tend the grass wherever you may be."
~Robert Fulghum

· How have I made the situation worse? Did I fail to cooperate with this person? Did I complain to a supervisor or co-worker? Did I wrongly blame someone else for some mistake I made?

_____

_____

_____

_____

· Are there things I could do to resolve the conflict? Apologize? Change my attitude? Accept responsibility? Do some favor for the person I wronged or in some way make amends?

_____

_____

_____

_____

Of course it's possible that you're a saint and none of this applies to you. (If you really believe that's true, then you don't have to read any sarcasm in that comment.) It's possible that you just got stuck working with some people who themselves have poor attitudes. **What's important, is to be certain that you're seeking a lateral move for the right reasons.** If you determine that *you're* the one with the lousy attitude, then for suggestions on overcoming that bad habit, refer to Page 183 in the next chapter.

> Again, this type of change may not require detailed planning like the path outlined later in this chapter. I do urge you to at least write a Job Action Memo (Page 140) just to clarify your idea and to have something in writing to give to your human resources department.

JOB SHIFT
LEVEL
FOUR:

Seeking a promotion

After doing some hard work on the exercises in this book, it may dawn on you that your ideal job already exists within the company where you work—and all you need to get it is a promotion. However, there are so many variables about going after a promotion, that the topic is beyond the scope of this book. In my resource guide in the back, you'll find some specific books that might help you with this, especially if you haven't been up this ladder before. I will, though, offer a few insights to get you thinking.

First of all, you need to plan to **be ready for the promotion should the opportunity arise**. By studying people who already hold that position in your company and learning as much as you can about what they do, you can place yourself at the head of the line when that door opens. A big issue to confront now is: **Are you ready on every level for such a big change in your life?** Learning a new job and taking on more responsibilities is stressful, that's certain. Have you considered how that would affect your personal life? What if you're expected to work longer hours or travel? Are you in a good place emotionally to take this on? (For example, a new job is rarely a good rebound relationship, because you're actually still distracted by the breakup and possible reunion.)

"I will prepare and some day my chance will come."
~Abraham Lincoln

If you work at a large enough corporation where there are multiple positions you'd like to be promoted to, then by all means, let your human resources department know. Ask them what you could do to become qualified for any of those positions. Is there more training you could take? It's also fair to ask if they know of any upcoming openings at that level. Perhaps a new position is even being added that would fit your dream job vision.

If it's your supervisor's job you yearn for, the tricky part is not to come off like a jackal licking your chops in the woods waiting to pounce. (No offense to jackals.) If you have a friendly relationship with the person you want to replace, and you think you can broach the subject tactfully, then feel her out and see what her plans are. Maybe she's hoping for her own promotion, and would be happy to mentor you to take over her job someday. If that doesn't feel comfortable, then do what you can to prepare, and subtly let it be known to whomever would be doing the promoting, that you're interested. It's perfectly okay to tell management that you want to pursue a career at the company and that you aspire to make greater contributions. **Just don't be so eager that you appear to be trying to overtake your supervisor.**

> Seeking a promotion is actually a fabulous way to get your dream job. Rewards do accrue with seniority, as does self-esteem, when your efforts and growth are acknowledged in that manner. Therefore, I say go for it! Though you DO need to do some detailed planning, as outlined a bit later in this chapter. When you're discussing your ideal job with anyone in a position to help you, offering them something in writing helps them visualize your dream job and gives them something to keep as a reminder that there may be things they can do on your behalf.

JOB SHIFT
LEVEL
FIVE:

your
added
value is
the key to
success

Creating an all new and improved job

The last level of job shift is to completely reinvent your position and create a whole new job for yourself where you now work. Throughout the book, I've shared quite a few examples of this, but let me give you another dramatic one. Alanna had a very satisfying administrative job at a non-profit organization that worked to save endangered species. She took great pride in knowing she was making some small contribution for the good of the planet—but that was also her problem. Her contribution felt too small.

"After three years of working there, I saw so much more that could be done to save the animals, but we needed more money than the amount that was currently being generated by freelance fundraisers," Alanna confides. "I had picked up quite a bit of knowledge about the process, and I came to believe I could do a better job—and see that all the money raised actually went to the organization. I wrote up a detailed proposal for the executive director, in which I suggested major developments to our volunteer structure, identified our potential donor base, outlined three major events we could put on annually and generally promised to be responsible for tripling our income in the first year alone. I was able to make that promise, because I was aware of the high fees we'd been paying to outsource most of our fundraising. Mostly, by the way, because the director had no stomach for it."

The director jumped at the chance to look so good to her board of directors. In fact, after just a year of great success, Alanna was promoted to replace her boss, since the board correctly realized who deserved credit for the significant advances in fund raising.

Inventing a new job for yourself often means someone else has to be hired to take over your former duties. You might get lucky, and the company may already be in an expansion mode, and therefore, adding another staff person is already in the budget. Otherwise, **the key to success is convincing management that your new position will add value to the company**. This might occur in several ways. You might convince management that your new position will result in greatly enhanced customer service or more publicity for the business, or any number of other benefits that are less quantifiable. In most cases, you will need to demonstrate how your position will pay for itself, whether in increased sales, productivity, reduced man hours in another department or by some other measurable means. Also, you'll need to put something on paper—at the very least a memo, and at most, a full-blown proposal outlining your job description and exactly how you will generate the equivalent of your salary—or more—to cover the cost of creating your new position. (There's much more on how to do that later in this chapter.) In the example above, Alanna knew she could cover it, because moving the fundraising in-house automatically meant increased revenue for her organization.

Again, I don't tell you this to make it seem daunting, but rather to make you aware of what to expect. If this is the direction you choose to go, pay close attention to the section on enlisting support for your idea. I designed the detailed path in this chapter especially for you, so please give it careful study. You may be getting antsy by now, wanting to get on with enjoying your dream job, but if you can just hang in there through this chapter, you'll end up with a solid proposal you can present to your boss. (I'll explain the best way to do that in Chapter Six.)

I think understanding these five levels of job shifts will help give you clarity about your own dream job. Let's move from theory to practice and build your path.

Creating a P.A.T.H. to your garden
To get to your ideal job, you need a PATH:

Planned

Actions

Toward

Happiness

Your **P.A.T.H.** needs to be well thought out, be constructed of stepping stones that are action steps, bring you closer to your dream job (not off on tangents) and it needs to lead you to find more joy in your job. Of course, there are too many variables to account for, so take whichever steps fit your situation.

There are ten stepping stones for you to follow:

1. Outline your specific path to your ideal job.
2. Determine what will enable your plan.
3. Prepare for objections.
4. Enlist support.
5. Measure the added value of your plan.
6. Write a Job Action Memo.
7. Be accountable for achieving your plan.
8. Present your plan to management, be prepared to revise.
9. Implement your plan.
10. Gather feedback and measure your success.

"The secret of getting ahead is getting started."
~Sally Berger

We'll cover the first seven stepping stones in this chapter, and the rest in Chapter Six. **First let's do a quick review.** By this point, you have:

· assessed your readiness for change and decided to explore your possibilities.
· identified your values and seen how your purpose fits with your dream position
· developed a list of your unique abilities and discovered the importance of working with, not against, your instinctive problem solving style
· discovered the possibilities at your current job and completed the job possibility charts
· examined your limiting beliefs
· designed a dream position that's fulfilling and satisfying and takes advantage of your skills

Stepping Stone #1

Outline the route to your ideal job.

Do this on a computer so you can add to it as it evolves. List and organize everything you can think of that you'll need to do to land your dream job. Don't worry about the order of it at first, just start making a list, then rearrange it in some sort of chronological order. Once you have that, certain tasks will form natural groups, so you can move those to a section with that heading. Please don't make this harder than it may sound. If the word "outline" makes you shudder and think of term papers on Middle English Literature, try calling it a To Do List instead. **Your natural groupings of tasks may include (but not be limited to):**

· **Research:** What new things would you need to know to perform your job? How much do people in comparable jobs earn? What other duties could you offer to take on that might be currently outsourced?

· **Supporters:** Who can help you with your plan? Do you need a mentor?

· **Skills:** What training do you need to prepare for the job? How will you get it? Can you read a book, take an online course? What about financing your dream—do you need to apply for a student loan? Empty your basement on eBay?

· **Testing:** Are there ways to test your ideas? Could you suggest a trial period? If it's complex, what about implementing your plan in stages?

Stepping Stone #2

What will enable your plan?

Items on this list are basically the opposite of obstacles, because they move your dream closer to actuality. In general, they make your life easier as well as make it easier to convince management your plan has merit. Here are some examples:

· Getting your supervisor to coach you in preparation for your new role

· Receiving a scholarship from a professional women's group to pursue night classes

· Securing a mentor to advise you on navigating company politics

· Devising cost-cutting measures, which in turn will fund your idea

- Finding better daycare arrangements to accommodate a different schedule
- Connecting with people in the larger business community who may be able to provide needed resources

For example, Rory works as an administrative assistant to the owner of a mortgage brokerage in Washington state. Because of what she learned working there, she was able to buy her first home. However, in her semi-rural area, real estate prices have soared crazily in the last few years, leaving many people on the sidelines believing they no longer qualify as home buyers. Rory knew this, because many of her friends were floundering in that boat, so she came up with a plan to offer free classes in home buying along with a free evaluation of financial readiness. Her theory was that if people liked her classes, they would naturally be inclined to apply for loans through her company, which specialized in helping people with less than stellar credit obtain mortgages.

"My boss loved the idea, so I immediately set out to make all the arrangements," Rory explains. "Through my contacts at the chamber of commerce, I was able to secure a good location for the classes, and a friend who's a teacher agreed to coach me on my course outline and presentation. Another friend helped me design flyers for the class. Word began to spread about the classes, and we had people calling to register before we even announced them."

This is a great example of how you might network to put the pieces of your plan in place. Rory had never designed a flyer, but she had a friend who knew how. Nor had she ever taught a class, but she knew someone who taught for a living. **Instead of seeing obstacles, Rory figured out what she needed to make happen to enable her dream. What things would enable yours?**

imagine
what you
could do
if you
saw no
obstacles

_____

_____

_____

_____

_____

_____

Stepping Stone #3

Prepare for objections.

By objections, I don't mean the obstacles that you may see between you and your ideal position. We'll do a thorough job of uprooting those in the next chapter. Objections are reasons your boss may give for not wanting to okay your plan. They are points of resistance where your plan may stall—unless you're prepared in advance to counter them.

The more you can think like your boss and predict what he wants or needs, the more receptive he's likely to be.

I know, I'm asking you to be a mind reader and figure out what your boss will say to your grand plan. You probably already do this instinctively all the time. If you're conscientious about pleasing your supervisor, you've already got a handle on what he or she is likely to prefer on most topics. Here's a chance to use that knowledge to further your goal of getting a green light. If you have trusted co-workers you can share your plan with, they are likely to have ideas about this, too.

Carmen works as a stylist at a fairly new Chicago salon and had an ambitious idea to revamp the whole place and set their business apart from their well-established competitors. "I knew I was suggesting some expensive changes, but I also believed it would work," she explains. "I wanted to cater to busy businesswomen who never seemed to find time to pamper themselves. I figured if we added enough business services, they could multi-task and wouldn't feel like they were missing much time at work. When I first laid out my plan to my boss, she just about choked on her laughter," she recalls.

Carmen's plan was to provide wireless Internet service, flat screen TVs tuned to business news, meal delivery, business magazines and newspapers, foot and shoulder massages while customers had their nails done, and so on. In short, the star treatment for high-powered executives. It's no surprise that Carmen's boss felt

"Imaginary obstacles are insurmountable. Real ones aren't. But you can't tell the difference when you have no real information."
~Barbara Sher

overwhelmed. "Every time she objected to one of my ideas, I had four answers ready, and eventually I convinced her it was doable. Now we're very trendy and on all the hot lists. I'd like to tell you who comes in, but I can't. Let's just say I've worked on some famous heads."

To boss-proof your plan, check it against these criteria:
· How much extra work will your plan create for your boss?
· How much extra work will this create for other team members?
· What will be the effect on productivity?
· What's this going to cost to implement?
· What other resources will be required to do this?
· How will your boss be assured you're qualified to hold this position?
· Realistically, how likely to succeed is your plan?
· What are your backup plans if this one fails?

Of course, there are many more potential objections, but **the big ones will always be: time, money, effort and likelihood of success.** In the space below, write each possible objection you could meet, then write your solution for each one. By being prepared in this way, you'll impress your boss with your foresight and planning, and you'll greatly increase your chance of achieving the go ahead.

Objection _____

Solution _____

_____

_____

_____

Objection _____

Solution _____

_____

_____

_____

Objection _____

_____

Solution _____

_____

_____

_____

Objection _____

_____

Solution _____

_____

_____

_____

Stepping Stone #4

Enlist support.

In order to make meaningful changes in your position, you will need to inspire co-workers and management to share your vision of your ideal job. If you're working through this process as a team at your company, then this will all be much easier, because everyone will have a similar motivation to improve their own jobs and cooperate with one another. If you're a lone wolf reading this book on your own, you'll need to proceed cautiously as you gather support for your dream. As I mentioned before, it may help to get at least one other co-worker to go through the process at the same time. That way you can help each other, and in presenting _two_ new, good ideas to management, you may reinforce one another. Then again, it could backfire and overwhelm your manager who only wants to deal with one unhappy worker at a time.

Did you catch that? I purposely cast you as an unhappy worker, because if you aren't careful, that's the first—and possibly the last—thing your boss will think about you and your plan. **It's critical that you present your idea as coming from someone who wants to make a larger contribution to the company—not as someone who is complaining about her job and wants her boss to fix things.** Let me say it another way: **your goal is to solve**

problems for your boss and the company—not bring him new problems to solve. This is where having team members review your concept and presentation would be invaluable.

What kind of support do you need? The more the merrier, but you could probably use help from all of these types:

Team members: your peers, especially those affected by your idea

A role model: someone who holds a similar position, either within your company or elsewhere

A mentor: someone inside or outside your company who can lend perspective and wise counsel

Resourceful people: friends or acquaintances outside your company with connections to resources that will advance your dream

Key allies: influential people in your company not on your immediate team

support comes in many different forms

"Never doubt that a small group of thoughtful, committed citizens can change the world. Indeed, it is the only thing that ever has." ~Margaret Mead

Let's start with your team members. In order for them to support your ideal job plan, it must also be good for them. As you undoubtedly know, there are oodles of books out there on teamwork, and you've probably seen at least one at some point in your career, so I won't write a whole chapter on this. (I could though, so don't get me started!) I do, however, want to make some key points about working with your team as it relates to creating your ideal job. If you have a history of difficulties in this area, then I encourage you to crack open one of those team spirit books.

When you envision your dream job where you now work, you have to evaluate the impact on your associates. No one wants to be left behind doing all the busy work, getting stuck with the thankless tasks you dumped in a pile. Are you going to suggest that your boss simply hire a new person to do your old job? Is there someone on your team who wants the position? If so, who would replace them, and so on? Maybe you envision a whole restructuring of your department? That would really need to be team effort. A good way to figure that out, would be to **list all your current duties that you no longer foresee doing and then state who will take them over.**

Duty:_____

Who would become responsible:_____

Duty:_____

Who would become responsible:_____

Duty:_____

Who would become responsible:_____

Duty:_____

Who would become responsible:_____

Of course, the best way to enlist the support of your team, is to also give support to *their* dream job plans. Perhaps you can make some adjustments to your job description to help someone else out. It's all about playing to your individual strengths. If you did your Kolbe A Index, you may have discovered you have an unbalanced

What wins
for your
team
could you
build into
your plan?

team—for example, too many Quick Starts and not enough Fact Finders or Implementors to get anything done effectively. If that's the case, a reasonable approach to your boss would be to point that out, and suggest that he hire as your replacement, someone who fulfills that missing skill set on your team. A team that is comprised of all the appropriate index types is a beautiful thing and will accomplish so much more than a team where people are forced to adjust to tasks they are not well-suited to do. Who wants to be a square peg in the proverbial round hole? Oh the splinters and the chafing!

Unfortunately, there are usually some sticks in the muddy waters at most companies who don't see the value of growth and change and who resist any attempt to be helped out of their own quagmire. They're the people who never have anything good to say about anyone. They probably shouldn't have been hired in the first place, but there's really not much you can do about them. Just be aware if you have such people on your team, and don't allow them to undermine your enthusiasm or commitment to your dream.

One other potential—and not uncommon—challenge in enlisting support from your associates occurs when you are something of a rising star in your firm, and your team finds it difficult to suppress their envy (or worse). If this sounds at all like you, then take some extra time to encourage your co-workers in their own pursuit of better jobs. Downplay your own excitement in front of them. What wins for your team could you build into your plan? Find ways to be sensitive to those you may be leaving behind. Even if you're moving on to another team or department, you never know when a former team member will reappear in your experience, so play nicely.

Next on your list of supporters might be a role model. I suggest looking for someone who has successfully navigated this route before, either within your company or elsewhere. Start networking and ask friends if they know of anyone who has created her own new job where she already worked. If there is someone else in your firm you can trust who is higher up the food chain than you are, you might consider confiding your dream to him or her and ask for guidance.

Then you might seek a mentor. Time and again, successful

"As we let our own light shine, we unconsciously give other people permission to do the same."
~Marianne Williamson

women in business reveal that having a mentor made all the difference. Often, what you see, you imitate, and what you imitate, you become. The higher your aspirations are, the more you'll benefit from knowing someone who's been there and done that. A good mentor can teach you how to land an assignment you want, what to do when you meet bias, or how to get people who can help you on your side. She could also show you how to build your professional credibility and take charge of how you're perceived. Some professional organizations have formal mentoring programs, so be sure to research that. If your city is large enough, you may even find groups especially for women, such as the Soroptimists. A mentor doesn't have to be a woman, but in either case, **beware of situations with an implicit expectation that you'll do something in return for someone else's help**. A true mentoring situation is without strings, and the only expectation is that one day you'll offer similar guidance to someone else.

Next, be aware of key allies in your firm. Don't be afraid to approach people in the organization who have considerable influence. They may seem like gatekeepers to some, but you can reach out to them and build productive relationships. They're not always managers. They might work in a different department. Never forget that management *wants* you to succeed. Developing these relationships will take time, so if you're in it for the long haul, don't overlook this category of support. It may be years before you can call on it, but it's invaluable to have. **In the space below, list the most important relationships you have at your company**. Below each name, describe why they're important, and then how you might nurture the relationship.

Ally_____

Important because_____

_____

I can nurture this friendship by _____

_____

_____

_____

_____

"The way is long, let us go together. The way is difficult, let us help each other. The way is joyful, let us share it. The way is ours alone, let us go in love.
~Joyce Hunter

Ally _____

Important because _____

_____

I can nurture this friendship by _____

_____

_____

_____

Ally _____

Important because _____

_____

I can nurture this friendship by _____

_____

_____

_____

Ally _____

Important because _____

_____

I can nurture this friendship by _____

_____

_____

_____

Finally, look for people you know who can help in other ways—or who _know_ people who can help. It's networking, plain and simple. I realize that the busy moms among my readers may balk at this suggestion. _How am I supposed to fit this into commuting, grocery shopping, skating practice carpool , piano lessons, homework supervision, cooking, laundry and all the things I'm too tired to remember?_ When you put it like that, maybe you can't. It depends on the scope of your dream and how much help you perceive you may need. If your ideal job seems attainable without a lot of help beyond your immediate co-workers, then hooray for you.

"It's your belief in your dream and in yourself, that will allow you to see possibilities and attract the resources that can help you. Find a way to believe in your dream."
~Marcia Wieder

However, if you really want to reinvent your company wheels and promote a sweeping change, then don't overlook the value of outside help—especially if your idea involves community interaction. Also, in my humble experience, busy moms are often the ones who benefit most from making new professional connections, because it can give them a sense of belonging to something other than a carpool. (Not that I'm anti-carpool!) Networking may unite you with other working moms who find ways to support one another. I would never underestimate the power of a woman with a cell phone and a wi-fi connection.

It's really quite amazing who your friends and family members know that you didn't realize they knew—until you ask. I've been amazed myself at how many wonderful contacts I've made just by mentioning to friends that I was writing this book. Don't be afraid to share your enthusiasm for your dream with others—it's contagious! Tell everybody you know and everyone you meet exactly what your dream is, and then be open to things happening almost magically.

I don't want to go all woo-woo on you, but there's a **law of attraction** that states: If you focus on the outcome of your dream in a

positive way (as opposed to worrying that it *won't* come true) you will draw to you people and opportunities that will help bring your dream to life. Try to get really excited about creating your perfect job—enthusiasm is catching. I've seen this over and over in my own life and in the lives of loved ones. A woman tells a friend she wants to become an advertising executive, and her friend has a college roommate who does exactly that. Another woman confides to her sister that she'd like to move into hospital administration, and her sister's mother-in-law works in that field. When you pursue those "coincidental" contacts, they lead to many more, and so on, until you're surrounded by people who have expertise in the area that attracts you.

Guess what happens if you don't share your vision with anyone? Nothing happens.

How can you expect people you don't know to help you, if you don't at least ask the people you **do** know?

If your dream is really huge, a dream with greater good for others infused into it, a dream that captures the imagination of others and inspires them intellectually and emotionally, then it's just a numbers game. The more people you tell, the greater the odds that others will buy into your vision and want to be part of it. **Never let the size of your dream stop you from pursuing it.**

In the space below, note what you need help with and who you will ask. (Notice I didn't say *could* ask or *might* ask or *can* ask—this is something you *must* do!)

_____

_____

_____

_____

_____

_____

_____

Stepping Stone #5

Measure the added value of your plan.

This could actually be the key to the whole thing, because if you pile on enough added value to your job proposition—indeed make it irresistible—then why wouldn't your boss approve it? So what exactly is added value? I thought you'd never ask. Admittedly, as a boss, I get really excited by this subject. I can't tell you how much it warms my heart when someone in my office has a great idea that would add value to our company, but I'll try. It's like getting an unexpected gift just because it's Tuesday. It's like finding out someone else cares enough to make an extra effort or when your son cleans his room without being nagged. (I guess that would be more in the miracle category.) It's like stumbling into your own surprise party wearing something nicer than ripped jeans and an old tee shirt. Here are some business world examples of adding value to a job:

· Your team doesn't have a resident techie, and you anticipate that your company will need to upgrade all office computers to Windows Vista, so you install it on your home computer first and perhaps do some online tutorials. Then, when the time comes, you're already an expert and can facilitate the transition with a minimum of distress.

make your plan irresistible

· You know your boss is struggling to raise productivity in the manufacturing sector of the company, so you volunteer to start and manage a program of rewarding employee ideas for innovation. This leads to all sorts of improvements in productivity, but even more important, it involves associates in creating their own job realities and demonstrates that their input is valued.

· You notice certain supplies are being wasted and you figure out how to be a better steward of raw materials.

· You institute a program of in-house cross-training so your team can better adapt to absences, maternity leaves, vacations and so on—all in the name of providing better customer service.

· You observe that customer refunds are bogging down in several places and find ways to speed up the process and enhance customer satisfaction. You follow this up with a study of all returns in the past year and identify *why* people are returning your products, which leads to new ideas to reduce returns.

· You suggest surveying your clients to find out how *they* think your company could better serve them, and you brainstorm with your team several ways to implement the best suggestions.

I could go on forever on this topic, but I think you've got the drift by now. It's really about just taking a step beyond your own pre-defined role in the company and seeing what else you might be able to do. It's doing the unexpected. It's having a larger vision. It's asking what you'd do if this was *your* company. **By the way, learning how to present new ideas from a larger perspective than just what's in it for you, is a very valuable and portable skill well worth mastering.** In the space below, I'd like you to **list some ways your ideal job could bring added value to your company.**

_____

_____

_____

_____

_____

_____

Stepping Stone #6

> "Failing to plan is planning to fail."
> ~Effie Jones

Write a Job Action Memo

I hope by now you're excited about your possibilities for a new position where you work. Results don't come from being excited or even motivated. Results in life come from taking action. **Just make sure that when you set a goal, it's S.M.A.R.T.:**

Specific

Measurable

Action-oriented

Realistic

Time-Focused

For example, Nadia works as an all-purpose administrative assistant at a printing company in St. Louis, and she's hoping to shift her job completely by creating a whole new position. Here's how her dream job description reads with all the **S.M.A.R.T.** criteria applied:

·   I want to create a job as the assistant to the sales manager, where I will be trained to become a part-time salesperson. I see my job as her assistant taking about half my time and the other half being

"All the flowers of all the tomorrows are in the seeds of today."
~Nancy Castleman

devoted to sales. I would like to have my own area to develop. I suggest targeting horse breeders, since no one is doing that yet. They actually have needs for high-end printing, and I have some contacts I can pursue. I want to begin this job within two months. I'm willing to study sales courses and other materials on my own time, and would like to be able to start making sales calls within two months after I start.

That's specific and realistic. It also shows that Nadia knows something about the sales department, because she's already picked a new territory she'd like to pursue. She has also stated some action steps she's willing to do on her own, and now has a timeline to begin her training and one to start actual sales calls. With all that clear in her mind, Nadia is ready to fill out the following form.

Job Action Memo

Use this memo to refine your vision and as a template for one you'll create and present to management. Just telling someone your idea gets the least results. Giving someone an idea in writing increases your results. Explaining your plan while your boss also has a copy in his hand is even better. Adding visual components (charts, maps, etc.) if your plan is complex, will enhance your chance of success even further.

With the above example from Nadia in mind, the first step is to summarize your ideal job here. (Refer back to your Dream Job Declaration on Page 108.)

Job redefinition _____

_____

_____

_____

_____

_____

Does it meet all five **S.M.A.R.T.** criteria? Good. Now fill in your date of significance, the no-matter-what date you will start your wonderful new job.

Target date to begin my ideal job _____

Write below a thorough description of all the main problems your plan will solve. For example, the problem solved is not: *I'm bored and need a new challenge*, but rather: *My unique skills are under utilized and you could be getting more for your money if they were put to good use.*

Problems that my plan solves_____

_____

_____

_____

_____

_____

_____

Next, write out all the added value your plan brings to the company, keeping in mind that this (and the cost analysis) will be what is likely to be most important to your boss.

Added value to the company _____

_____

_____

_____

_____

_____

_____

"What we must decide is perhaps how we are valuable, rather than how valuable we are."
~Edgar Z Friedenberg

Note below who else would be affected by your getting this job and how.

Who else is affected_____

_____

_____

How my team is affected_____

_____

_____

_____

What will be required of them_____

_____

_____

_____

Who has agreed to be part of this plan_____

_____

_____

_____

Add below what you need in order to accomplish your plan: equipment, software, training, space, more team members, etc.

What is needed to implement this plan_____

_____

_____

_____

_____

_____

_____

Be sure to answer this all-important question:

How long before my plan is profitable?_____

Next, detail all the relevant skills you plan to bring to this new job. Don't assume your supervisor knows all your abilities. Attach and refer to your resume, if appropriate.

Skills I bring to the job_____

_____

_____

_____

_____

_____

_____

_____

_____

Write below how you expect to grow as a team member if you are able to move into this new position. For example, *I expect to develop further abilities to mediate conflicts and grow as a negotiator.* Or *I expect to enhance my supervisory skills and ability to delegate appropriately to my associates.*

How I expect to grow in value as a team member_____

_____

_____

_____

_____

_____

_____

Note any other items in these categories.

Additional positive impacts and benefits to the company_____

_____

_____

_____

_____

_____

_____

> "You can't just sit there and wait for people to give you that golden dream, you got to get out there and make it happen for yourself."
> ~Diana Ross

Things that will be easier or better because of this plan_____

_____

_____

_____

_____

_____

_____

Show some foresight, and acknowledge potential problems in implementing your plan, as well as ideas for handling them.

Potential problems_____

_____

_____

_____

_____

_____

_____

Possible solutions_____

_____

_____

_____

_____

_____

_____

I'd like you to answer the question: Why do you want this job change? Refer back to the **Possibility Charts** you filled out beginning on Page 100. Find the chart that corresponds to your dream job outlined above, or if your vision has changed since then, do a Possibility Chart for your revised dream now. Then transfer your desired results to the space below, adding in any other features you now envision.

My desired results from my new job are _____

_____

_____

_____

_____

_____

_____

Note any changes in structure you might want, such as different hours, a new schedule, flex time or working from home.

Suggested new schedule_____

_____

_____

_____

_____

Be prepared to say what change, if any, you expect in compensation. Consider both salary and benefits.

What I would like in compensation for this new position_____

_____

_____

Finally, answer this question: What exactly does management have to agree to for you to move ahead with your plan?

Approval that I seek_____

_____

_____

_____

_____

_____

_____

> "I change myself, I change the world." ~Gloria A. Anzaldua

As an example, I'll continue with Nadia's dream of shifting to a sales/administrative hybrid position and show you how she filled out the Job Action Memo. The **problem that her plan solved** was: Audrey, the sales manager, has expressed feeling overwhelmed by administrative duties, and I know I can relieve her of those, thereby freeing her to do more actual sales. I also believe there is an opportunity for increased sales by expanding the sales force, at least with a half-time position, and I would like to move into that.

For **added value**, she wrote: I already have special knowledge of an underserved potential customer base and contacts in that industry.

In the category of **who is affected**, since Nadia's current job was an entry-level position, she suggested: The company will need to hire a replacement for me, but I promise to train her well, so there will be no service gap.

Under **what is needed,** Nadia wrote: I would like Audrey to train me in sales, but I am also eager to do a lot of studying on my own at home. As to **profitability timeline**: I expect that within three months of beginning to make sales calls, I'll be able to bring in enough income to offset my salary.

For her **skills** section, she wrote: All the skills I've developed in my current position are transferable to this new job, including: computer expertise in Excel and Word; phone handling and customer service; report generating; organizational abilities and knack for creating smooth-flowing systems; tact in dealing with difficult people (who shall be nameless, though certainly known to all).

Her expected **growth in value** was: As an added member of the sales team, I expect to substantially increase my value to the company. Whenever another sales person is out on vacation or sick leave, I could hop in and service their accounts. I also expect to add new administrative skills working specifically for the sales manager.

What problem does your plan solve?

What would be **easier** because of this plan: I foresee lightening the load of the sales manager by relieving her of mundane chores so she can concentrate entirely on sales, which should add to the bottom line. The same goes for the other salespeople. That, combined with the added revenue I can bring in, ought to generate more operating capital for the company.

Under **potential problems/solutions** Nadia noted: Although I have no sales experience, I am motivated to learn and I'm a quick study. I have no fear of making cold sales calls, in fact, I believe I would thrive doing just that.

Her **desired results** from her new job were: I want to feel more challenged, try something new, spend part of my time outside the office and have more variety in my work day.

For her **new schedule**, Nadia suggested: Subject to discussion with Audrey, I would propose doing my administrative duties in the mornings and making calls in the afternoons. This would make a clear distinction and prevent the administrative portion from creeping up and overtaking my time for sales calls.

As to **compensation**: I would not ask for a raise.In fact, to offset the cost of implementing my plan, I would be willing to take a pay reduction during the two months of my training. I would expect the standard sales commissions on any sales I make.

The **approval** she sought was: If you find this proposition agreeable, I would like permission to begin discussion with Audrey immediately, as well as permission to write up and place a help wanted ad for my current position. Upon the hiring of my

> "Are you more committed to your dream or your reality? The evidence lies in whether you are in action on your dream."
> ~Marcia Wieder

replacement, I would begin simultaneously training her and transitioning into my new job.

I hope all you Quick Starts can appreciate the positive impact such a thorough, well-reasoned memo might have on your boss, and how many good qualities it would demonstrate about you for having done it. I know it may seem like an overly complete document, so don't hesitate to adjust it to fit your situation. Don't overlook the value of writing this memo for your own clarity and as preparation for your actual discussion with management.

Just a reminder—we'll walk along the last three stepping stones on your **P.A.T.H.** to your dream job in Chapter Six—but first, I have a few more points to make. Only a few, really.

Put negativity in its place

Writing your Job Action Memo may well have stirred up some obstacles to your plan. Though we'll tackle them in the next chapter, note here any specific roadblocks you believe may stand between you and your dream job. Just putting them on paper and knowing you'll get to pounce on them in just a bit can help reduce anxiety.

_____

_____

_____

_____

_____

Also, do you notice any limiting beliefs rearing their ugly heads? You remember, those are the critical voices that try and derail your dreams, over and over. Look back at what beliefs you wrote down on Page 93 and see if any of them are active, now that you're working on manifesting a specific dream. Note any current limiting beliefs here.

_____

_____

_____

_____

"Aero-dynamically, the bumblebee shouldn't be able to fly, but the bumblebee doesn't know that, so it goes on flying anyway."
~Mary Kay Ash

_____

_____

Now, write down what you are going to do to counter those limiting ideas.

_____

_____

_____

_____

_____

Finally, to ensure you don't allow negative thoughts to hold you back, **write your first action step and take it.**

_____

_____

_____

_____

_____

Nadia identified three **possible obstacles**:

1. Audrey, the sales manager, may not believe I can do sales, and she may need proof of my ability.
2. My boss may not want me to leave my current role as a general administrative assistant, so he may nix the whole idea.
3. I'm not sure I will be good at sales, since I've never done it—though the idea of it doesn't scare me, I just don't know what to expect. My confidence is shaky.

Nadia's strategies for **overcoming** these potential problems were:

1. I could read some books and/or take a class BEFORE I approach management about my idea, which might convince them I'm serious. Audrey ought to respond well to my offering to help the salespeople with administrative needs half-time.
2. I can show my boss how adding a half-time salesperson will pay for the other half of my job, as assistant to the sales manager. I

know the sales department needs help, because they're always behind in their reports and other paperwork, so creating a new position for me will also make the salespeople more productive.

3. I can practice my sales pitch on my friends who also happen to be real prospects. I can rely on them for honest and constructive feedback, which should boost my confidence.

Under **limiting beliefs**, this is what Nadia wrote: The voice I hear in my head tells me I'm not ambitious enough to be the kind of self-starter a salesperson needs to be. I also doubt whether I can enlist enough support. To **counter that idea**, she wrote: I may have lacked ambition when I was just out of school and quite insecure, but now that I'm nearly 30, I feel ready to push myself a bit more. I want to increase my income so I can buy a house, and I realize I need to move beyond simple, safe jobs in order to afford that. For my helpers, I will enlist these colleagues:

1. I'll ask Irina, a friend who's in sales, for advice on getting off to a good start. Since we aren't in the same field, I think she'll be willing to help me.

2. I'll ask Dorothy in accounting, who I know is pals with Audrey, for advice on how to create a job proposal that will appeal to Audrey. I'll find out what she values most, what problems she needs solved and what work habits matter most to her.

Finally, Nadia answered the last question: My **first action step** toward my dream job is: I will call Irina tonight and make a lunch date for this week. While I have her on the phone, I'll ask if she can recommend a book on sales. I'll also look on Amazon.com for books and order at least one tonight.

> **"Coming together is a beginning. Keeping together is progress. Working together is success."**
> **~Anonymous**

Nadia did, indeed, take her first steps. "I really liked having a template for figuring out how to proceed in a logical manner. Besides, it got me started in the right direction," she recalls. No surprise, Nadia got her dream job and is now having a ball visiting horse breeders and selling them expensive printing for catalogues and show programs.

As you move through this process, I'd like you to consider this—**most people accept the limits of their dreams to be real and finite.**

But a few open-minded people
allow room for
expansion.

Which group are you in?

Congratulations—as soon as you take the first step you noted above, you will have planted the first seed in your garden of possibilities. Of course, there are many more to be planted, and we'll get to those soon.

Stepping Stone #7

Be accountable for achieving your plan.

Have you ever hatched a good idea, kept it a secret, then never followed through with it? I think we all have. What can make a big difference—especially for those of you who prefer to fly solo—is sharing your ideas with at least one otherperson who will hold you accountable for taking action on it. Ideally, in a team situation, you'll hold each other accountable for your individual goals. I encourage you to make this an important part of your dream job planning. Really stay on one another—nudge, nag, encourage—whatever it takes to keep the fire lit within. No matter how grand your intentions, it's easy to lose sight of them when life gets messy, as it has a way of doing. Have regular check-ins with one another. Send reminder memos. Put sticky notes on your team's monitors. Adopt some silly item as a mascot and pass the bulldog statue or whatever you choose from person to person as a symbol of your determination. Keep it fun, but keep going. If you don't, **the dream you lose could be your own.**

Journal exercise

How does your garden grow?

This is a good point to discuss how you'll mark your steps toward your dream job. Instead of comparing yourself to some impossible standard of perfection (or to someone else's idea of accomplishment), give some thought to creating a new way of evaluating your progress. Ask yourself these questions:

· How will I know when I'm making progress toward my goal?

_____

_____

_____

_____

_____

_____

· What signs could I be looking for?

_____

_____

_____

_____

_____

· Can I expect others to acknowledge my progress? If so, who?

_____

_____

_____

_____

_____

· Can I ask someone for feedback along the way? Who?

_____

_____

_____

_____

· What rewards can I plan into my process so I get some satisfaction as I go? What kinds of rewards would enhance my values and make me even happier in my job?

_____

_____

_____

_____

_____

_____

_____

· Can I commit to reviewing my progress with myself, weekly or at least monthly?

_____

_____

_____

_____

_____

_____

Checking in with yourself is essential to keeping your dream alive and staying on track to reach it. Course corrections are easy if you've only veered off for a few days.

Keep your dream in sight

This is a critical moment in the course of manifesting your ideal job. You have clarity on what you want and you have your plan to get it. But for the action-impaired among my readers, whatever you do, don't stop now! In Chapter Six I'll guide you by the hand and show you how to approach your boss with your ideas. Just don't descend into fear in the meantime. One thing that will help with that, is keeping visual reminders of your dream all around you. If you never made or purchased something in that regard, take another look at Page 109.

"You really can change the world if you care enough."
~Marian Wright Edelman

I also suggest you set aside five minutes every morning (on your way to work is a good time) and every night before you fall asleep to visualize yourself enjoying and thriving in your perfect job. This is a proven technique for everything from winning tennis tournaments to destroying cancer cells, so please don't dismiss it as some new age nonsense. Countless studies have been done with MRIs of the specific regions of the brain that control different thought and motor functions, which prove that visualizing an apple has the same effect on the brain as seeing a real apple. Since your brain can't distinguish between your dreams and reality, to your brain, your dream already exists. This is a powerful tool to keep your plan for your ideal job fresh and vibrant.

Keeping your dream alive in your heart and soul and mind makes it impossible to forget.

Applause, applause!

Imagine confetti falling (and someone else cleaning it up)

Now it's time to encourage you to reward yourself for making it halfway through the book. Good for you! **Do you know how rare you are to have this much sticktoitiveness?** (Yes, that's really a word—it's in the dictionary and everything.) Since you're now all ready to present your idea to management, for this bouquet why not consider some pampering? If it's going to be a big whoopdedo, perhaps you want to buy a new outfit to wear when you present your plan. Maybe you'd like a trip to the salon or spa. Of course if it was me, I'd buy a new putter, but that's just me. That's the cool thing about these rewards—they're all about you, and only you get to decide what will make you feel nurtured.

When you're finished with that, come along to the next chapter, where together we'll rid your garden of all those nasty weeds and pests that seem determined to destroy your dream before it ever has a chance to take root.

I'll bring the weed whacker!

"A weed is no more
than a flower in
disguise."
~ James Russell Lowell

Chapter Five
ELIMINATING WEEDS, PESTS AND OTHER OBSTACLES

Chapter Five At A Glance

- Don't give up along your way
- Do you know where your obstacles are?
- What's your excuse?
- What do you need help with?
- Learn to say no to naysayers
- Who's got time? You've got time.
- Assessing your messes
- How to survive being overwhelmed and confused
- Low self-esteem is the crabgrass of your life
- Don't let fear choke the life out of your dreams
- Transforming bad attitudes, even yours
- More garden pests that want to destroy your dreams
- What else is bugging you?

You know how you're at the mall, and you can't find the last store you want to go to, so you hunt down the giant map and locate the big red dot labeled: YOU ARE HERE? (Not that I, being a guy person, would ever consult a map!) Anyway, you read through the long list of stores, find the code number for the place you want to go, then peruse the map until you find Yellow Store Number F-19. Of course it's as far away as it could be. And your feet hurt. And your three-year-old is fussy because the stroller is full of packages. And you can see by the map that you'll have to pass through the food court to get to the store, and you know that will trigger demands for ice cream from your toddler. (Or maybe your own resolve will weaken as you pass Mrs. Fields.) And then you look at your watch and wonder if you even have time to make it to Yellow Store Number F-19 and still get home in time to fix dinner. Then you talk yourself out of going there, because, hey—they probably won't have anything you'd like, anyway. You release a long sigh, feel your shoulders droop in disappointment, turn around and head for home, while another attempt at doing something nice for yourself dissolves in defeat.

That's exactly what countless women do every year with their precious dreams. Their well-thought-out visions of a better life. Their carefully designed ideal jobs. Their lovingly planted gardens of possibilities. They just let them succumb to crabgrass invasions, to fungus and other plant diseases, because they can't see how to rid their gardens of all the obstacles they see in their way. The woman at the mall even had a map—she knew the route from the big red dot to Yellow Store Number F-19, but she still didn't get there. Because I don't want that to happen to you, this chapter is all about **overcoming the different things that block your dreams** as preparation for the next step in the process—which is implementing your ideal job.

Are you on your way, or are you sidetracked?

Later, we'll delve more deeply into your own perceived obstacles, but first let me share with you the ones I see most often and offer some advice on dealing with them. Hey, I'm no therapist, but I do have nearly 30 years experience being the boss, listening to and solving people's problems, so sometimes I do feel like one. Besides,

"Never fear the space between your reality and your dreams. If you can dream it, you can make it so."
~Belva Davis

in presenting my workshops around the country, I've witnessed all sorts of behavior and heard thousands of reasons why people don't think they can achieve their goals. I haven't met an excuse yet that stands up to real scrutiny. That's right. A reason is just an excuse in a nicer dress. An excuse is just a rationalization you tell yourself to keep from making an effort, from taking a chance on yourself, from stepping outside what's safe and familiar.

If you have excuses, you're resisting your bright future.
If you have solutions, you're on your way there.

To be fair, many of these common obstacles come in various colors, patterns and depths. Some of them can be severe enough to warrant professional counseling, or at the least, reading a book totally devoted to dismissing your troubling obstacle. As you work through this chapter, if one challenge sticks out and jumps up and down to get your attention while sirens go off in your head, then don't just rely on my advice to tame it.

I believe all obstacles can be divided into three groups:

1. Obstacles that are **external.** These are always about practicalities and therefore fairly easily solved. These include issues around education, hardware and software as well as gathering support.

2. Obstacles that involve your **reaction to situations.** These are more challenging, because often you can't control the cause—but you can control your response. These include feelings of overwhelm and confusion, being crunched for time and dealing with negative influences.

3. Obstacles that are **internal.** These are by far the toughest to manage, because they are the most invasive and deeply rooted. The good news is, their source is also their solution—what you created, you also control.

GROUP ONE:

EXTERNAL OBSTACLES

Let's start with the easy ones. Here are some examples, along with some solutions.

Lack proper skills. Let's say you've decided your ideal job is creating your company's newsletter, updating the company website and other tasks all involving software programs for which you don't yet have the skills. Many businesses offer in-house training or will pay—or least contribute to—outside classes to develop your job skills. You don't have time for classes? Most software can be learned at your own pace in online, self-directed study programs. Those are great because they eliminate fears of doing poorly, appearing stupid or asking so-called dumb questions. Check with your community college, as those classes are often real bargains. Perhaps you work for a small business and no one's ever asked for training before. There's no reason why you can't be the first to ask—and receive it. Don't let lack of precedent hold you back. Somebody somewhere knows what you need to learn and is willing to teach it to you.

Lack of materials. Maybe you need a laptop to be able to work while you're on the move, or a new software program. Instead of seeing this as an obstacle, see it as something to include in your Job Action Memo (Page 140).

Lack of support. Suppose you realize that to get your dream job, you're going to need a lot of your co-workers' support in various ways. That's a good realization, because it's often true—which is why I'll be going into that topic in great detail in the next chapter, so stay tuned!

That's it. I told you this group was simple. Practical problems are easy to solve, because there is less emotion attached. If you have a practical problem that you can't figure out, you can always ask a guy to help. That's how we're wired, and it makes us feel important to fix things.

Journal exercise

What do you need help with?

Make note here of any external things you need to do, or could do, to further your dream along.

_____

_____

_____

_____

_____

_____

_____

Where will you find them? Who can help you get these resources?

_____

_____

_____

_____

_____

_____

GROUP TWO:

REACTIONS TO SITUATIONS

Let's move on to the second group of obstacles, the ones that involve how you **react** to situations. Sometimes these are circumstances you can't control and sometimes these are choices you make. Once you grasp how critical it is to manage your response to things, life gets so much simpler and less stressful, I promise you. For example, you can't control getting stuck on the freeway ten cars back from an accident, but you can control your reaction. Do you spend those 20 minutes tensing up, pounding your fist on the dashboard and feeling your blood pressure rise through your sunroof? Or do you pick up your cell phone, let your husband know you'll be late and ask him to start dinner, then open up the morning paper (which you didn't get around to reading) and make good use of your time? Can you view the delay as an unexpected gift of a pause in your busy day?

Say no to naysayers

By far, the biggest challenge in this category is learning how to respond to negative influences, especially the people in your life who may, intentionally or not, try to destroy your dream. These are the **naysayers**, and I liken them to crows in your garden of possibilities. Like a mob of noisy crows heckling you from surrounding trees, naysayers want to distract you and talk you out of pursuing your ideal job. They are very likely to be friends and or family members who would swear they have your best interests at heart (though naysayers can also be colleagues or even your boss).

It could be your mother-in-law, who worries that if you become too involved with your work, you'll have less quality time for her son and your children. She may subtly (or not so subtly) discourage your ambition: *Now why would you want to go and take on more things to do at work...aren't you busy enough at home?* She'll use guilt and a whole bag of tricks to try and put you where she thinks you belong.

Maybe your naysayer is a friend who can't help being jealous of your desire to better yourself. Like a crow stealing berries right out of your garden, she pecks away at your plans, tearing them apart and eating away at your self-confidence: *Aren't you scared that if you take this promotion you might not be able to handle it? What if you get in over your head and have to slink back to your old job...or worse, what if they fire you?* Because she fears change, your friend wants to keep you on her level, where she never has to confront her own dead-end job.

Just as crows are opportunists who'll eat the seeds and seedlings in your garden before they can ever take root, naysayers often love the secret thrill they get from trouncing someone else's big ideas. They often live such small lives themselves that they really do derive pleasure from derailing dreams. Oh they are sly, too. They fail to show up to babysit so you can take

"No person is your friend who demands your silence or denies your right to grow."
~Alice Walker

a night class, or they don't return home in time for you to use the car. They keep forgetting to lend you a book you need, or they talk you down behind your back, betraying confidences. I don't want to make you paranoid, but most people have a few of these crows lurking in their lives.

How do you handle naysayers?

Remember, you can't change the naysayers, but you do control how you respond to them.

You remain clear about your dream and your plan to achieve it. You keep reminding yourself what you know is your truth, and you turn away from their bad advice. You may quickly learn who you can trust with your dream and who you need to protect it from. Be firm. It's okay to reply to questions by saying, "You know, my plans aren't firm yet, so I won't go into them right now." Then change the subject—and always have a Plan B for important situations. Your friend bails on babysitting? Call your backup sitter. Find the book you need at the library. Don't divulge plans for your ideal job to anyone who could use them against you.

What value is a friend who does not want for you your highest good?

Your response may even need to be more drastic, such as ending destructive friendships. What value is a friend who does not want for you your highest good? Perhaps you need to limit your exposure to family members who don't support your goals—at least until you have achieved them and are happily settled in your dream job.

Sylvia couldn't exactly avoid her biggest naysayer, because it was her husband. "I know he didn't intend to be so non-supportive, but that's how it felt," she explains, recalling her first days of exploring an expansion of her job at a trade association. "I worked in member services, and I had my own ideas about how to dramatically increase our membership and revenue. I wanted to invest a couple of evenings a week in researching my plans, but my husband revolted," Sylvia confides wearily. "Much later—after a number of teary fights—we got to the real issue. First, he didn't like having his applecart rearranged at all when it came to his home life. He counted on me to listen to *his* tales of woe from work, but he had little patience for my restlessness. Second, he feared what might happen if I excelled at my job and really made a career out of it. He didn't want the status quo to change: that he earned more than I did and that his needs came first."

I hate to slam my gender, but despite advances in women's rights over recent decades, there are still a lot of guys out there who feel threatened when their role as chief provider is challenged in any way. They rationalize that's it's okay for their wives to augment the family income—as long as they remain king of the hill—and the castle.

"I did manage to get my husband to back down and let me pursue—and achieve—my dream, mostly by reassuring him that the process would be short and that I didn't expect my altered job would impact him much at all. Except, of course, to make me a heck of a lot happier to be around," Sylvia says, smiling discreetly.

The bottom line is, **if you allow naysayers to deter your efforts, you give them your power—your power to improve your life and grow as a human being.** So just say no.

> "What do you pack to pursue a dream, and what do you leave behind?"
> ~Sandra Sharpe

Journal exercise

Build yourself a scarecrow

While this idea is fresh in your mind, take a few minutes to jot down any naysayers you can already identify in your life. Decide how toxic their influence is and what you're going to do about it. Putting up scarecrows in your garden *before* the crows arrive, is the best defense.

_____

_____

_____

_____

_____

_____

_____

_____

_____

When time is not on your side

This next pest in your garden of possibilities is as ubiquitous as those tiny green bugs called aphids, the ones that suck sap from your plants and can cause new growth to be stunted and distorted. # This pest is a <u>false</u> belief that you don't have enough time.

I can hear the uproar all the way out here in Oregon. *Who do you think you are, Pat Healey, to tell me I <u>do</u> have plenty of time for everything in my busy life!* Since you asked, I'm a guy who's studied the Pareto Principle, and if you'll swallow your indignation for a few minutes, I bet I can show you where to find a lot more time in all your days. Yeah, I moonlight as a magician. Okay all you aphids out there, here comes a blast of bug spray.

There's a scientific law in business and economics which states: **the great majority of results come from a small minority of causes or effort.**

It's known as the Pareto Principle, but is also called the 80/20 Principle, because it reflects the fact that about 80 percent of results flow from 20 percent of the causes. Put another way, 20 percent of the customers provide 80 percent of the profits in a business. It's also been proven that 20 percent of the employees create 80 percent of the results in an office.

One out of every five people in an office will be much more productive—that one person just seems to get more done in a day than the other four. It's just the way it is. It's really tough to find those great achievers, and yet **it doesn't take all that much effort to shift yourself into the achiever column**. It boils down to keeping your commitments and following through on your ideas. Implement them. Don't just say you'll do some outside sales at new locations—get out of your swivel chair and actually do it. What's the spark that ignites the brains of those who do? I wish I knew. If I could figure that out I'd be one big bazillionaire. What holds people back? Perhaps it's peer pressure. Maybe you don't want to outshine your parents. There are all kinds of psychological bugaboos. I do know if you can figure it out, you can change. You can join the 20 percent club.

What does this mean exactly? Shockingly, it means that **most people waste 80 percent of their time on things that don't bring them closer to their dream**. You can probably think of ways you misuse your time away from the office, but here are some dandies.

Time sappers:

· Mindless television…don't you know by now how *Wife Swap* will turn out?
· Disorganized errand running…how many trips to the store did you make last week for milk or Oreos?
· Sleeping in is overrated…besides, too much sleep makes you sluggish.
· Nagging your spouse, your kids, your golden retriever and your cat (now there's a colossal waste of a good nag).
· Complaining to your pals on the phone every night.
· Complaining to your pals on the phone every night.
· Complaining to your pals on the phone every night. (Monotonous, isn't it?)
· Drinks after work, crossword puzzles, jigsaw puzzles and other leisure activities. If you have that kind of free time, you have time to invest in creating your ideal job. *But Pat, I need time to unwind after a hard day at work.* **It'll take a lot less unwinding if you manifest a job you really love.**

> "Time is a created thing. To say *I don't have time* is to say *I don't want it.*
> ~Lao Tzu

From welfare to faring well

Here's a story about someone who had everything stacked against her but still managed to join the 20 percenters through sheer grit. Monica was a stay at home mom with three young children living in a comfy ranch house in rural Kansas, and she was still recovering from cervical cancer and a heart attack. Then just as she was starting to feel healthy again, her husband left her. "Emotionally, I felt like scrambled eggs," she recalls. Her next stop: a dark day in a welfare waiting room full of toddlers with tantrums.

After moving to a cramped apartment, Monica took stock of her situation and decided she had to take responsibility for making a better life for herself and her kids. "My dream had always been to go to college and become a teacher, but I didn't see at first how I'd find the money or the time to manage that. The challenge was too tough to

I believe in myself, and that's all that matters.

grasp as a whole, so I just took it one year at a time. I got student loans, cut out all extra expenses, left the kids with my mom and did my first two years at a nearby community college," Monica explains, still sounding amazed at what she accomplished. In the evenings, she read bedtime stories to her kids, fit in her own homework after they fell asleep, then crashed on the couch.

Then it got really tough. In order to complete her last two years of college, Monica had to drive 150 miles round trip every day, five days a week. In addition, her homework got a lot more challenging, which meant she got a whole lot less sleep. Inspired by one of her son's favorite story books, taped to her dashboard were the words: **I can do it, I know I can. I believe in myself, and that's all that matters.**

Monica did indeed do it—she graduated with honors and has been teaching happily ever after back in her home town. "I don't regret how difficult my life has been, because I learned how vital it is to fall in love with life and how precious each minute I have with my children is. . . . as the saying goes, it's about the journey, not the destination."

Monica is among the 20 percent of people who don't waste their valuable time. She really gets it, and she's earned a great life to prove it. Time really is the ultimate leveler. It's the one and only thing that everyone is given equally. **What will you do with your next 24 hours?**

Your Mess Assessment

By now, you probably have your own dream well in mind. To free up more time to implement your plan, let's see if you can identify some of the things in your 80 percent column. **Clearing up the messes in your life that waste your valuable time, will free up all sorts of energy to attain the life you want.** Here's a good example. Do you still pay all your bills by check? Have you considered paying them automatically by direct debit to your checking account? Not only does it take a lot less time, it prevents you from forgetting a bill or being late, which has a negative impact on your credit ratings, which in turn can increase other rates.

Okay, let's get real here. Let's inspect the undersides of the leaves on your plants—how many aphids have infested your garden of possibilities? Think about your current job and everything you do in any given week that's a **waste of time** or that you'd classify as a **bad habit** that sucks time out of your work days. For example: stopping by Starbucks every morning for a scone and a soy latte, or how about surfing the Internet on company time, planning your next vacation? What about all that complaining to your co-workers during every break and lunch hour. (Don't make me repeat that five times!)

Time wasters and bad habits on the job:

_____

_____

_____

_____

_____

_____

_____

_____

Just how messy are you? C'mon, really?

Admit you're responsible for the **messes** that slow you down at work. For example, your work space at your current job is so disorganized you're afraid to call in sick, because your associates would never be able to find anything they needed. Are there stacks of filing waiting to be done, or invoices to be sent? Only you know your dusty little—or not-so-little—secrets.

Work space chaos:

_____

_____

_____

_____

_____

_____

_____

_____

Next, I want you to examine these two lists and see which of your time wasters, bad habits and messes you are willing to cut out. Take a bright marker and circle the ones you are now ready to eliminate. Now that you're more efficient and have found so much extra time, devote some of it to creating your ideal job!

To really mine for gold, **repeat the process with regard to your personal life.** If you're like most people, you've got at least one closet—or maybe a whole garage or basement—overflowing with piles of stuff. **Chaos in your environment reflects a chaotic mind.** Sure, some of us are more instinctively organized than others, but that just means you may have to try harder to get it done. Do you need motivation? How much time do you waste every month looking for your keys? Have you dashed to the store for cornflakes, when you already had a box hiding under a pile of laundry? Ever found your checkbook under the front seat of your car? I could go on, but then you'd think I've been spying on you.

> "It's not so much how busy you are, but why you are busy. The bee is praised; the mosquito is swatted."
> ~Marie O'Conner

_____

_____

_____

_____

_____

_____

_____

_____

Getting over being overwhelmed

The next pests in your garden may be swarms of fruit flies, those annoying insects that feed on overripe fruit—a perfect way to think of what happens to your dream when you become **overwhelmed with too many demands on your time, too much chaos** and too many perceived steps to reach your goal. You feel surrounded by buzzing flies and they cloud your vision, making you unable to move in any direction, so you just give up. Meanwhile, your dream lays rotting, enticing even more fruit flies.

Of course the rest of your life can contribute to feeling overwhelmed with it all. When the unexpected happens, you may have to shelve your plans for a bit while you restore some order to the rest of your universe. It's *good* to have a life outside of your job; it's healthy and reveals that you value balance.

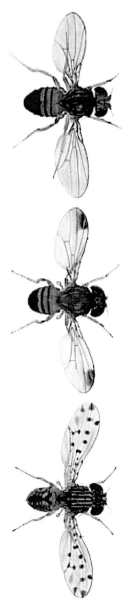

The worst response you can have to feeling overwhelmed is to push yourself harder to somehow struggle through it.

Instead, stop everything you can. Sort out your life. Make a new plan, and resume pursuit of your ideal job when your zeal for it returns. Just don't forget about it!

If you're simply overwhelmed by the perceived enormity of the tasks you face to get into your dream job, then you need a new approach—and a better flyswatter. Maybe you're just disorganized, and all you require is an hour or two with a notebook and some snazzy purple file folders.

Or perhaps you need to learn the art of chunking.

Here's how Gayle dealt with it when she sought to reinvent her administrative job at her rural Montana electric company. "I realized one of the big things I did all day long was answer the same 20 or so questions from customers about how to conserve energy and save money on their bills," Gayle says, still sounding upbeat. "I wanted to write a proposal for a revised job description that focused more on customer education. I had big plans to offer classes on alternative energy, making homes energy efficient. Then I wanted to create brochures and take them to home expos, and on and on. I had so many ideas that I lost sight of my goal."

Enter the chunk. "One Saturday I had my notes spread out all over the family room floor, when my teenage daughter took pity on my frustration and taught me how to chunk. All I did was convert my notes into a giant outline made up of ever smaller items, and then I broke those items down into the smallest action unit—a chunk. The point is, **if I only had 15 minutes to work on my plan, I could turn to my outline, choose a minor chunk and do it in 15 minutes.** Then I got to check that chunk off. Not only did I *not* waste my spare quarter hour bugging my kids or something, I moved one tiny step closer to completing my project."

Gayle did finish her proposal, and it was received with great enthusiasm by her supervisor. She's now helping to educate her customers about the advantages of green energy and takes enormous pride in her work, because she knows she's actually doing something beneficial for the environment.

What can you chunk today?

Have you stopped making progress toward your ideal job because you don't know which step to take next? Try making an outline on your computer and separating your tasks into the tiniest possible increments. List some things you'd like to try to chunk. Remember, we all get overwhelmed at times—it's how you respond that separates you from those who succumb to it and those who figure out how to manage it.

"Don't agonize. Organize." ~Florence Kennedy

Clarifying confusion

Closely related to feeling overwhelmed is being **confused**. The difference is, when you're overwhelmed you know what you need to do, there just seems to be too much of it; but when you're confused, you don't have a clear path to follow. This situation reminds me of squirrels I've observed in my yard hunting madly for lost nuts they've buried. They know they're there somewhere, and they race around from planting bed to planting bed, feverishly digging and making a mess until they finally find one sorry hazelnut from last fall's harvest—very inefficient. All you need is a better plan. If the one you made in Chapter Four isn't detailed enough to give you clarity, then get a bigger piece of paper and go nuts—so to speak. For Pat's sake, keep the darn plan where you can see it. **You'd be surprised how many people write out perfectly good plans to manifest their ideal jobs, then never look at them again.** Is it any wonder those are the ones who get lost in the woods digging for buried hazelnuts?

GROUP THREE:

INTERNAL OBSTACLES

If you're still with me, good for you! It isn't easy, I know, to stare down weaselly obstacles with nothing in hand but a metaphorical scarecrow. Now we come to the biggest selection of common obstacles—your own inventions, the ones you've concocted in your own mind. If this concept troubles you, that's good—it should! People who prefer to blame all their problems on other people can have difficulty accepting responsibility for their own situation. If you find yourself balking at some of the ideas in this section, journal about it and see if you can discover your underlying truth. For now, please approach these with an open mind.

Some of these challenges are lifelong companions, others may be finely honed coping skills. It doesn't matter. For our purposes, these mental attitudes don't move you closer to getting your ideal job, so let's root them out. Remember:

Believe in your dreams and they may come true; believe in yourself and they <u>will</u> come true.

Get high on yourself and end low self-esteem

Of the internal obstacles, the most insidious and harmful is **low self-esteem**, which behaves exactly like that gardener's bane: crabgrass, so named for its prostrate growth habit. With a bit of imagination you can think of it scuttling off like a crab on the ocean floor. As much as I like to think I can solve anything, if you have a serious issue with low-self esteem, a few paragraphs in this book aren't going to cure it. The best I can do is help you diagnose it, and encourage you to do some serious self-examination in your journal. If you decide this is a problem that has held you back in your job as well as in the rest of your life, then I urge you to seek some form of counseling or coaching to overcome it. If you don't get low self-esteem under control, it will prevent you from clearing your other obstacles, too. Just like crabgrass, it's invasive, and left unchecked, will spread farther and deeper until your garden of possibilities has been choked to death.

Have any varieties of these weedy symptoms of low self-esteem sprung up in your mind lately?

- I'm a loser for ending up in a job that doesn't make use of my abilities.
- Oh, my job's not so bad . . .I should be happy just to have a job.
- I know the marketing manager needs a new executive assistant, but she'd never want me for the job . . .what do I know about her department?
- I'm just unlucky. Nothing good ever happens to me.
- I wish I hadn't agreed to shift to this other position, and now I don't dare tell anyone how much I hate it.
- Who am I to think I could have such a great job?

I could go on and on and on—these are all typical indicators that you've lost the ability to stand up for yourself, to **take your life in hand and accept responsibility for making it stellar**. That's right, star-like. Remember those starring roles you came up with in Chapter Two? If your self-esteem is a little wobbly, please fill out the chart on the next page, then make a copy and put it where you can look at it often as a reminder of your highest capabilities. From your AWEsome List on Page 46, simply pick your favorite starring role for the center of the star, then add your other skills and hidden talents to the rest of the page.

Deanna is a classic case. She started her career in a top Atlanta ad agency, and over the course of three years, she worked her way up to a solid administrative job assisting the media director. As a Kolbe Fact Finder, she was well-suited to her job, but her low self-esteem prevented her from rising any farther, especially to the job she had her eye on. "I was always a bit intimidated working at a flashy agency, being a small town girl at my core. But that was also the allure. I've always been fascinated by the media, and there are some fun perks—especially for the actual media buyers. But I knew that media buyers need great negotiating skills, must work well under pressure and have fantastic money management skills. All things that scared me, for sure," she admits now.

Self-esteem depends on how you feel about yourself, as well as how you believe other people think of you. How Deanna ended up with hers in the dumps doesn't concern us. How she raised it up, does. "I started to consciously take more risks at work," she explains. "I began making small suggestions in staff meetings. When those were well-received, I gave myself a gold star on my internal chart. Then I got bolder and started doing some media research on my own and making real buying suggestions to my superiors. Again, they were receptive and appreciative. Over time, I could see my confidence growing. Being timid by nature, I also took assertiveness training, and that was time and money very well spent. Now I don't even hesitate to shoot my hand up in a meeting if I have an idea, whereas the old me would've mulled over my idea so long that the topic would've passed me by. I'm so much more relaxed at work, because worrying all the time takes a lot of energy. Oh yeah, I got the job!"

How I Am A Star

my best starring role

Six solutions for low self-esteem

The best defense against crabgrass is having a healthy lawn, one that out-competes with weeds and prevents crabgrass from establishing itself. It's exactly the same with self-esteem, so here are some proactive tips for keeping your self-image green and healthy. Okay, maybe not green, exactly, but vital and flourishing.

1. Learn the power of NO.

Getting roped into things you don't really want to do, whether at work or not, never makes you feel good. When it happens over and over, you begin to feel like the doormat you are becoming. One great exercise to reclaim your own power of choice, is to say "No" for one entire week to every opportunity or request that you can. Keep in mind, this may not work at your job! Use common sense, and don't jeopardize your position. However, this can be a great tool to develop if you are plagued by co-workers pushing candy bars for their kids' baseball team or pals who want you to go off your eating plan. In your personal life, if you are run ragged by other people's needs, then this will be revolutionary for you. Say "No" to things no matter how much you really want to do them. Above all, don't explain or offer an excuse. Just politely decline. You'll be shocked at how much extra time you have. This is the key: **Until you can say "No" whenever you want to, "Yes" means nothing.**

2. Have an opinion.

In a similar vein, the next time you're asked what you want to do or eat or where you'd like to go on a date, and so on—give an answer! This is not the same thing as people who always have to have things their way. Having an idea about what you really want in any situation and expressing it is empowering.

3. Do your To Do list.

Nothing feeds self-esteem like accomplishment, especially when you manage to do something you didn't think you could. As you work through your plan for your ideal job, you'll have lots of opportunities to try some new things. These will be things you may have a little—or a lot—of fear about doing, but doing them anyway is the direct route to soaring self-esteem. Recall an example from your past when you did something difficult and did it well. Remember how good that felt? Well, you can feel that good every day! Just do something challenging and then applaud yourself.

4. Acquire a taste for praise.

If you feel less than fabulous about yourself, you are less likely to stand out at work, to do things that would draw attention to you. As a result, few people pay attention to you or have reason to offer you praise—which of course perpetuates the cycle. You can break it by intentionally doing the opposite of what you normally do. There are always opportunities to excel, to volunteer for a project that would allow you to play a starring role, to work on a task at home, to go the extra mile for your boss. You've seen others around you do it and reap the rewards, I'm sure. Just try it, and see how it feels to earn positive attention and gratitude for a job well done. **Excellence is a choice you can make.** (And by the way, well-earned praise tastes like a four-layer chocolate fudge cake with chocolate chip Haagen Dazs on top.)

5. Stop hiding out.

Does your job deserve you? People with chronic low self-esteem often end up in jobs where they can hide out, where not much is asked of them and not much is given. Take a long, hard look at your current job. Is it allowing you to be the best you possible? Does it bring out your best traits and use your full range of skills? If not, then get busy and redesign a better job for yourself. No one should feel like work is just a place to hide from life.

6. Celebrate you.

You're the only <u>you</u> who has ever lived and ever will. No one else on earth has your exact collection of genes, personality, experience and knowledge. Even though some days you may feel anonymous and like just another cog in the corporate wheel, it isn't true. What's special about you that you can nurture and promote as part of your ideal job description? If birthdays are celebrated in your office, by all means put yours on the calendar, and when it rolls around, be sure to enjoy it. In fact, find other occasions to celebrate yourself.

Journal exercise

"Instead of thinking about what you're missing, try thinking about what you have that everyone else is missing."
~Unknown
(was it you?)

Why I'm worth celebrating

If low self-esteem is a problem for you, then this will be a good exercise in pushing your boundaries. **Name at least ten things you could celebrate about yourself during the next month.** That's right—month. What? You don't deserve to celebrate yourself every three days? Sure you do. Here are some ideas to get you started, but **DO NOT STOP until you have at least ten items on your list.** You could celebrate: your new haircut, the favor you did for a neighbor, that your daughter got a good report card (you must have had something to do with it!), the acknowledgment you got from your boss for a new idea you offered, that you got up early and went to the gym, that you walked right past Krispy Kreme without a second glance—okay, without a third glance. You get the picture. Give yourself permission to celebrate the special moments, the small wins that

can get forgotten in your hectic life. When will you find time to do all this celebrating? I'm glad you asked. If you skipped over it, return to the **Mess Assessment** exercise on Page 167, and you'll gather plenty of time, I assure you.

1. _____
2. _____
3. _____
4. _____
5. _____
6. _____
7. _____
8. _____
9. _____
10. _____

Don't be afraid of fear

That may sound odd, but this internal obstacle shuts you down, makes you second guess yourself and absolutely will destroy any dream if you give fear a chance to feed on it. Some people allow fear to rule their lives to such an extent that they are never fully alive. **Fear is like a fungus which grows in the dark of your mind when you're lying awake at night stressing over your job.** Like a fungus, it spreads quickly, is pervasive and can make you sick—or worse. Living in fear is also giving your power away, which is demoralizing and allows all kinds of other obstacles to grow in your path. More dreams have probably been strangled by fear than anything else. To eradicate fear requires strong measures, so consider some of the ones I've used during my many years in business.

Common fears and some tips for confronting them:

· *I'm afraid to tell my boss what I really want—what if he gets angry at me?* How much of your fear is just insecurity? You need to allow **trust** to develop in yourself, your co-workers and your boss. I know it can be tough, but you have to be vulnerable enough to take some risks—that's how you change and evolve. Remaining in your comfort zone will not move you closer to your ideal job. Besides, how can your boss give you what want you want if he doesn't know what that is?

· *I lay awake at night, my stomach churning with anxiety over going back to school nights, and how that will affect my family.* All you need is a plan, a **system** of steps that will organize your life so you can further your education and move into your perfect job. Break down your fears into separate pieces and solve each one individually. Then make sure you're getting help from your family— you're not trying to be that mythical Super Mom, are you?

· *I'm such a chicken about trying new things. I've had so many disappointments that I'm afraid to push myself into new roles at work. I feel safe in my boring job.* There's nothing wrong with craving safety, it's a natural human instinct. However, if your desire for something better than boring is strong enough, it can fire up your enthusiasm for change. Try building your **confidence** by thinking of times in your past when you did try something new and succeeded. Then start very small. Baby steps will still get you to your goal…it may just take a bit longer.

· *I'm afraid of loving my job too much! I know women who live only for their careers and never marry. I'm 32, still single, and I'm at a point where I could take on a lot more responsibility and get a lot of satisfaction from it I'm sure, but I'm afraid of falling down that rabbit hole and waking up at 52 and wondering where my life went.* You do have a tough choice to make. But **clarity** will be your best friend as you navigate your career. Always keep your larger life goals clearly in mind, then ask lots of questions about extra hours and expectations for any opportunity you're considering, to ensure you preserve enough time to have a personal life. Personally, I think devoting half your waking hours to any job is plenty. Save the other half for yourself.

· *If I don't like my new duties, my boss will never let me out of them or ever listen to me again.* Analyze your fears and find the irrational ones—then trash those immediately. You know what I mean, those ideas that are just plain silly or over-the-top or very unlikely to be true. Any boss worth her weight in memos will **listen** to her team—at least some of the time! Besides, in order for you to get your new and improved job, she had to listen to you, didn't she?

· *I'm reentering the workforce now that my nest is more or less empty. (Those birds do return, don't they!) I'm afraid I won't fit in with an office full of younger people, and I fear that even business behavior has changed while I was busy driving carpools.* Don't sweat it for a minute. You bring something to the office uniquely yours, something every office needs—the voice of wisdom, experience and **maturity**. You're not afraid of hard work and you're a pro at juggling five things at once. Youth can be overvalued in an office. I'd rather hire a 40-something than a 20-something any day. Besides, you know how to bake the boss a birthday cake!

I know applying for a transfer to another department would be a wonderful change for me, but what if I'm not up to the challenge and fail? Sometimes you just have to grit your teeth, take that proverbial **leap of faith** and do whatever it is you're afraid of doing. Fear can be paralyzing, and sometimes it just takes getting upset enough about your current reality to fuel your desire to leap.

> "Do one thing every day that scares you."
> ~Eleanor Roosevelt

Fear is often false

Jennifer already had a job that was darn close to her ideal, working for an Indianapolis custom home builder—only she didn't realize it. She single handedly ran the office, had lots of autonomy and even peace and quiet to do her work, because much of the time

everyone else was out on job sites. Yet after four years of contentment, she felt her enthusiasm for work draining out of her day by day. "I knew I was getting bored with how easy my job had become, and some days the hands on the clock seemed stuck," Jennifer says, easily recalling her frustration. "I was also annoyed because my boss was having lots of problems with subcontractors. He was making mistakes getting the right fixtures to the right job sites, which had set off a chain reaction of delays and wasted man hours. I knew I could help straighten out his mess, but I was afraid to suggest changes, because he'd always taken care of that part of the business himself. In fact, he'd make jokes about how no one else could manage subs the way he did. On top of that, my husband and I had just bought a new house—thanks to a great deal from my boss—so I had to keep my job to meet the mortgage, and I was afraid of upsetting him."

"You gain strength, courage, and confidence by every experience in which you really stop to look fear in the face. You must do the thing which you think you cannot do."
~Eleanor Roosevelt

When Jennifer finally got up her nerve to discuss the problems with her boss, the solution for both of them became clear. "When I offered to help him by setting up some systems for tracking the components for each project, he almost cried with relief. He'd been ashamed to ask me to help because he knew he'd screwed up, and he assumed I was already overworked. But actually, I welcomed a new challenge. Now we're super organized and have been able to increase the number of houses we can work on at one time."

What Jennifer encountered is very common in small companies where the owner is heavily involved with the business. Most entrepreneurs start out doing everything themselves and are reluctant to let go of certain duties as the business grows. They just don't believe anyone else would do as good a job as they do, but they stretch themselves so thin that *they* aren't doing a good job. If you suspect this could be the case where you work, think about what things you might be able to remove from the owner's plate—tactfully of course—you can't just grab the chicken leg, er, spreadsheet and run. **The real point here is:**

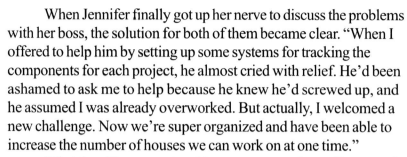

both the boss and his valued employee were afraid to talk to each other about what was wrong with the company.

I'm not talking about the justifiable kind of fear you feel when you encounter a grizzly bear in your backyard. (Where do you live, anyway?) For the fungal kind of fear, one of my favorite ways of breaking it down is to think of it like this:

False

Evidence

Appearing

Real

Journal exercise

Think about it. Jennifer's fears that her boss would resent her offer were false, and her boss was wrongly afraid that she was too busy to take on more work. Yet they were both convinced that was the reality of their situation. It took Jennifer facing her fear to break the illusion, and then the solution—which was already in place behind the illusion—could be seen.

Facing your fears

When it comes right down to it, you're left having to confront your fears, face to fungus. Not a pretty image, is it? Neither are your fears, but the sooner you expose them to the light of day, the sooner you can dissolve them and move on. Please don't avoid this exercise…it can do you so much good. **Write any fears you have about your plan for your new job here.**

_____

_____

_____

_____

_____

_____

_____

_____

How bad is your attitude?

The next internal obstacle to achieving your dream may be the roughest one to read about, because you may not want to admit that blight has affected your mind and your life. Blight is a strong word, almost biblical in its implication, because it means destruction and ruin. In your garden of possibilities, blight is a systemic disease that causes browning and then death of the entire plant. The blight I'm referring to is a **bad attitude**.

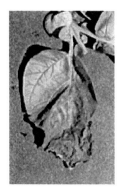

Maybe you only have a mild case of blight. Maybe you only fake being sick once a year, and you figure: *Hey, I work hard, I deserve an extra day off.* Your blight may be more advanced if you believe you're much smarter than your boss and think you can get away with goofing off on the job. You rarely do the best work you're capable of doing, and you believe: *At this salary, they're lucky I show up most days.*

Further symptoms of a bad attitude:
· You interrupt others and are disrespectful of your co-workers.
· You feel no remorse when you're late or when you waste time.
· You spend more time criticizing the work, attitudes and views of others than evaluating your own work, attitudes and opinions.
· You never want to be held accountable for your mistakes, and you have lightning fast excuses for any mistakes you make.
· You spend more time than anyone registering complaints.
· You have little or no passion for your work.
· You never volunteer for extra assignments or to fill in for someone who is out sick.
· You are good at making messes, but rarely clean up after yourself or others.
· You show no interest in taking personal time to increase your skills in order to improve performance.
· You almost always leave work on time and never stay late to help others.

Another symptom of a bad attitude—gossiping

That list was harsh, wasn't it? As a boss, I've been on the receiving end of a lot of bad attitudes. You should see the list before I pruned it! The truth is, if you're reading this book, then you probably don't have a very bad attitude. Still, blight can show up when you least expect it, and it can be passed from person to person. Take gossiping, for example. Would you say you've spread gossip at work during the last month? Or have you listened to any gossip at work in this last month? Then guess what—you're a gossip. **If you didn't put a stop to the gossip, then you're a silent conspirator, as guilty as the person who spreads rumors, lies and hurtful words.** Gossip is one of the most insidious and destructive forces in any company, and I challenge you right now to help stop it where you work. It infects the minds of all who listen and contributes to a decline in overall attitude toward your work.

Here's the good news—you can turn it around in an instant. The next time you overhear someone gossiping, simply join the group and redirect the conversation toward something positive: *Say, did you guys hear about Sally over in accounting? She had her baby yesterday and everyone's doing really well.* Or how about this: *Have you thought about what you're bringing to the company potluck dinner?* Or maybe this would do it: *Does anyone know of a class I can take to learn QuickBooks?* What you divert the discussion to doesn't matter, as long as it's away from gossip. You don't even need to admonish the others for gossiping. Just lead by example. Before you know it, your co-workers will be wondering why you're so nice to be around, why you always leave them smiling.

Journal exercise

"I discovered I always have choices, and sometimes it's only a choice of attitude."
~Judith M. Knowlton

How bad have you been?

Hey, confession is good for the soul. However, this is a serious problem in the workplace, so I urge you to honestly search your soul and see if you've been guilty of even minor lapses into bad attitudes. Acknowledging them is the first step toward correcting them. Besides, as you'll soon see, you're going to need help to realize your ideal job, and the only people who enjoy bad attitudes are other people equally blighted. So fess up, and then journal about ways you can erase this blight from your garden.

_____

_____

_____

_____

_____

_____

_____

_____

_____

_____

The best cure for a bad attitude

To illustrate my point about attitudes, I'm going to tell you about an inspirational man who had the best attitude toward life—and death—I've ever encountered. His name was Art Buchwald. Even if you've heard about his story, please read it again, as I doubt you'll ever meet anyone with a better understanding of the meaning of life.

"Would you like some strawberry rhubarb pie?" the woman asked. "Later on in the day I'll probably have some," Art Buchwald replied, "but at this moment in my life, I am so happy, I can't do anything different."

This conversation was quoted in the *New York Times*, next to a picture of Art playing the ukulele with his two grandchildren at a lunch with his daughter and son-in-law. Art Buchwald didn't make that comment in 1986 when he was elected to the American Academy and Institute of Arts and Letters. He didn't say "Hold the pie" when he won a Pulitzer Prize. He certainly didn't say it in 1994 when he lost Ann, his bride of 44 years, to lung cancer. Nor did he make that comment in February 2006, when he checked into a hospice in Washington, D.C., because kidney failure put him at death's door. Two weeks later, one of his legs had to be amputated, and three weeks later, Art Buchwald refused dialysis. His doctor said he would be dead in a few weeks, if not days, but he didn't die. In early July, he checked out of the hospice and moved back to his old home on Martha's Vineyard to go on living. The I'm-too-happy-for-pie moment occurred during that summer of 2006 when Art was too busy living to die. Against all odds, Art Buchwald thrived until January 18, 2007.

The next time you think you're having a bad day, remember Art Buchwald and the lessons he taught us.

Put on a happy face—and keep it that way

So how does someone attain that sublime level of happiness? Like most things, you work at it. Art Buchwald didn't have an easy

"The way I see
it, if you want
the rainbow,
you gotta put
up with
the rain."
~Dolly Parton

childhood and he had plenty of misfortune in his later years, but as he sat teetering on the edge of death, he was still too darn happy for his favorite pie. Man, I hope I'm that happy when my time comes.

Did you know that happiness has become an area for serious scientific research? What's been discovered so far, is that while to some extent we are either pre-wired genetically to be happy or we're not, there is also a lot of room for us to consciously *choose* to be happy. I'm not alone in believing that **in order to create the life of your dreams, both at home and at work, you need to nurture the habit of being happy.**

Recent studies reveal that our adult brains continue to change with experience. You can actually increase your capacity for happiness with the right exercises. Why is this important to know and understand? Simply put—to avoid joining the growing number of people succumbing to depression and other psychological problems. It's predicted that within 20 years, depression will be the number one illness afflicting the women of the world.

I thought that'd get your attention.

How can you make happiness more of a habit in your life?

Here are some basic tips:
- Be grateful for the good in your life. Some people enjoy keeping a separate gratitude journal that they can read when they hit a rough patch.
- Be deeply involved in all facets of your life—don't just phone it in.
- Engage all your senses on a regular basis, get out in nature, listen and look more acutely at the world around you.
- Nurture relationships, be a giver as well as a receiver. Visit friends in the hospital, practice random acts of kindness, don't take your loved ones for granted.
- Be involved in your community—volunteer for civic projects, at your kids' schools, check up on elderly neighbors, take pride in your home and neighborhood.
- Live with a clear heart. Purge yourself of regret, anger and other negativity. Forgive anyone who needs it and move on!
- Learn lots of way to handle stress, before it handles you. (Having a

job you love is a great way to reduce stress.)

· Cherish your body—despite the trend toward spare parts, it's still the only one you're going to get.

· Monitor your thoughts and what you allow into your brain. If you catch yourself indulging in negative thinking, have a new thought! Does incessant war coverage give you nightmares? Don't watch! What's negative in the world is always available on cable news. Choose instead to put joyful thoughts, inspiring stories and good news into your mind.

Finally, scientists found that optimists suffer half the incidence of heart disease as their pessimistic counterparts, and having a sunny disposition reduces your risk of early death by 50 percent. What are you waiting for? Go pet a puppy or smell a gardenia!

Getting rid of remaining obstacles— speedy pest control, at your service

Here's a reason to be happy—you've made it through all the biggest obstacles that I've noticed when it comes to making dreams real. I just covered the big three in the self-created category: low self-esteem, fear and having a bad attitude. The ones that are left in that category are not quite as imposing, so I won't go into so much detail with them. Nevertheless, these pests can still wreak havoc in your garden of possibilities if you don't watch out for them. **Put a check mark (or draw a bug splat if you're artistic) next to any that you've caught in your garden.**

_____ **Self-doubt** is a relative of low self-esteem. I think of it as a mole in your garden, working unseen and underground, chomping away at the roots of your plants and those tender tulip bulbs you planted. What you need is more self-confidence, and you earn that by **taking gradual steps in the direction of your dream**, doing ever-more-challenging tasks. Then presto! One day you'll arrive at your destination and your self-doubt will have vanished.

_____ **Self-sabotage** is a nasty obstacle, one you aren't always aware of inflicting on yourself. It reminds me of quack grass, which spreads underground and then pops up in your garden when you least expect it. An aggressive perennial grass, it easily regenerates from very small broken pieces left in the ground—as does self-sabotage. It feeds on shreds of self-doubt lurking in your mind and attacks your dreams, often just before they bloom. Why? Because at your core, some part of you doesn't believe you deserve to be happy.

Awareness is the solution. You have to track your history with this one and be ever-vigilant for it to erupt again, because quack grass is stupid. It just keeps repeating the same pattern over and over until you finally notice it and decide to eradicate it. (Yes, you can borrow my weed whacker—why do you think I've been lugging it around?)

_____ **Self-criticism** is another member of the insect family. It behaves like those annoying gnats, whose larvae devour plant roots. Then here's the really bad part: before you realize you're indulging in destructive self-criticism, the gnat larvae sprout wings and fly away, leaving you with an empty, itchy, picked on feeling. I'm not talking about useful self-evaluation, where you honestly assess your weaknesses for ways to improve yourself. No, I'm talking about holding regular, all-out hate fests for yourself. Pity parties where you can be heard moaning: *I'll never get my ideal job, because I'm not smart enough, or talented enough, or clever enough or ambitious enough. Besides, only the young, attractive women get promoted around here. And then there's my age—I'm too old to get the kind of job I want. What a dumb idea this was to even get my hopes up.* Yikes! If you have voices like that running rampant in your head, tell them to get out! Now! Again, awareness is the answer. Learn to **monitor your thoughts** and quickly swat gnats like that before they can sap your sprit. You could also ask trusted friends to let you know if they hear you talking trash about yourself.

_____ **Limiting beliefs** were already covered in Chapter Three, but I want to point out an additional feature they have. Just like dandelions, limiting beliefs send their seeds far and wide to plant themselves in other gardens. Once you give in to a limiting belief, those around you can also adopt your belief. As pretty as dandelion seeds are to watch, don't spew your limiting beliefs all over your co-workers and friends.

_____ **Procrastination** ought to be on the hit parade of obstacles. I hate to think how many productive hours are wasted by

this virulent pest. Procrastination is like a caterpillar, who eats away at your days and your energy, then poof, it morphs into a beautiful butterfly and disappears, leaving only your half-eaten dreams as proof it was there. The only other evidence the caterpillar was there are phrases like these escaping from your mouth: *pretty soon; I'm going to get started on that; maybe tomorrow; it's going to really be great; yeah I'll have that to you tomorrow.* Thankfully, this one's a snap to catch. Just quit goofing around and **do whatever it is you need to be doing**. In the time you spend procrastinating, you could have it done. Few things in life will give you as much joy as ending this bad habit. Just decide to do it!

_____ **Distraction** happens to the best of us. A friend calls it the Bright Shiny Object syndrome. She's forever getting diverted from her projects by the specter of an even more appealing one, all sparkly and pretty, just over *there*. This obstacle reminds me of a tree cricket, whose chirpy song distracts you while it chews your garden down to the ground. This same friend battles it with signs, engraved stones on her desk and post-it notes all around her computer monitor reminding her to FOCUS. That is the antidote: a **disciplined, determined focus on your goal** combined with a learned ability to ignore whatever comes along seeking to lure you away.

_____ **Low energy** infects some people because of health problems, but for the rest of you, sorry to say it, but you're just like slugs. They're slow-moving, but eventually they'll decimate your garden. I'm not going to dispense healthcare advice, except to say if this really is your problem, get a checkup and find out why you don't have more zip in your step. Of course, some of the previously mentioned obstacles could be slowing you down and dragging you into depression, which is another good reason to get checked out. Finding **joy in what you do** is a surefire way to increase your energy. When you're in love with your life, then you can't wait to spring out of bed in the morning and see what cool thing is going to happen today. *Staff meeting in the park—great!*

_____ **Weak will** is really sneaky. Like the bark beetle, it's known as a secondary invader, feeding on already decaying plant matter. No surprise, beetles are the most successful creatures on earth, causing untold destruction year after year. Like the beetle, your weak will to succeed waits until your dream is already sidetracked by one or more of the other obstacles, a naysayer, for example. Then, once you start to lose enthusiasm for pursuing your ideal job, weak will takes over and finishes off your dream. The best solution is to clear away all the other obstacles, then weak will dies of starvation. In the meantime, practice **affirmative thinking and behavior**. Weak will shudders at the sound of phrases such as: *I am pursuing my ideal job no matter what! I know exactly what to do to reach my goals, so get out of my way! I deserve and accept all the good that I can imagine and create!*

     Impatience is a toughy, and I'll admit it, one of my own (few!) shortcomings. Just like pesky grasshoppers, my thoughts hop around too much, destroying opportunities for deeper reflection and relaxation. I don't think there is an easy answer for this one, and you need to beware of the power of impatience to disrupt or derail your dream before it can come fully to life. If you are prone to rash behavior and quick judgments, **try counting to ten before you open your mouth and ask yourself: Is what I'm about to say or do going to help me reach my goal?**

"Don't be pushed by your problems. Be led by your dreams."
~Anonymous

From nearly fired to dearly beloved

Let me tell you about Meagan, because her situation exemplifies how your dream can fade—and then be reanimated. Meagan had always loved art and earned a degree in art history hoping to work at a museum. She wasn't sure in what capacity, she just knew she wanted to be surrounded by beautiful things and work in an inspiring environment. When she landed a position at a famous Manhattan museum, she was ecstatic.

"I couldn't believe my good fortune," she says, bubbling over with joy. "I actually got what I thought was my dream job right out of college. Even though I was at the very bottom of the administrative team, I was overjoyed just to work there. All was fine during the first six months or so, but then the thrill wore off. In truth, I was stuck in a windowless office in the bowels of the building and only glimpsed any art when I had to deliver something to another department. Sure, I could wander around the galleries on my lunch hour, but that didn't feel any different than being a member of the public. I kind of lost my enthusiasm to excel, and my mind started to wander during the day to my personal life and my plans for after work with friends. One day I realized with much pain, that my dream job had become just an ordinary, dreary job."

What happened to Meagan is very common. When you idealize a job in advance, especially one in what seems like a glamorous field, you set yourself up for disappointment—at least until you can work your way up to the level where people are, indeed, enjoying exciting and glamorous jobs. It's also a symptom of youth and inexperience. But for Meagan, things got worse before they got better.

"I just didn't see how I was going to ever be happy at the museum. I didn't have the advanced degrees needed to participate in the curatorial department, where the interesting work was done, and my lack of further education started to chip away at my self-esteem. I told myself I should've gone to graduate school instead of being in a rush to leave. Yet once I had a taste of life outside college, I really didn't want to go back for another three or four years. I became cranky and ill-tempered at work and lost all desire to be there, though I was still on the lookout for some kind of solution. When it came time for my one-year evaluation, did I ever get a shock."

Meagan was told bluntly that her supervisor was disheartened by her diminishing enthusiasm for her job and was ready to let her go. Still, she was given one last chance to turn things around, since they'd already invested a year's worth of training in her. "Panicked, since I didn't see how I was going to get excited about the job I had, I asked if there was another department I could transfer to. I was told there was an opening in the museum store, but that it was considered a lesser job. I didn't care. I grabbed it. Maybe it was just the relief of having a second chance, but right away my energy level shot up."

That was six years ago, and now Meagan runs the museum store and couldn't be happier with her job. "What I realized, is that my satisfaction was tied to feeling like I worked in a museum. I needed to be surrounded by beautiful things. I was never going to get promoted to curator in my other job or even get a window in my office. Now I can be part of the life of the museum without feeling

Have you set yourself an ideal trap?

"You can't expect insights, even the big ones, to suddenly make you understand everything. But I figure: Hey, it's a step if they leave you confused in a deeper way."
~Jane Wagner

deficient about my lack of an advanced degree. I get to travel and interact with all kinds of fascinating people. Now the only problems I have are good ones, like having too many artists to choose from for our limited edition prints. Life is good."

What saved Meagan was that she already had awareness about her dissatisfaction, and she'd been trying to think of a solution on her own. She wasn't just ignoring the problem. When an opportunity appeared, she didn't hesitate and latched right onto it. She trusted her instincts—which were right on target—and she's perfectly suited to the creative challenges of running such a department.

More on obstacles—a gift and a surprise

Okay, that's it. That's my catalogue of weeds and pests to banish from your garden of possibilities. If you take action on these now, then the implementation phase we'll begin in the next chapter will be a cool summer breeze. Ahhhhhhh. You may have noticed that I didn't include as obstacles any problems you may be having with co-workers or your boss. That's because I wanted this chapter to just focus on you. In Chapter Four we discussed resolving issues with co-workers, and ahead in Chapter Six, we'll play with fire and jump into problems you may be encountering with management. I know, you can hardly wait!

Journal exercise

What else is bugging you?

I want to give you space to record any thoughts this list of obstacles has stirred up for you. Go back and review any pests you check marked (or splatted) and think about how you're going to get rid of them. In addition, **if you can think of other challenges you already see ahead, note them here, then determine which of the three categories they fit in:**

1. external obstacles
2. reactions to situations
3. internal obstacles

Remember, obstacles in the first group just need mechanical solutions,

ones in the second group require you to alter your response, and
those in the third group are all within your control, since you invented
them to begin with.

Also, give some thought to your instinctive coping style.
How do you normally react when problems rear their pesky heads?
Do you look for the lesson, are you thankful, do you fight back, do
you seek help or do you retreat? If whatever methods you've been
using aren't working so well, then I challenge you to try some new
responses. I know, I'm always giving you something else to do! I'm
done for this chapter. It's time to give yourself another bouquet.

Applause,
applause!

Is it your nature to nurture yourself?
I hope so. Most women are instinctive nurturers, but their
biggest challenge is making the time to do it for themselves. You notice
I said *make* not *find*. Now that you've assessed your messes, you <u>do</u>
have more time in your days, don't you? For doing this chapter's
really difficult work, you deserve a fabulous reward. Remember the
exhausted woman you met at the mall in the beginning of this chapter?
The one who even had a map to yellow store number F-19, but still
couldn't drag herself over there to find some reward for herself? Let's
give her story a happy ending. *Your happy ending*, by figuring out a
fitting way to nurture yourself after what I've put you through in this
chapter. Only you know what will be appropriate for you. A Spa day?
A nice, long massage? A vacation day at the beach? A romantic
weekend with your honey? I wouldn't dream of telling you what your
reward should be—I've learned a few things about women during my
spins on this planet. Whatever it is, really enjoy it, because you are

among the tiny percentage of people who ever make an effort to improve their lives. Now don't you feel special?

After you finish with that, follow me to Chapter Six, where you'll learn the best way to present your plan to management, tips and tricks on dealing with your boss and bringing your dream to life. **Come on, this is going to be fun!**

"I'd rather regret
the things I've done
than the things
I have not."

~Lucille Ball

Chapter Six
PLANTING YOUR GARDEN OF POSSIBILITIES

Chapter Six At A Glance

- Understanding your supervisor
- What do bosses really want?
- What you wish your boss knew about you
- How to handle difficult bosses—the Top Six Nixers
- Taking the longer way
- Boss protocol 101
- Making the meeting go your way
- Watch out for this sinkhole
- Climbing over the wall of resistance
- How much can you compromise?
- You deserve a change of scene

Doesn't it feel good to confront your pests and weeds?
This is where it gets really exciting, because now you're finally ready
to show your plan for your ideal job to your boss and plant the seeds
for your garden of possibilities. As a reminder, here are the ten
stepping stones from Chapter Four. By this point, you'll be familiar
with the first seven steps. **I suggest you use this as a checklist to
be sure you're completely prepared for the next step.**

**The ten stepping stones of your PATH (Planned Actions
Toward Happiness)**

___ 1. Outline your specific path to get your ideal job.
___ 2. Determine what will enable your plan.
___ 3. Prepare for objections.
___ 4. Enlist support.
___ 5. Measure the added value of your plan.
___ 6. Write a Job Action Memo.
___ 7. Be accountable for achieving your plan.
___ 8. Present your plan to management, be prepared to revise.
___ 9. Implement your plan.
___ 10. Gather feedback and evaluate your success.

Stepping Stone #8

Present your plan to management, be prepared to revise.

Since there's a good chance your boss or supervisor gave this
book to you, your approaching him or her with a new vision for your
position will be expected, so that's one step made much easier. Even
if you have no concerns about this step, I still suggest you read this
section, because it also offers tips for dealing with different kinds of
bosses, even difficult bosses—just in case you have one of those. If
you did the Kolbe Index (see Page 52), then consider sharing your
results with your boss. If this is something you did on your own,
perhaps you can demonstrate how it could help your whole team to
do them. Of course, having your boss do his index too, would be very
helpful. It can actually be fun—and very enlightening—to explore how
each of you instinctively solves problems.

However, if you found this book on your own, listen carefully and you'll hear a big round of applause from me! That shows initiative on your part and a true desire to improve your job—and your life. Though in your case, you'll have to plan exactly how you'll approach your boss with your new ideas. One way would be to keep her in the loop from the beginning. Share your excitement over what you're learning as you work through the chapters—c'mon, you are excited aren't you? Tell your supervisor you believe this new process will help you make a greater contribution to the team and the company. Perhaps your enthusiasm will inspire management to pay for Kolbe indexes for your whole team.

What I know about bosses

As preparation for presenting your plan, let's talk about bosses. After 29 years of experience, evolving from a less-than sensitive boss into an all-around good guy (sure, go ahead and ask my team!) who genuinely wants my own team to prosper and enjoy fulfilling jobs, I believe I can decipher *Bossus Expeditus*. What I hear over and over as I travel around the country presenting my workshops, is that

bosses know their people are unhappy, but they don't know what to do about it—in fact it's a major source of their stress, too.

They know many of you feel disengaged from your jobs and are just putting in your time, but they can't figure out how to connect with you—partly because they're often buried in day-to-day crises that demand their attention. They're also frustrated because they realize communication between you isn't as good as it could be—and few of them have specialized training to make it better.

What do bosses really want? Here's what my research reveals, and if you can consistently relate to this list and fulfill many or even some of the items on the list, you'll gain an important piece of the job happiness puzzle. If you please your supervisor, and together your team is productive, then it's a big win for everyone. So here goes—just for fun, mark ones that you believe are true of you and see how many you have at the end.

What bosses want their teams to know:

· We want to know that you're committed to your job, that you believe in what we're trying to accomplish, that you actually want to be here.

· We want you to contribute your ideas and enthusiasm; when you participate, we know you're involved.

· We want to believe that you bring your best attitude to work, that you care about giving good service to our clients or creating the best possible products. We want you to be proud you work here.

· We want to trust you to work productively without micro-managing; we want to encourage you to make good decisions on your own.

· We want to see you flourishing as part of a healthy team, cooperating, knowing when to bend and when to stand firm in your position.

· We want you to give us honest feedback, yet allow room for us to be human and make mistakes; we want honest, open communication.

· We want you to evolve as employees, to learn new skills, to welcome new challenges, to thrive as the business grows.

On the flip side, I've listened to what associates have wished their bosses knew about them. Since so few people seem to ever tell their supervisors how they really feel, I'm suggesting it would open up new lines of communication if you could do just that. You probably

few
people
seem to
tell their
boss
how they
really feel

won't agree with all of these, **so just put a check mark by anything on this list that resonates with you.** In the space that follows, write down some things you'd like to share with your boss that she probably doesn't know about you.

What team members want their bosses to know:

· ___ We want you to know that showing us appreciation for the work we do is our greatest reward. We value days off and soccer afternoons, too, and of course, we also like seeing your appreciation reflected in our paychecks. But simple, honest, timely praise for a job well done costs you nothing, yet to us is priceless. It's also the most direct route to inspiring loyalty.

· ___ We are willing to extend ourselves and go the extra mile for you—as long as it isn't a pattern of abuse and as long as you acknowledge our special efforts. We get tired of bailing you out of jams without you even noticing.

· ___ We want you to know that ongoing cash incentive programs are often counterproductive. While we don't mind short-term fun incentives like trips for contests, etc., what we don't like is the constant pressure of feeling like we have to produce at a certain level to receive a certain benefit. As dedicated employees, we don't need to have golden carrots constantly dangled in front of us.

· ___ We want to earn your trust and once we have it, we'd like to rely on it to adjust our schedules when appropriate. We'll work hard for you and give you our best, but we'd like options such as: flex hours, job sharing or telecommuting.

· ___ We want your respect. We want to be treated as individuals, and we don't want to be pitted against our co-workers.

· ___ We want to be included in making plans that affect us. We want to be part of the action, involved in figuring out strategies for our departments, we want to know our input is valued.

· ___ We love having control over our own days, being trusted to manage our time well and prioritize our tasks.

· ___ We want you to understand that we can't always do everything you need or want. Please take a moment to assess our work load before you bounce in with one more great idea to implement. We can feel overburdened when you come in with big, sweeping goals and changes without first asking how it will impact our team.

"The problem with communication, is the illusion that it has been accomplished."
~George Bernard Shaw

· ___We'd like you to abide by the same rules you require us to follow. We feel demeaned when you set behavior rules for us and then turn around and break them. We're in this together, so please, show us some courtesy.

· ___We love it when you're as engaged in the work as we are. We like it when we know we can count on you, when we know where to find you to ask questions. Please don't make us handle jobs that are obviously yours to do.

· ___We want to be given room to grow. If you allow us to be more, your business will be more.

· ___We love goals, but make them attainable based on the talent and resources we have. We're already working at full speed. When you don't hire enough people to do the work, something— and someone—always suffers.

· ___We truly want to do a great job for you, but we don't always know what you want, because your instructions aren't clear or you're too rushed to explain things to us. Then when we fail to meet your expectations, we don't like it when you fail to share any responsibility for the situation.

· ___We want to be able to talk candidly with you, but you often seem unapproachable because you're so busy. We would love occasions for our team to spend time with you away from the office, so we could get to know each other better.

"We cannot teach people anything; we can only help them discover it within themselves."
~Galileo

I bet that felt good! **Here's your chance to jot down some ideas you'd like to share with your boss.** Where have you disagreed in the past? How have your approaches to problem solving been at odds? On which topics would you like to see the two of you communicate more effectively?

_____

_____

_____

_____

_____

_____

_____

_____

_____

_____

_____

_____

_____

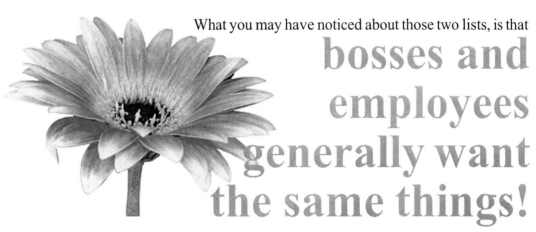

What you may have noticed about those two lists, is that

bosses and employees generally want the same things!

That's probably a shock to many of you, but it's true. You want to do good work and be valued for it, and your boss wants nothing more than to reward you for doing excellent work. You are indeed on the same team. You might want to put this on a sticky note and press it to your wrist . . .er, monitor: **We're all on the same team!**

How to handle a Problem Boss

Though it pains me to admit it, I know there are difficult bosses out there. Gee, I even used to be one! Statistics reveal that the Number One reason people quit their jobs is a poor relationship with their supervisor. They don't feel appreciated. They don't feel they are heard. They're misunderstood. You know the litany, I'm sure. There are as many types of difficult bosses as there are thorns in a rose garden, but below you'll find a rundown of some of the worst offenders, along with **strategies for coping with them in order to get them on board with your new job plan.** In fact, sometimes just resolving a poor relationship with your boss is all you need to find more joy in your job. HOWEVER, as a boss myself, I am required to

> "So much of what we call management consists in making it difficult for people to work."
> ~Peter Drucker

tell you that everything I say about troublesome bosses can also be said about difficult employees. If you're reading this book, you probably aren't one, because you care enough to want to improve your job experience. All I ask is that as you read about problem bosses, check in with yourself to make sure none of it could apply to you—perhaps on a bad day?

While it shouldn't be your job to "fix" a dysfunctional boss, the reality is, if you work for one, you have only three choices:

1. Continue on and suffer the consequences.
2. Switch to a different department or company.
3. Work with your supervisor to see if you can't improve the quality of your life at work.

Keep in mind, if you have a difficult boss, she's probably not happy either. Solving the underlying issues won't be easy, but if you've seen enough goodness in her to merit the effort, then it can be very rewarding to help another person evolve—and you'll grow right along with her, since as we know, none of us is perfect. Even me. *Sigh.*

Meet the Top Six Nixers

These are my picks for bosses to watch out for—along with some strategies to get them to help foster your dream job.

Nixer #1

Felicia Flitter

This type of boss is really quite benign, because she means well and wouldn't dream of intentionally making your life more difficult. Unfortunately, that's exactly what she does with her scattered, unfocused, messy approach to business. She's often the business owner, and it's only because of reliable people like you that she's still in business. Every day brings a new panic. Reports need to be rushed because she forgot a deadline. Meetings are missed because they didn't get on your calendar. The Flitter operates (and probably thrives) on the adrenaline caused by crises. It makes her feel important. It makes you feel sick. You just want to be able to do your job in peace and quiet, on time and without stress.

Caroline, the executive assistant to the owner of a yacht brokerage company in Florida, knew she had to do something before her boss drove her to drink. "She's really very sweet to me on a personal level and never complains when I need time off to do something related to my kids, but the rest of the time she was driving me nuts, and I wasn't sure it was worth it," she confides. "Before I could ever finish one assignment, she gave me five more that were even more urgent. Then an hour later she'd wonder why the first task wasn't done. She had no clue how long things took to do."

That was actually the key to working better with a Flitter. Caroline had to teach her how to be a good boss—not something in her job description, of course, but that's what was needed. "I decided to keep a log of every task my boss gave me during one week and indicate how long it took to complete each item. I also managed to convert that data to a chart that showed how often I was interrupted by her, how long it took in real time to accomplish the tasks and how bottlenecks got created.

Ultimately she was able to see how the only way I was able to sort out her chaos was to work overtime when she wasn't around."

Happily for Caroline, her Flitter of a boss appreciated the visual demonstration of her behavior, and used the information to reform her management style. Now she plans ahead more and saves up new tasks to give Caroline at certain points in the day, rather than interrupting her every few minutes.

How could you use Caroline's experience in your situation?

chaos is
also
stressful
for the
one who
creates it

- Stop being a martyr and cleaning up your supervisor's messes without comment.
- Document your chaos so that your boss can grasp what she's doing to you.
- Work with her to create a scheduling system, so deadlines for reports and meetings don't get lost in the hubbub.
- Set specific times to review new assignments when there is also time for questions.
- Make good use of wall planners, white boards or whatever tools help you keep your workflow visible to you <u>both</u>, so she isn't tempted to dump too much on you.
- Develop good boundaries, so there are no hidden bad feelings; state what's true for you about your work.

Getting a chaos queen to say Yes. If you aren't by nature well-organized, is there someone else in your work group who could step in and offer advice and help with systems design? Most disorganized people adapt well to systems they understand and that are easy to use. Chaos is also stressful for the one who creates it. If you can help your Flitter reign in her pandemonium, you'll be her hero for sure. Once order is restored, you can move ahead and present your ideas for your ideal job. Note some ideas here to help rectify the situation.

Nixer #2

The Absentee is fairly harmless— except to your ego, your potential and your future!

Absentee Abe

This boss is often a middle manager, someone who became bewildered in the corporate sea and lost sight of land. He just doesn't seem to care about much of anything and certainly not you. He rarely listens to what you have to say, never wants to hear your plans and ideas and avoids mediating department conflicts. Most days, he drifts in late then schedules long lunch meetings (some of which you suspect are with his barber). Though he barely meets the standards for his job, somehow he always slides by unnoticed and unscathed. He's as bored with his job as you are with yours. The Absentee is fairly harmless—except to your ego, your potential and your future! You might be a perfect match—if you hadn't decided to dream up something better for yourself.

Shakira had just landed her first sales job lining up corporate travel accounts. At the bottom of the food chain, she was given leads that were long considered dead, in a territory no one else wanted, but she didn't let that stop her. With great creativity (born partly out of inexperience) she soon realized the standard techniques she was taught in her brief training session were not going to heat up her cold leads. "I had some previous experience in video production, so it didn't intimidate me to think of ways to use short videos as presentation and lead generating tools," she explains. "I wrote up a quick proposal and tried to get my supervisor excited by it, but he just rolled his eyes and wouldn't even let me finish. He said there was no budget for that sort of thing and just walked out of his office, leaving me standing there with my mouth open."

Realizing she had nothing to lose, since she'd be fired anyway if she couldn't get some sales happening, Shakira turned to her pals from her previous job at a local TV station. "I went back after hours and one of the editors let me work at a computer that wasn't in use at that time of night. With the station's advanced software, I was able to convert my power point presentations into cool little videos, add some stock footage, music and everything. The file size was small enough that I could email them to prospects as a different way of getting their minds on travel and off their usual headaches. It worked! After converting my fourth cold lead to a hefty sale, my previously uninterested boss took notice."

Is there
something
dramatic
you could
do to
get his
attention?

Because he knew it would reflect well on him, Shakira's Absentee boss finally encouraged her creativity. Next, she moved on to creating clever and inexpensive leave-behind materials, again tapping into her own outside resources when she couldn't get access to something she needed. Once she tasted success, Shakira was unstoppable, and thrived on the challenge of dead leads. Eventually, she moved on to training other salespeople and creating custom sales materials—a job she adores.

What can you learn from Shakira?

- Dare to try something entirely new at your company.
- Don't believe the negative things you hear about your job.
- Reach out to a network of associates to help you do what others consider impossible.
- Research new ways of delivering old messages.
- Always question what's been done before; innovate.
- Don't let a lack of funds deter a good idea.
- Results speak for themselves—get the sale and you get the job.

How to get your plan through to an Absentee boss. Think of things he has responded to in the past—is there anything that gets him focused? Can you tie into that somehow? Is there something dramatic you could do to get his attention? Is there a way to implement your plan in small stages? Write your ideas here.

Deanna Demander

This boss is sadly too common. She has high standards for herself and just assumes you share them, without ever thinking what that would look like from your desk. Unlike the Absentee boss, the Demander is always there when you arrive and never gives you a moment to settle in, before she starts adding to the stack on your desk that she began making hours earlier. She expects perfection and speed from herself and from you. She never has time to talk, and when you don't understand something, your stomach does cartwheels when you have to ask her to explain anything twice. Gratitude is not part of her makeup. She finds her job highly rewarding and just assumes that you do, too. Insensitive sums her up.

To survive in the elite world of high net worth estate planning, Ellen knew she'd have to figure out a way to get her boss to pull back a bit and relax her controlling management style. "I had great credentials when I took the job as her executive assistant, but she treated me like I was fresh off the hay truck," she remembers with exasperation. "As a Mississippian, I'm used to a mellower approach to life, but here in Dallas I feel like I'm running all day long without ever catching my breath. Finally, I took a stand and told my boss that if she didn't schedule a full hour meeting for us by the end of the week, I was going to quit. That got her attention," she recalls, now able to laugh a bit.

At the meeting, Ellen presented a one-page summary of her requests, in descending order of importance. At number one, was a plea to let her do what she knows how to do well. "I knew my boss was creating her own stress by wasting time hovering over me unnecessarily. I simply asked her for a one-week trial of my ideas. I figured we'd both see the difference immediately, so that's all it would take to prove my point. Or not. I also explained that I'm not wired like she is, but that my calm was something she could rely on when she got over-stimulated by her work. She especially seemed to like that concept. Once I saw her smile, I even suggested that the time she saved by not micro-managing me, she could spend getting a massage. I could see that equation also getting through to her."

Ellen's boss, being a sharp cookie herself, easily agreed to the trial arrangement. By the end of Day Two, she made it permanent.

> She finds her job highly rewarding and just assumes that you do, too.

Ellen kept her job, but her neck aches and acid stomach episodes were history. In time, she even took on prospecting leads for her boss, something that fit right in with her interest in the comings and goings of the rich and near-famous of Texas.

What can you take away from Ellen's experience?

- Don't be a doormat! Use common sense about reasonable workplace behavior and insist on being treated with respect and as something more than an office machine.
- Don't be afraid of issuing ultimatums (as long as you're prepared to take action on them if they don't go your way). Sometimes it takes a strong statement to get a Demander's attention.
- Don't waste a high-powered boss's time—be fully prepared with a concise written statement of your requests.
- Gently explain that you are different from your boss, which is a good thing, and let her know how your difference is her asset.
- Let her know you want to find a solution that works for you both—that you aren't complaining, only trying to improve efficiency by having each of you do what you do best.
- See if you can suggest ways to unwind your high-strung boss.

How to present your plan to your Demander boss

What will she respond to? Is your plan for your ideal job going to pass her standards of excellence? Can you frame it in such a way that it's all about you being even more wonderful in your job, as well as making her look even better? Work <u>with</u> her personality, not against it. Jot your ideas here.

_____

_____

_____

_____

_____

_____

_____

_____

_____

Nixer #4

Toxic Tom

This guy likes to snarl and growl and control every situation. He rarely lets you think for yourself and loves to sneak up behind you and peer over your shoulder to see what you're up to. He doesn't know the meaning of trust. His pleasure comes from berating you in front of others, and he seems to look for ways to upset you and demean you. Undermining your confidence at every turn, he loves to find fault—even where there is none. Busy work is his middle name. (Busy work for you, that is.) He may be able to survive in a large company by treating his own boss very differently than he manages you, but he's more apt to be the owner of the company—probably taking out the frustrations of his recent divorce or other unhappiness on his team. Whatever his reason, this toxic fellow can be just plain mean—if you let him. "Let" being the operative word.

While it's never professional to bring your religious practices into the workplace, you may instead be able to approach your job with a more forgiving attitude and a more generous spirit. Lucy had been feeling depressed because she worked for a toxic boss, ironically in the U.S. Department of Health and Human Services in Washington D.C. He was always making what she felt were excessive demands on her, and Lucy was fed up with her work at what she called Inhuman Services. "I was sick and tired of being belittled in staff meetings for not doing things he'd never even asked me to do! It was like he was from the *Twilight Zone* or something. He had me doing so many versions of every report cycle that I know I did get mixed up sometimes, but he was the source of the panicky behavior, for sure."

Yet by having an open discussion with him and finding out what kind of pressures he was under from *his* supervisor, Lucy was able to better sort out what she was being asked to do. "I realized I was doing a lot of busy work, preparing back-up plans for situations that never happened, just so my boss would feel more secure and ready for any eventuality," she explains. "He seemed to believe that picking on me in front of his boss made him look like he was in charge. I gently suggested that it made him look like he couldn't manage his staff well, and that he'd appear more competent if he was seen *praising* his team members for their good work. It was a huge shift of

> "We are all faced with a series of great opportunities brilliantly disguised as impossible situations."
> ~Charles R. Swindoll

"Kill my boss?
Do I dare live
out the
American
dream?"
~Homer
Simpson

perspective for him to make, and it took several months, but finally he began to soften his ways."

Applying her beliefs to the situation, Lucy forgave him for his previous actions and became determined to find a mutually beneficial solution. "I was able to convince him that we could handle anything that came our way without all the extra work." Once he saw that he could rely on Lucy, he agreed to end his over-the-tops demands. She now feels more valued as an employee, and her boss treats her with more respect and sees her as a partner with a common purpose.

What is there to glean from Lucy's experience?

- Even the most unpleasant boss can be rehabilitated.
- Try fighting meanness with kindness.
- Have compassion for his pressures.
- Find solutions that are mutual wins. Be sure to meet him at least half way.
- Don't argue in front of others.
- Have suggestions ready for alternate work styles.
- Demonstrate a reasonable amount of patience while he evolves.
- Be sure to let him know how much you appreciate his willingness to try something new—especially if his ways are entrenched.

How to win approval from a toxic boss. No doubt, this is the toughest challenge. If you take this on, some sort of sainthood is assured. You'll have to figure out why your boss is so toxic, which is a tall order. Trying to get him to talk about himself is a good place to start. We all need to be heard, and sometimes a patient listener can work

try being the calm eye in the center of the hurricane

wonders. Ask co-workers for their advice. Does he get along with anyone in your office? If so, ask that person for help. Try being the calm eye in the center of the hurricane. If he can't rile you up, he may stop trying. This type of boss instinctively goes after others' vulnerabilities in order to make himself feel better. Are there genuine, positive traits or actions you can acknowledge in him? I hate to say it, but it's a bit like training a puppy—reward the good behavior and give no attention to the bad. As for getting him to approve your plan, the best advice I can give you is to hold your discussions in private. Without an audience, the toxic boss is often just a pussycat. Note any ideas you have for taming him here.

_____

_____

_____

_____

_____

_____

_____

_____

Nixer #5

Selma Squelcher

Insecurity is her middle name, because she can't stand it when anyone she supervises seems ready to outshine her in any way. Without many talents herself, she relies on dimming others' abilities to maintain what little starshine she has left. The squelcher will rarely approve new ideas or anything outside company rules as she sees them. Then when she gets pressured about performance, she feels justified in berating her team. Her big fear is being exposed as incompetent, and she can be a difficult person to get an idea past.

Rachel came up against a Squelcher when she hatched an idea to improve customer service at the large, Virginia art supply chain store where she worked. A classic starving artist, Rachel was professionally trained but needed her clerk's job to pay her bills. "I figured at least I'd enjoy the employee discount, meeting artists who came in and generally being in a creative environment," she explains, still shaking her head over the difficulties she soon encountered.

"Though the store offered some classes on various topics, I saw right away that customers had lots of questions about using materials that were never going to be covered in a class. Besides, they wanted answers on the spot, not in some class three weeks from Sunday."

Rachel approached her supervisor and suggested that she could do product demonstrations everyday from noon until 2 p.m., each day focusing on a different type of project. By posting a schedule of her demonstrations and asking for requests, she could meet customer needs in a more timely manner. "Boy did that idea get shot down in a hurry," she remembers. "I could tell by my supervisor's reaction that she thought my idea was just an excuse for me to play instead of work.

After getting a loud 'No' I sort of gave up, until I saw that maybe I could just start by offering answers one-on-one. I stayed alert for customers with questions and jumped at the chance to give them as thorough an explanation as I could without actually doing a demo. Soon my co-workers redirected all questions to me, and I became the resident expert on just about everything we sold. While this made my job more gratifying, it still wasn't the best I knew I could do."

"Go within every day and find the inner strength so that the world will not blow your candle out."
~Katherine Dunham

As often happens in such cases, eventually the store manager saw Rachel in action being super helpful to customers. Her explanation of the difference between acrylic and gouache paints had even drawn a small crowd, as shoppers in that aisle drew near to listen to an obvious expert. No dummy, the store manager pulled Rachel aside and asked if she'd like to teach classes at the store. "When I told the manager my original idea, he loved it and wasted no time in giving his okay. Within a month, I was doing product demos all day long and absolutely loving my job. Instead of dragging myself home with little energy for my own work, I arrived eager to apply what I'd been doing at work to my own paintings. Now there doesn't seem to be much difference between my two jobs—I make art at both of them."

No surprise, sales at the store rose dramatically. The Squelcher didn't last long after that and got to throw her wet blanket somewhere else.

What can you learn from Rachel's experience?

you can always suggest even more ways that your plan will make her look good

- If your supervisor won't give you the okay for your grand plan, is there another way you can begin to implement small parts of it?
- Sometimes an idea just needs proving.
- Sometimes it needs to take enough form so that it can get noticed by someone other than the Squelcher. This approach will require tact and planning.
- Don't be afraid to seize an opportunity to share your idea with upper management.
- Work really hard to make your plan a success—don't just let the opportunity slip away with a half-hearted effort. Rachel did *not* know everything there was to know about all the products in the store, but she made it her business to learn. She contacted manufacturers for training videos, she taped craft programs on the DIY Network, checked out books from her library, joined a knitting club and pestered friends to teach her techniques that they knew. In short, she made a career out of becoming an extraordinary expert on arts and crafts supplies.

How not to get your plan squelched. It's no fun having your parade rained on time and time again. One approach is to have such a grand idea and gather so much support for it from your associates, that it becomes a giant snowball your supervisor can't hold back. Another is to form strong alliances at all levels of your company in case you need their support. If you think there is any chance of honest communication with your Squelcher, you can always suggest even more ways that your plan will make her look good, and if there are enough wins in it for her, perhaps she'll put her stamp on it. Note your strategies here.

_____

_____

_____

_____

_____

_____

_____

Nixer #6

Phony Phil

This boss can be difficult to identify—until you've been cheated by him. Lazy at his core, he thrives in middle layers of large companies where he can coerce others to do all the work. His specialty is taking all the credit for your hard work and innovative ideas. He's as phony as the rubber slug your six-year-old son leaves lying around to annoy you. This guy lies when it suits him, and it often does. He can ooze charm if it'll get you to help him. It's all part of his big act, designed to disguise his incompetence.

Jayne got along well with her boss—until she realized how he operated. Assistant to the regional sales manager of a pharmaceutical company, she brought enough corporate experience to her job to think she could handle anything. "I'd never encountered a boss like this before," she confides. "The first thing I noticed about the company was lots of bloat—enough layers of red tape to reach around our region."

Jayne quickly figured out a superior tracking system for their large sales force and presented it to her boss. He agreed and told Jayne to put it into action. She was able to slice the field rep's paperwork in half, thus making them much more efficient. Two months later, when the quarterly figures were in, their region came out

on top—and guess who took all the credit and never mentioned Jayne once? "Since my boss had nothing to do with it except to okay it, I knew right then I had to shift to another department," she explains. "Besides, I could see it was part of an ongoing pattern of behavior that included lying and back stabbing. I had documented the entire process, and Human Resources was great about understanding my concerns and recommended me for a position in the national sales office. Now my ideas are welcomed and acknowledged and I feel valuable. I work hard and really try to innovate, so I need to believe that ability will be both utilized and rewarded."

What can you learn from Jayne's situation?

The challenge here is to be open and honest in your dealings

- If your boss does not value integrity, he is not likely to change. Try and make him see the light if you like, but behaving unethically is usually an entrenched core belief.
- There is no need to sink to his level—cling to your own truth and positive approach and you'll thrive.
- Keep a paper trail that documents important ideas and projects you suggest and implement.
- If you find yourself working for an unethical boss, talk it over with human resource folks if possible. If it's not, then you're in a precarious position, because you can't be sure where his alliances are. Whistle blowers usually end up leaving the company where they report unethical behavior, and that may be for the best. Jayne had the last laugh though, because she ended up working for her supervisor's boss, and over time, was able to demonstrate exactly who had designed the new tracking system.

Getting a real plan past a phony boss. This is no picnic, either. The challenge here is to be open and honest in your communications without calling him dishonest. You'll have to be a true diplomat to get your plan past this guy. Sad to say, your best bet may be a lateral move or a promotion. Note your ideas here.

_____

_____

_____

_____

_____

_____

_____

> "The magic formula that successful businesses have discovered is to treat customers like guests and employees like people."
> ~Tom Peters

I hope these stories of successful coping will inspire you in dealing with your own supervisor. Keep in mind that you don't have to *like* your boss to enjoy your job. Perhaps you are just different temperamentally or view the world through different colored glasses. Maybe she doesn't fit your image of how a good boss should behave. Can you let some of your own judgment go and look for the good qualities in her? Of course it makes for a jollier workplace when you get along well with your boss. That can also be a trap if you aspire to greater things, yet cling to the safety of a familiar, secure situation.

Just remember: the one thing you always control is your response to your boss and what she does.

Happily, I believe that conscientious, caring bosses are more prevalent today, especially as companies look to trim their corporate fat. Life's too short to work for an ineffective boss. If that's the wild card you were dealt, and you can't see a sure route to improve the situation, then no one would blame you for moving on to a healthier pasture. If that is, indeed, your current challenge, don't miss Chapter Seven, where we'll examine how to make a graceful exit—and make a better choice next time.

Reaching your dream the long way around

Some supervisors just can't seem to make room for their associates to make progress, have goals or move forward with their careers. Valerie remembers all the hoops she had to jump through to redesign her job, but she's not complaining. "Gee, I sure thought I was in a job with no future, after six years doing pretty much the same support work for a top executive at a consumer testing company," she explains. "I don't know why it took so long for me to realize my ideal job as a product tester was in the building next door. One day after watching another woman cooking eggs in various skillets, I quizzed her about her job. It sounded like my kind of omelet, so I asked my boss if I could transfer to that department. To my surprise, he said he couldn't spare me! That sent me on a four-month crusade to find people in the company who would back my switch. Finally, after being very insistent and persistent I got the okay. I love my new job, even though I took a small reduction in pay, because now I'm having a ball! I was so cut out for this, and every day is completely different….no boredom now! The days just fly by—some days I'm sad to see that it's time to go home."

"Just go out there and do what you have to do."
~Martina Navratilova

What Valerie encountered is not uncommon. Because she was such a good employee and had become one of those executive assistants who does just about everything for her boss, he really didn't want to let her go. Selfishly, he dreaded the inconvenience of training a replacement, because he knew he had a loyal, dedicated associate in Valerie. He failed to recognize her stagnation and didn't have her best interests at heart when he refused her transfer request. While it's natural for a boss who has grown accustomed to a great right hand assistant to want to retain her, I really hope managers wil realize that

it's in the best interests of the company when all employees are working at the level of their highest potential.

Now for some self-serving advice

Who doesn't like to be appreciated and catered to? I know I do. I ranted a bit earlier about how bosses need to show more appreciation for their employees, but it works both ways. If you can find opportunities to show genuine gratitude for the good things your boss does, he will notice, I promise you. (He may even be inclined to do them again.) If you feel comfortable giving him sincere feedback, too, then so much the better. We all want to hear that we're doing a good job—even us boss types.

Just how much genuine appreciation can you show your supervisor without seeming like you're trying to bribe your way into his esteem? It depends on so many variables that only you can answer that question. How long have you worked together? Do you feel like you are genuine friends? Do others share your level of admiration, or are you a one-woman cheering squad? **In general, I would err on the side of doing less, but here are some broad guidelines.**

· Appropriate birthday cards are great; leave the R-rated ones on the rack.
· If the whole team wants to make a fuss and do a cake, or even a simple gift, that's probably fine.
· Be wary of personal gifts, especially for no apparent reason. Be especially afraid of giving anything too personal—ask this test question: What would a spouse think about it? Also be careful of giving anything too valuable, as it could definitely be misconstrued.
· Homemade baked goods rarely miss (unless he's trying to drop some pounds).
· Showing genuine concern when your boss has a personal or health crisis will be appreciated. Pitching in to pick up her slack, will be remembered for sure. If the team wants to send flowers to the hospital or to a funeral, also fine.
· Surprises can work, but be really sure it's something he'll like.

Olivia had a job she absolutely adored in the marketing department for a chain of eldercare facilities, but a difficult boss

modeling
how a
caring
person
behaves,
Olivia
brought
out the
best in
her boss

almost ruined it for her. Her solution was to kill her ornery boss with kindness. "I had spent the weekend painting my office (with his permission, of course) and making my space welcoming and a place I could be happy spending most of my quality hours," she recalls. "On Monday, he kind of whined about wishing *his* office felt as nice as mine now did, so I offered to spend the next weekend doing the same for his space. He was very surprised, but took me up on my offer. I made sure he gave me an ample budget, then I brought my boyfriend and my dog along to help, ordered pizzas and made a party of it. We built shelves, brought in plants, hung up the awards gathering dust in the corner, framed some of his photos and made it a friendly environment. You know what? I actually noticed his mood improve from then on, as if the cheery yellow of his walls seeped into his heart."

Now for sure, that's going way beyond the call of duty, but one weekend of effort turned the tide for Olivia. She continued to do other thoughtful things for her boss, including taking care of the new plants in his office, making portfolios of all the many articles he had written, dog sitting for him on occasion (which she actually enjoyed) and so on. By modeling for him how a caring person behaves, Olivia brought out the best in her boss and was able to really enjoy her dream job.

"When people go to work, they shouldn't have to leave their hearts at home." ~Betty Bender

How nice do you want to be?

How much effort you feel good about making on behalf of your boss is entirely up to you. If a better relationship with your boss is all that stands between you and really loving your job, then consider how you might go an extra mile or ten to get on her good side. What heartfelt actions could you take that would make your boss happy? What special challenges is she going through that you could help with? How could you demonstrate that you admire your boss as a human being? List some ideas here.

_____

_____

_____

_____

_____

_____

_____

_____

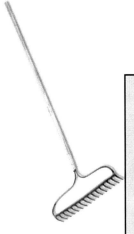

Tips for making your meeting go your way

      This list is plain old common sense, mostly written for those of you who hate to plan anything too carefully. In your enthusiasm (and possibly haste) to present your idea to management and get that garden planted, don't jab yourself in the foot with a rake.

- Make an appointment to talk to your boss, don't just barge in on him. This is important to you, isn't it? Unless you're proposing a plan that directly relates to other team member's plans (and is in fact a team plan) meet with your boss alone.
- Dress professionally, especially if you're hoping for a promotion or to interface more with your customers.
- Be professional. Take the meeting seriously, and let your boss know right away that this request is important to you.
- Hand him a written proposal or Job Action Memo to read while you present your ideas verbally. Show enthusiasm for your plan as you stress how it will benefit both him and the company.
- Bring any visual aids that will help make your case.
- Stay focused on your one goal; this is not an excuse to air all your stacked up grievances.
- Be rehearsed in what you want to say, perhaps even carry a small card with key points if you tend to get nervous in these situations.
- Listen very carefully to his reactions. Take notes. Ask questions. Depending on the scope of what you propose, he may well need time to review your plan, discuss it with others or just think about it. **The absence of an immediate Yes is NOT the same thing as a No.**
- Read that last point again! Rather than thinking of this as a one-time meeting, think of it as <u>beginning</u> a dialogue.
- Be prepared with alternate ideas. If you meet with immediate resistance, see the tips on Page 224.
- Regardless of the outcome, remain polite, professional and thank him for his time.

Watch out for this sinkhole!

Keep in mind as you prepare to approach your boss with your plan for your dream job, that its chance for success will have a lot to do with your current standing and track record. Be ready to discuss that too. You might even do a quick self-review beforehand, so you can speak about your strengths and accomplishments and how this plan will capitalize on those. If you have obvious weaknesses or challenges that your boss has been critical of in the past, be prepared to address those too. Does your new idea eliminate those challenges altogether, thereby making it a non-issue? Are there old issues you need to resolve before management will green light your plan?

Remember in Chapter Two (Page 51) how I urged you to keep a sunshine folder documenting your ongoing accomplishments? Now would be a great time to pull it out and have it ready, in case your boss tries to dismiss your readiness for more responsibilities or in any other way shatter your dream.

> "New ideas pass through three periods: It can't be done. It probably can be done, but it's not worth doing. I knew it was a good idea all along."
> ~Arthur C. Clarke

What if the wall of resistance is too high?

Despite all your best efforts at boss psychology, despite all your thorough planning, your boss may for any number of reasons simply refuse to approve your plan. She may not even tell you why. What then? You may remember, the name of this stepping stone is actually: Present your plan to management and be prepared to <u>revise</u>. In the **Job Action Memo** you created in Chapter Four (Page 140), you were

advised to have a few back-up plans in your hip pocket in case Plan A didn't fly. Do you? Now would be the time to whip them out.

Here are your options as I see them:

1. Before you leave the meeting with your boss, ask why he didn't approve your plan. Ask if there are things you could change in your plan that would allow him to agree to it. What aspects of your plan are most bothersome? The more you learn about his objections, the easier it will be to handle them.
2. Ask if you can present one of your alternate plans.
3. Seek common ground—what points can you both agree are worth considering or even agreeing to at this time?
4. Suggest a trial period—a month or a quarter.
5. Suggest phasing in your idea in stages.
6. Ask him to approve part of your plan to give you some way to at least begin the process of creating a more ideal work situation.
7. Avoid ultimatums, displays of bad temper, pouting or any other unbecoming behavior.
8. See if there are modest portions of your plan you can test quietly on your own. It may be that you'll have to create your perfect job one tiny step at a time—more like a glacier than an avalanche.
9. If you are determined to see this through or else, then you'll have to gather other allies. This is always risky, and if you fail, you may alter your relationship with your boss (and not in a good way).

How much can you compromise?

If it seems like your boss is some big dog digging up your carefully planted garden of possibilities and is just not going along with your initial vision for your ideal job, then you have to reevaluate your design and ask yourself some tough questions. Review your original notes and ideas as well as the exercises you did in Chapter Three to see how you might reconfigure your dream job. How can you address his concerns? What new varieties of flowers are you willing to plant in your garden? **Now would be a great time to ask for help**—from your team members, from other allies in the company, from your mentor, heck, ask your mom! Just get other perspectives. Perhaps you asked for more than your boss could handle at one time. (Few of

"Before I built a wall, I asked to know what was I walling in or walling out."
~Robert Frost

"The most successful people are those who are good at Plan B."
~James Yorke

us really embrace change.) What's the one aspect of your dream job that you'd most like to manifest? Would just getting the go ahead for that one thing create a starting point you could live with for awhile?

Above all, don't give up—

revise!

Is it all about your bottom line?

What if you actually like your job, but it just doesn't pay well enough to meet your needs? That's a great question with an even better answer: read Barbara Stanny's book, *Overcoming Underearning*, which offers a detailed plan for addressing that issue. I will share a few thoughts, though. If you work for a small business, it all comes back to added value (see Page 138). Sit down and talk with your boss, share your concerns and see if there are ways you could contribute more value to the company, which in turn would earn you greater rewards. If you work for a large firm, that's a fair question for an advisor in your human resources department. They may well have specific guidelines you can follow to advance through the company, or advice about what you'd need to do to qualify for a higher-paying position.

As with most issues, it's all about communication. Hinting won't help. Complaining to your co-workers won't help. Feeling overworked and underpaid won't change anything but your attitude. You need to have a candid discussion with someone in a position to help you do something about it.

You're only stuck if you choose to be stuck.

Another bouquet—with a hitch

Ring some bells, light some sparklers, have some whipped cream on your mocha latte, roll around in rose petals. You deserve it. You did it! You got management to agree to at least some version or aspect of your plan, and you're ready to tend that garden of yours. I'm proud of you. Now the fun really begins. We'll get into implementation in the next chapter.

If you've done the hard work of this chapter, then you deserve a supreme reward, and I've got a good idea for you. Quick, close your eyes and envision your work space. What do you see? What does it say about you as a person and as an associate of your company? Is it inviting and well-organized? Are there images to inspire you and remind you of your purpose? Do the colors stimulate you or put you to sleep? Is it comfortable and ergonomically correct for your body and any physical challenges you may have? Are there any points of connection to the outside world, to nature, or do you feel locked inside an interior cubicle? Do you smile just seeing your space when you arrive each morning?

Applause, applause!

For your reward, and to celebrate attaining at least some aspect of your ideal job, **I urge you to give your work space a makeover.** I guarantee it will give your attitude a big boost and set the right tone for your new endeavor. **Here are some ideas:**

· Ask if you can paint the walls or perhaps some of the furniture. For example, ugly old metal file cabinets can be hauled outside and spray painted quite nicely. If it's allowed, have the whole team come in some Saturday and have a painting party. Cheerful wall colors go a long way toward creating a happy place to work.

· Clear out the clutter and all those secret spots where you stash stuff to do later. Reacquaint yourself with the bottom of your inbox. Catch up on your filing. Make room for new energy.

· Get organized. See if your boss will spring for whatever you need

having a
beautiful,
well-
organized,
efficient
work space
is a huge
component
of finding
more joy in
your job

to contain the chaos: file crates, more shelves, stacking file trays, hanging baskets, cable wranglers, whatever you can think of to help restore order. Don't forget to add some color. These days there are stores in every mall that specialize in storage devices, and all that cool stuff comes in every color of the rainbow.

· Set up your space for efficiency. Put things you use all the time within arm's reach. Is your phone in the optimal position for you? How about your computer? If not, ask your tech person to help you adjust things for your best use.

· If you have an office with enough room, consider making it a friendly place to hold informal meetings or work with another colleague. Do you have a visitor chair? Is it actually something someone would want to sit in for more than five minutes?

· Bring things from home that express your personality. Family photos of course, but don't forget a picture of Dingo the Dachshund, snapshots from a great vacation, images of your prized roses—whatever symbolizes to you some of the reasons you are motivated to come to work. How about bringing a bowling trophy or a blue ribbon from the county fair? Don't be afraid to let people know who you are outside of work.

· Invite the outside in. Plants are one of the best ways to liven up an office and they help cleanse the air by emitting oxygen during the day. There are plenty of varieties that will grow in windowless rooms, just ask a knowledgeable plant person. Bring some fresh flowers from your garden, or how about some shells from your last trip to the beach or feathers from your bird watching jaunts? We all need to be reminded of our connection to the real world beyond our business lives, and this is a great way to do it.

· Decorate your space with things that remind you of the purpose you've chosen for your work. Maybe it's a motivational poster, a favorite quote you had framed, an encouraging card from a good friend, an embroidered statement of your personal mission. Only you know what will inspire you and help remind you of your larger reasons for being at work.

There now, doesn't that feel better? I know, for this reward I made you work, but I promise you that **having a beautiful, harmonious, well-organized, efficient work space is a huge**

component of finding more joy in your job. If you don't consider yourself a visual person and you're clueless about how to fix up your space, that's a perfect opportunity to get to know a colleague who is inclined in that direction. She'll probably be flattered you asked her advice. Plan a shopping trip some day after work and bond over potted ferns and picture frames.

Brenda took this idea and ran wild with it. As the office manager at a small literary agency, she loved working surrounded by books. Still, the walls were drab and the furnishings were a hodgepodge of things from who knows where. Before the business owner left town for a conference, Brenda asked if she could overhaul the entire office. Her overworked boss was delighted and gave her an ample budget to play with. "Over the course of the next two days, the whole staff pitched in like crazed workers on speeded up footage from HGTV," she recalls, shaking her head in amazement. "We painted everything in sight, added lots of beautiful art prints, covered funky old cabinets with nice textiles, brought in lots of plants and best of all, we made a treasure map on the back of the door where no one but us would see it." When the boss returned from her trip, she was blown away by her team's creativity. "Even she felt more inspired to come to work, and I know I sure do," Brenda says.

"Life is change. Growth is optional. Choose wisely."
~ Karen Kaiser Clark

This chapter has shown you how to handle problem bosses, how to present your plan to management and how to overcome resistance to your ideas. I'm so proud of you for making it to this point in the process, because it takes a lot of courage to walk away from familiar and safe situations and to seek something new. **There's no point clinging to safe jobs that offer no higher meaning to your life.** As scary as change can be, some sort of change is always happening anyway, so why not seize control and direct it toward your ideal job?

In the next chapter, we're going to nurture that new garden of yours and get your new job off to a good start. We'll look at ongoing challenges you may have with your associates or your supervisor and ways to possibly repair broken intra-office relationships. If all else fails, you'll learn how to move on to another job with grace, integrity and without burning bridges. **Come on, I've got the watering can.**

"Don't compromise
yourself. You are
all you've got."

~ Janis Joplin

Chapter Seven
TENDING YOUR GARDEN OF REALITIES

Chapter Seven At A Glance

- Will you know your job when you get it?
- Get off to a great start
- Who will you thank?
- Are you a skilled communicator?
- What to make from bad apples
- Can't we all just get along?
- How's it going so far?
- To go or not to go
- Rebirthing your job
- Five new ways to change your job
- Knowing a good job when you find one
- Leave a lasting impression
- The best place to work

Whew! Presenting new ideas can make anyone nervous, so it feels good to have that over, doesn't it? In this chapter we're going to walk the last two stepping stones along your **P.A.T.H.** (Planned Actions Toward Happiness). I mention that to remind you that's what this has been about all along—helping you find more joy in the job you already have—or at least at the company where you already work. I'll share some thoughts on ensuring that your ideal job actually turns out that way, as well as what to do if it doesn't.

Stepping Stone #9

Implement your plan.

First, answer this: **Will you know your dream job when you get it?** *Well, duh, Pat, of course I will!* Don't be so sure. Even if your boss approves your whole plan, the actual form your job takes will undoubtedly differ from your vision—and that's fine. Your dream, after all, was merely a tool to spur your change and growth. All through the book I've been talking about your garden of possibilities—well guess what?

Now it's your garden of realities, grown from the *seeds* of your possibilities.

(You didn't think I was going to abandon my garden metaphor did you?)

Look around. Have some volunteer flowers popped up that you didn't plant? Did your boss add his own desires to your plan? Did you have to compromise with team members to get an okay? None of these outcomes is bad. They're just different and perhaps unexpected. Can you be open to the idea that maybe, just maybe, their input made your dream job even better? Perhaps having your boss delete a few items from your plan will turn out to be a blessing. Maybe you were overly ambitious in your design. Maybe he knows about opportunities coming your way that you're unaware of, and he wants to be sure you can handle those, too. My point is this:

Can you accept the form your new job is taking, even if it doesn't look much like your original design? I hope so, because that's part of the magic of this process.

Well, gee, Pat, if it's all magical anyway, why did you make us go through all those darn exercises? It's a critical part of the process that you have some vision for your future in order to have something to pursue. You need a clear dream to pull you along the stepping stones on your P.A.T.H. **The magical part is simply how all the forces at play co-create your actual job.**

Molly would agree with that, I know. A customer service rep in a big city, east coast insurance office, Molly didn't get a green light for her job plan—partly because she was still quite new to the team and hadn't yet proved herself. Still wanting to help her out, Molly's boss asked what one thing would have the greatest impact on her happiness at work.

"That was easy," she replies with a laugh. "I told him I wanted to bring my aging toy poodle to work with me. Worrying about her home alone all day was causing me a lot of stress. I knew she'd be thrilled to sleep all day under my desk. After consulting with the rest of the office, he gave me the okay for a one-week trial. Of course my sweetie passed, and here's the funny part—my little pup turned out to be quite an asset. When potential new customers come into the office and see my dog, many of them comment on how nice it is that I can have her with me. I can see it in their eyes that they think well of a company with such a big-hearted attitude—and my boss agrees. He admitted that more than one person has told him on the way out the door that they knew they could trust anyone with an office dog."

Here's the really amazing part from a business owner's point of view—that one simple "Yes," which cost him nothing, will very likely ensure that Molly remains a happy, loyal associate for years to come.

> "Choose a job you love, and you will never have to work a day in your life."
> ~fortune cookie
> (Hey, I'll take wisdom wherever I find it!)

What's the golden wish that would rock your world?

Get out your watering can

It's taken me six chapters to guide you toward landing your ideal job, but that's just the beginning of your real journey. Now you have to deliver on your promises. Don't be one of those people who begs for an opportunity, gets it, then blows it off. **In order to actually find joy in your new job, you have to do it.** That may sound simplistic, but for some people the thrill is in the hunt, the securing of the job—not in the day-to-day reality of it. Now it's time to water and care for your garden of realities. If you find your enthusiasm waning, review Chapter Three and your journal entries about your dream job. Reconnect with your passion and your purpose. Remember that experiencing more fulfillment in your job is the direct route to de-stressing your life.

Here are some tips for making a good impression during the first weeks of your new position (especially important if you're going through a trial period). Yeah, I know, these may sound self-serving coming from a boss, but I want you to know how we evaluate our team members.

· **Over-deliver**. No, I don't mean bring in extra donuts. Actually, the expression is under-promise and over-deliver, meaning you can dazzle your supervisor by being even better than you said you'd be at your new job. Demonstrate how excited you are to have this opportunity. Get your team revved up, too.

· **Spare her the gory details**. This is tricky to do well, but worth learning. When your boss asks you how your new project is going, she probably doesn't want to hear a detailed rundown of all the problems you've encountered. She might interpret that as whining on your part, or perhaps as a cry for help or even as the first hint of failure. Instead, it's fair to say: "There are a few kinks, but I'm working them out." It's fair, that is, if you believe you *can* work them out and still meet your goals. That sends the message that you're on top of the situation and able to handle challenges that arise. We bosses expect there will be problems—and we love it when you handle what you can on your own.

· **Get help if you do need it**. On the other hand, if you and your team are floundering and your project is on a downward course, don't wait until the last minute to call in reinforcements. Really big problems do land on your supervisor's desk—that's her job. Be prepared to move forward into solution mode; don't linger in blame-land and excuse-ville.

> "Next to excellence is the appreciation of it."
> ~William Makepeace

Thanks—pass it on

As you go about settling in to your perfect job, remember to thank all the people who helped you get there. As you saw on the lists from both bosses and employees in the last chapter, it is sadly uncommon for busy managers to regularly acknowledge the assets their team members contribute. Sincere appreciation is one of the most cost-effective tactics anyone in the business world can utilize, because it's free! Think about it. Can you recall the last time you were thanked for a job well done? Didn't you feel fantastic? When's the last time you told someone else she did something well?

Here's my challenge to you: the next time you're with co-workers and the conversation starts to turn negative with griping about the same old stuff, try turning it around.

Boldly change the subject by telling the group about someone in your company who did something well. It's even better if that person is present. They'll probably be startled at first, but see if you can't reverse the cycle of gloom by focusing on good things that happen at work.

Though Julie was becoming invested in her company and its purpose, she failed to share that shift with anyone.

Julie's story illustrates the power of appreciation. She dropped out of college after two years, because she just never found her niche. Nothing really sparked her passion. Exceptionally attractive, she'd always been wary of trading on her looks. She drifted from one unrewarding job to another for about six years, until she landed at a Boston architectural firm as their receptionist. "I took the job because it didn't seem too demanding," Julie confides, "and that was true. They clearly hired me for my appearance and ability to be well-spoken on the phone. I was the only woman on the staff, and no one paid much attention to me, but then a funny thing happened. I started to absorb the texture of the place, to understand their mission as a company that specialized in historic restoration. Before I knew it, I was spending my lunch hours looking at old buildings with a new appreciation."

So far, so good, right? Well, not exactly. Though Julie was becoming invested in her company and its purpose, she failed to share that shift with anyone. "The architects were always so absorbed in their designs, and I was frankly intimidated by them. I felt embarrassed by my lack of education on the subject, so I was afraid to say anything. I didn't want them to laugh at my beginner questions, and I didn't want to waste their valuable time, so I started reading books on architecture and I became totally hooked."

However, in her desire to please her bosses, Julie unfortunately became their doormat. Their beautiful, actually quite bright, doormat. She didn't complain when they asked her to stay late and deliver plans after hours. She didn't resist when they piled more duties on her desk. She didn't seem to mind when they got her to run errands on weekends. But eventually Julie had enough.

"One day, after skipping lunch because they needed me, and then missing dinner, too, I finally snapped. I had a full-blown meltdown, and it wasn't pretty," Julie confides. "However, in the process, I let it slip that I'd become obsessed with architecture— which of course flabbergasted my bosses. Long story short, we had a marathon heart-to-heart talk and realized we hadn't known each other at all. My bosses were so thrilled with my interest, that they offered to send me to night school to study drafting. **That one act of appreciation and recognition proved more belief in me than**

anyone in my life had ever shown before. It made me absolutely devoted to them—as people and as a firm."

The happy ending for Julie is, she now has her ideal job working for the same company in their drafting department and is considering continuing on to get her degree in architecture. All this happened because she began to take an interest in her company—and finally told them about it—which in turn, startled them into fully appreciating her.

Here's another quick example from many years ago—which is part of the point. "When I first started out in publishing," Samantha remembers, "I worked at an entry-level job as an editorial assistant at a big, famous magazine. To my surprise, on the day before my birthday, someone delivered a bottle of champagne to my desk with a card signed by the head of the company, wishing me many happy returns and giving me my birthday off. I just about fainted—it turns out this was company policy. I was already obsessed with my glamorous-to-me job, but that gesture made me even more joyful about my position. I was so touched by that generous spirit, that I've never forgotten it, nearly 40 years later. Of course, it also spoiled me, since no other boss ever followed suit," she says, laughing.

Journal exercise

Creating a circle of gratitude

How many times a day do you say thank you? Play a game, and see how many times you *can* say it in one day. **Thank you. Pass it on.** Jot down some names and recent good deeds of your associates, and make a point of letting them know you noticed. What goes around will, indeed, come back to you.

"Feeling gratitude and not expressing it is like wrapping a present and not giving it."
~William Arthur Ward

_____

_____

_____

_____

_____

_____

_____

_____

Talk is cheap—great communication is priceless

There's a good chance your new position has you interacting with some new people, or perhaps with the same people in a new way. If you recall, good communication ranked high on both the list that bosses made of qualities they value in their staff members and on the list of things team members say is important to them. Conversely, poor communication ranks as the number two reason employees disconnect from their jobs emotionally. Just what does that mean, anyway? I believe quality communication is an art form, and a critical skill for any associate to master. As much as I like to pretend I'm omniscient, bosses are not mind readers. You have to tell us exactly what you want. We're busy. We have a lot on our minds, and we won't pick up on your subtle hints. (Just ask my Office Manager!)

Here are some aspects I find essential for good communication with all team members:

- You always tell the truth, even if it makes you look bad.
- You know when to speak up—and when not to. Timing is everything.
- You understand tact and how to wield it with clients as well as with co-workers. Your mother was right. If you can't say something nice, don't say anything.
- You know which topics are better discussed in private, and you don't violate that.
- You develop patience—interrupting is rude and shows you aren't really listening to the other person.
- You defend your boss and your teammates when you can truthfully do so. You never belittle people—it always makes you smaller in the process.
- You don't talk just to hear the sound of your voice, no matter how much you love it.
- You consciously look for positive things to say to people and think twice before saying something negative. Always wait to be asked for criticism, then find a way to make it constructive. Instead of telling Sam his presentation put everyone to sleep, tell him his content was good, but his presentation skills could use some brushing up and offer to help him.
- You don't email someone on the other side of the wall, when

no matter
how
cute, an
emoticon
is not a
substitute
for the
real thing

asking a question face-to-face will expedite your work. As a rule, don't just email your team members who work in the same office. Person-to-person contact has been greatly eroded by technology. No matter how cute, an emoticon is not a substitute for the real thing. When you smile at another person, you literally change your own brain chemistry in a good way.

· You stop what you're doing and give visitors to your office your full attention. Multi-tasking should not include listening.

· You show an interest in your associates as human beings with lives beyond the office, but without prying or getting caught up in personal dramas. Even if you're not a dog person, it won't kill you to admire photos of Jim's new schnauzer. You spend more time with your co-workers than you do with your family, so you might as well get along with them and reap some benefits of human interaction.

· You understand that communicating well is as much about listening as it is about talking. Study active listening skills and watch how popular you become in the office.

Communication can break or make your plan

Vera's story shows the value of great communication. She wears many hats (office assistant, customer service, some order taking) at a small health food company. While she liked her job well enough, Vera knew it could be even more rewarding—for her and their customers. "I knew I had a great idea, but my problem was a boss too busy to give me his undivided attention. Instead of waiting until a better time, I kept on talking, and of course all he heard was *more work*. He told me to save my idea for a later date, but I knew that meant it would never happen. Instead, I asked him if I could just whip up one example of my idea for him to see what I had in mind."

"The question isn't who is going to let me; it's who is going to stop me."
~Ayn Rand

When Vera approached him again a few days later (and at a moment when he was slightly less frazzled) she showed him samples of the recipes she'd developed using company products. Her idea was to eventually create a whole cookbook of ideas and put it on the company website. Whenever customers called to place an order—or for any reason—they could be directed to the recipes as a nice added bonus. "This time, he loved the idea, as I thought he would all along. I just needed to do a better job of presenting it to him. I realized that my underlying purpose is to promote good health by encouraging greater use of our products, and creating these recipes fulfills that need in me."

If at first you don't succeed, review your communication skills, and see how you could improve your delivery.

What kind of apples are in your basket?

Okay, you're getting used to your new job, and you're feeling more joy—or at least you would be if it wasn't for *him*. Or *her*. You know who I mean—**the one bad apple in your basket**, the one person who just doesn't move in the same direction as the rest of your team. Sadly, a fair number of people are showing up for work every day and exhibiting unprofessional behavior. They're selfish. They disagree with everyone on everything. They're bullies. They're lazy. Do I need to go on? I didn't think so. If bad apples fall in every orchard, then what's a good gardener supposed to do?

Compost them! No, I don't mean you should toss the bad apple in the garbage, no matter how tempting that might be. I mean that you can find the bruised spots on this co-worker's personality and recycle just the damaged portions by showing him understanding and concern for his well-being. Now I realize you're not a therapist (and gee, neither am I) but most people respond to basic expressions of concern:

1. **Attention:** what does your bad apple need or want?
2. **Listening:** what are the views and opinions of your bad apple?
3. **Compassion:** what challenge—personal or professional—is your bad apple struggling with?
4. **Caring:** what's the last nice deed you did for this bad apple?
5. **Acknowledgment:** has your team found things to praise him for lately?
6. **Support:** when's the last time you offered to help him?

Before you dismiss this idea as too simple (or as too much work!) please think about your office dynamics. In most work groups, people take on roles that fit them naturally, often because they played the same role in their family. Someone rises as a leader, another as a caretaker and a third as the joker who provides comic relief. Other team members may act as tireless worker bees, while

another is the idea guy or the problem solver. However, sometimes people get pegged as a troublemaker, and before they know it, that's how they're always treated—whether they've been causing problems lately or not. That in turn can lead to the bad apple feeling unjustly treated, which makes him angry, which causes him to act out again, which proves he is at his core, rotten. Or does it?

Humor me. As an experiment, devote one full day—more if you can—to treating your bad apple as if he was the most valued associate you have. **Engage with this guy as if he's the best employee at your company.**

> "Could we change our attitude, we should not only see life differently, but life itself would come to be different."
> ~Katherine Mansfield

Actively practice the six concerned behaviors I listed above and see what happens. Obviously you can't keep that up forever, but if you see a shift in your troublemaker, if you see a spark of goodness shining through, note which behavior he responds to the most and focus on offering more of that. If the only thing between you and your full enjoyment of your ideal job is a bad apple, then I say it's worth some effort on your part to see if you can help him heal his bruises.

At the large Denver pharmacy where they worked, Mary Kay struggled with a co-worker who was always cranky and never wanted to do her fair share. "Whenever it was time to unpack new shipments, Amy vanished. When customers formed lines five deep, Amy was on her break," Mary Kay explains. "She had a real knack for avoiding anything she didn't want to do, and then if she got stuck doing it anyway, she grumbled the whole time, so it became easier to do things without her—or her attitude."

One day when talking with her supervisor, Mary Kay finally asked why Amy's behavior was tolerated. "To my shock, I was told that Amy had many personal challenges and that rather than complain about her, I should get to know her better." To her credit, Mary Kay did just that, and learned that Amy had her plate so piled high with trouble, that there was little room for any niceness on her part. She suffered from migraines, but as the sole supporter of her three young kids (one with ADD), Amy needed to save her paid sick days for

those times when she was *really* bad off. She had an abusive ex-husband who liked to show up to harass her, which is why she sometimes did a quick disappearing act. To top it off, she also endured chronic back pain, made worse by standing so long each day. Oh yeah, and her mother (and best babysitter) was dying.

"Over time, as I showed Amy that I cared about her situation, she warmed up to me and decided she could trust me. Now we have a good relationship, and I've learned to be really grateful for all the ease in my own life."

Journal exercise

Can't we all just get along?

Come on. See if you can't compost some of that negative energy on your team. It makes great fertilizer for your garden. Who could you surprise with a random act of kindness? Who could you ask to lunch for a good heart-to-heart talk? Who do you routinely dismiss as not worth your time or interest, and how might you practice compassion instead? What's cool is it's catching. Vicious cycles can reverse direction in a heartbeat. The best part about intentionally being nice, is it makes you feel better too, but then I think you know that. It's just easy to forget when we get caught up in our hectic lives. **In the space below note any ideas you have to be a more caring team member.**

_____

_____

_____

_____

_____

_____

_____

_____

Stepping Stone #10

Gather feedback and evaluate your success.

None of us works alone. Well, okay, there is a recluse I know, but she's wired way differently then you and I are. You and I work on teams, even though your company may not use that term. You rely on your co-workers all day long for input, help, advice and feedback. They are a standard against which you can measure yourself. As you begin your dream job, be sure to actively seek reactions from those you trust. (Asking someone you know who resents your new position is not the idea.) Ask your trusted colleagues how they think you're handling your new responsibilities, and of course, from time to time, ask your supervisor if she thinks you're meeting your new challenges. If she's unhappy with your performance, you want to know about it sooner rather than later.

Daring to ask demonstrates your dedication to doing a good job. Take some notes. Give the feedback some serious thought. Few people ace a job on the first try. Use the feedback to make course corrections. **You do want to do your very best, don't you?** I thought so.

After a fair amount of time, say a few months, set aside some time to evaluate your progress. Go back and reread your **Job Action Memo** (Page 140). Are there things you've forgotten to implement? Are there promises you made that you haven't kept? Discuss it with your boss. Make sure you're <u>both</u> happy with how your dream job has come to life. Take another look at the **G.R.O.W. Chart** (Page 25) and see how your new job rates now.

Remember, a garden never stops growing. It goes through spurts and cycles of life, including the harvest, a period of dormancy or rest, and the reseeding of next season's plants, but it's always there.

What if you're still unhappy?

Despite your best intentions and efforts, sometimes you have to consider that maybe there's a better place for you to work. The second most common reason, just behind poor bosses, people leave their jobs is poor relationships with co-workers. If you're starting to feel like leaving, I'd first like to suggest that you make a sincere effort

at repairing those relationships.

If that's not the reason things aren't working out, maybe you're in the right field at the wrong company, or you need to escape a toxic boss, or you just want to have a change of mental scenery. Perhaps your discontent is

rooted in a lack of belief in the product or service your company provides. Maybe your own values are not supported by the work you've been doing. For example, learning that your company has a less-than stellar environmental record, coupled with reluctance to institute green policies, may be deeply at odds with your personal beliefs. Such a rift would almost inevitably lead to unhappiness on the job. In such a situation, if you had the stomach for it, you could remain on the job and become a crusader from within to urge the company to change their policies. That kind of goal would be highly satisfying if attained, but might also be greatly disappointing if not met. Only you know if you have the temperament for that kind of mission.

Your only other recourse is to find another job that does reinforce your values. It's not easy to arrive at this decision and trust your instincts. Once your employer learns you want to quit, she may well try and talk you out of it. If she's a savvy boss, she knows **the cost of replacing you can be a staggering amount—up to one and a half times your annual salary**. Did you realize how valuable you are? A truly wise employer will also recognize when someone is no longer a good fit for the company and allow her to move on with grace and gratitude.

> **To help you decide, here are some of the common advantages of moving on:**
> · You'll meet new people, probably make new friends.
> · You'll have new challenges and opportunities for growth.
> · You'll be able to choose an employer who shares common values.
> · You may find a job that's closer to where you live.
> · You may earn more money or receive better benefits.
> · You may thrive and be invigorated by a clean slate.

Of course, nothing is guaranteed. People tend to be on their best behavior during job interviews, and that goes for bosses, too. The grass may turn out to be an ugly shade of brown. Your boss may not be such a swell guy, even after all your solid research. You may be incompatible with your new work group. You'll have to start over building seniority, vacation time and other benefits. Most important, you're going to have to prove yourself all over again and establish credibility and a good reputation in a whole new setting.

Don't get me wrong—I'm not by any means trying to scare you into staying in a joyless job. Not for a minute. Like all tough decisions, you need to give it serious thought and weigh the pluses and minuses.

Journal exercise

To go or not to go

Use the space below to **list the advantages and disadvantages of moving on.** Change is rarely easy, but attaining clarity on this will keep you from beating yourself up later on, if your next position doesn't work out for you. Make sure you've given yourself plenty of time to make your current position more viable. Consider all the work you've done on designing your dream job and realistically assess the likelihood that you'll be able to enjoy some version of it where you work now.

_____

_____

_____

_____

_____

_____

_____

_____

"Having a bad Monday is a lame way to spend 1/7 of your life."
~Unknown
(If it was you, do something about it!)

"You cannot fail at being yourself. A cat doesn't try to be a tiger and you shouldn't try to be something you aren't. You are a process, not a product. Your job is to discover what you are and to create that creature. You still won't be perfect, but success isn't about perfection, it's about authenticity."
~Bernie Segal

Maybe you need to rebirth your job

Let me tell you about Sarah, because her story exemplifies how you can lose sight of your dream—and rediscover it in another form. As far back as she could remember, Sarah had wanted to be a teacher, and she did, indeed, make that happen. For 15 years she found a lot of job satisfaction teaching high school algebra. However, she didn't adjust well to changing times, and in fact, began to feel classic career burnout. "It just crept up on me, and I was too exhausted to figure out why my attitude had deteriorated so much," she reveals. "Sure, fewer and fewer students were interested in math, and my resource budget kept shrinking. Finally, the rash of school shootings sent me into a deep depression. I just couldn't acknowledge that much rage could exist in these young kids. I lost my focus as a teacher and realized I had to do something entirely different. It was a wrenching decision to make, because I felt a real obligation to the kids and my whole self-identity was wrapped up in teaching."

On her summer break, Sarah researched other ways to apply her skills as an educator, and by the end of the season, she'd found a new career as a corporate trainer at a giant computer manufacturer. "Oh my gosh, I never knew I could have this much fun and get paid for it," she gushes now. "Dealing only with adults, after so many years of struggling with uninterested kids, has revitalized my zeal for teaching. I've lost twenty pounds and feel ten years younger. Every time I catch sight of myself in the mirror, I chuckle and wonder who that happy person is. Cool—it's me!"

If you're still wavering about whether to move on or not, talk to people in your human resources department if you have one. You may want to share your concerns with your boss, and give him a chance to rectify your issues. You don't have to reveal that you're on the verge of quitting. Ask if there's a new project you could work on, anything to reignite your enthusiasm for your job. That way, if you do decide to go, at least you'll have tried every other recourse first. It's important for your own peace of mind to know that you tried every approach to making the job you have work for you. Otherwise, you're likely to hop from job to job never finding satisfaction.

Sometimes external events pull you in different directions and

provide a boost to change jobs. Indulge me a moment while I brag about my talented son Bret. He loves the music business and began his career as a graphic designer creating CD packaging for many top stars, including Bon Jovi and Madonna. He was an integral part of the team that won a Grammy for their design work several years ago for the Dixie Chicks. Then along came MP3 players. Their popularity has had an extreme effect on the CD packaging business. Bret decided to leave that field and apply his skills to his second love, sports. As the graphic designer for the L.A. Dodgers baseball team, he landed another dream job where he found total fulfillment. A third job change came about when Bret and his wife Stacey had their son Jack. Living in Los Angeles with a new baby, finding schools and a child-friendly neighborhood, added another dimension to their lives—including the need for additional income. I'm delighted to say that Bret is now working for Disney, creating packaging for products in their movie division, and he's having a blast.

Replanting your garden in another pasture

Okay, so you've decided to go. Before you storm out in a huff or give your notice, I urge you to plan your exit so that you can **leave with integrity and dignity**. Besides, you're very likely to need a good reference from your boss at some point in your future. Perhaps not for years, but you'd be surprised how far back human resource department folks will look for evidence about your history.

In my experience as an employer, it's really almost like a divorce when people leave. Everyone thinks they need to blame someone for the position not working out. There is probably a little bit of blame to go around on all sides, from employer to employee. The bottom line is, sometimes people and companies are just not a good match.

Let's look at some ways of re-visioning your work life.
Here are five interesting ways of changing jobs to consider.

1. Repurpose what you know. Follow former teacher Sarah's lead and think how else your unique abilities could be applied. Which of your skills are portable? If you're a bookkeeper, would you like to try tax preparation and have more contact with the public? If you feel stifled in a corporate marketing department, would you prefer the lively pace and casual environment of an ad agency? If you're stuck in a cubicle as a customer service rep at a long distance carrier, could you switch to handling returns face-to-face at a department store? If you're a baker, could you become a candlestick maker? Okay, maybe not. But you get the idea. Think beyond the box you've climbed into.

2. Work for a one-man-band. If you have a toolkit overflowing with skills and you wish you could use them all, then consider working for an entrepreneur as his right- and left-hand Gal Monday-through-Friday. This is a demanding but exciting career, full of drama, creativity and nothing but variety. You may well be his entire team. You may be expected to be on call at odd hours. Then again, you may also get to travel with him to Jakarta or Oslo—or maybe just to Peoria, but hey, you get out of the office. While the job is intense, if you prove your loyalty, your boss is apt to reward you beyond your wildest imagination. This is probably a job for an adventurous single woman or perhaps a mature, empty-nester.

3. Follow your bliss. Make your avocation your vocation. Turn what you do in your free time into your career. Make your hobby pay. How? Do you love to travel? Work for an airline and enjoy all the free travel miles. Do you adore animals? Work for your local humane society and do some real good while you're at it. Do you thrill to dancing or swimming? Become an instructor. How about skiing? Work at a resort and get free lift tickets. If you find yourself watching the clock every day until you get to escape your job and go play, then you need to figure out how to get paid for playing!

"There are many things in life that will catch your eye, but only a few of these will catch your heart. Pursue these."
~Michael Knollin

4. Wear several hats. Maybe your personality is so complex and your interests so diverse that no one job can provide the fulfillment you seek. In that case, try having several part-time jobs. Roslyn juggles a part-time job as a researcher that she does from home, with running her own antique doll shop. That way she gets to exercise both halves of her brain and pursue all her interests. Lucy has three jobs. Mondays she works at her town newspaper as a proofreader, which meets her needs for feeling like part of a team. Tuesdays and Wednesdays, she's the relief innkeeper at a bed and breakfast, which allows her to interact with visitors to her area and indulge her love of gracious hospitality. The rest of the time she runs around hunting for treasures, which she sells on eBay. You won't meet a happier person anywhere. "How lucky am I? Three jobs and I love 'em all," she exclaims.

5. Start over and learn something new. This country is full of people who switched horses midstream and are much happier for making the hop. If you've been doing the same thing for a long time and have reached the burnout stage, maybe it's time to regroup. Could you go to night school or study online for a whole new career? There's no shame in rethinking your life, no matter what your father may tell you. The only shame would be wasting the rest of your life at a job that no longer feeds your soul.

Looking for a better pasture

As you look around for a potential new place to work, try applying the **G.R.O.W. Chart** (Page 25) to everyone you see. How happy do they look? How's their energy level? What tone is set by the physical space? Rate the possibilities of the new position—how high up the scale can you imagine yourself—will you blossom in this new environment or merely branch out a bit? How big of a change are you ready to make?

When auditioning new companies (and bosses) here are some positive signs to look for, indicators that you might love working there.

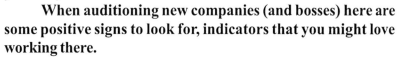

- · A boss who affords you opportunities to grow
- · An energized workforce where there is a lot of vitality
- · Evidence of a love of learning and an ethic of constant improvement
- · Employees are trusted to achieve the results in their own way
- · A leader who has genuine concern and interest for the people on her team
- · Contributions are recognized
- · High-caliber peers you'd want to work with—colleagues you could learn from
- · Individual differences are welcomed and diversity is cherished

Journal exercise

Be a good detective

I would suggest that you have at least ten questions written down and memorized before you go into your next interview. Look at your values list on Page 61 and form questions that will reveal whether or not your values would be honored in a new position. Will you find fulfillment for your job purpose as you outlined it on Page 64? Look again at your **Dream Job Declaration** on Page 108 and compare that vision to the opportunities before you.

_____
_____
_____
_____
_____
_____
_____
_____
_____
_____
_____

Saying GOODbye

Always take the high road when it comes time to say goodbye. Be professional, and leave them with a smile on their faces. I've even known people who gave parting gifts to their soon-to-be former associates. I know of another woman who had her own goodbye lunch catered at her last staff meeting. I'm not suggesting you make such grand gestures, but I am asking: **What could you do to leave a lasting** _positive_ **impression?** Especially in small towns or close-knit industries, you may well work with some of these people farther on down the road. Wouldn't it be swell if they greeted you with open arms like a long lost friend, rather than someone they wished would get lost?

Here are some tips for leaving with grace and style

- Above all don't leave your boss in the lurch—give whatever is the standard length of notice in your field or company. Two weeks is considered minimal.
- Be gracious about training your replacement if you're around for it, and be upbeat. Do not infect the new person with any regrets or gripes you may harbor. Let her make her own discoveries and assessments.
- If you won't be there to help with training, then by all means, make it as easy as possible for the person who will be showing the new person how to do your job. Make lists of where things are, suppliers, the likes and dislikes of your supervisor and so on. If appropriate, leave a weekly schedule of your activities. Make sure your computer file names are understandable by renaming them with logical names. *Cancun log sheet* won't mean squat to the new gal, but *2002 Annual meeting data* might.
- Delete all personal files and emails from your computer.
- Leave a clean work space. No one wants to start their first day at a new job surrounded by stacks of Pepsi cans, old magazines and piles of junk mail.
- If you must leave unfinished projects, make sure your team knows about them and what remains to be done. Try not to leave the new gal an overflowing inbox that she won't know how to handle.
- Leave a nice welcome note for your replacement, perhaps with an offer to answer questions via email, if you feel comfortable with that. (And if you do make that offer, be sure your boss knows just how cooperative you are being.)
- At the very least, write your boss a thank you note or letter, rounding up your most authentic expressions of gratitude. Surely there's something you can sincerely thank her for!
- Also consider doing the same for key co-workers. If there are items in your work space you know would be appreciated, such as a well-adjusted philodendron, then pass them on to your pals.
- When the final hour arrives, leave with a smile and good wishes for the success of your team. If you need to scream, wait until you've left the parking lot!

Even under the worst circumstances, a person can leave with dignity. For Geralyn, the challenge was huge, because she was convinced the owner of her company was emotionally unstable, which in turn caused his irrational behavior. One day he would praise her productivity and the results of her efforts, then on the following day he would reverse himself and berate her for the very same thing and insist that she increase her output. Even as he piled more and more projects on her desk—which she took home to finish in order to stay on top of her work load—he continued to complain that she wasn't working hard enough. This, of course, was crazy making for Geralyn, and she couldn't be faulted had she quit and simply moved on to saner pastures—which is what she ultimately did. First, she devised a **supreme exit strategy**.

there is almost always a way to leave with a smile

"Since my health was deteriorating at an alarming rate due to the extreme stress I was under, I conferred with my therapist, my doctor and close friends to make the smoothest transition possible," she confides. "First off, I got my doctor to call my boss and explain that I needed to work from home several days a week to reduce my stress. Then I increased my self-nurturing activities and booked a massage for every Friday at 5 p.m. The most important thing I did was find my own replacement and make sure she was on board with what she'd be up against."

Geralyn knew that her boss would be thrilled to see her go as long as she made it easy for him to replace her. "I was very close to many of my co-workers, so it was important to me to leave with as little disruption as possible. I didn't want to leave them in a bind. Besides, I needed an excellent reference from him, so making his life easier was one thing I could do to promote that. When I gave my notice, I told my boss I already knew someone who'd be great at the job and suggested that he meet her to see for himself."

It worked exactly as Geralyn predicted, and her boss was so happy with the change that he became a pussycat for her last two weeks. "Here's the amazing part," she explains. "Within a week of my leaving, my former boss called begging me to do some freelance consulting for him on the side. I was thrilled to have the extra work, but I made sure I was well-paid for my efforts."

No matter why you decide to quit, no matter how bad your job

may have been, there is almost always a way to leave it with a smile—even if it's really a smile of relief. Whether you're moving on or remaining in your perfect new job, I'd like you to ponder this for a moment: **What would be your proverbial candy store, the place where you couldn't believe they paid you to work?**

Where everybody wants to work

Could it be your company? Why not? Have you ever seen the *Fortune Magazine* list of the One Hundred Best Companies To Work For and wondered why they made the list? It's mostly about company culture, a trendy term for the overall mood, policies and style of the workplace. One definition of a great place to work is somewhere employees trust the people they work for, have pride in what they do, and enjoy the people they work with. This considers your relationship to management, to your co-workers and in a larger sense to the company itself. It's a universal desire to value your job and to feel valued in return. How do you think the majority of employees where you work feel about that?

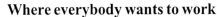

> ## What role do you play in making it a great place to work—or not?

How you might contribute to creating such a workplace:

- Inspire your team to excel. Take a leadership role.
- Advocate for more empowerment by demonstrating successful acceptance of more responsibility. Teams who steer their own ship run aground less often.
- Seek to earn increasing levels of trust.
- Show your team members how much you appreciate them. Often.
- Magnify what's working, instead of what's not.
- Honor thinkers who leap outside the proverbial boxes.
- Encourage younger and newer associates to share their ideas— innovation often comes from the mouth of, well, the new gal.
- Be a learner, embrace new systems, vault out of ruts.
- Volunteer to help others—and expect the same in return.
- Solve problems as they arise—stashing them away never works.

"It's kind of fun
to do the
impossible!"
~Walt Disney

> **My challenge to you is to see what you can do on your own, and what you can suggest to management, that would elevate your company onto such a list.** This is a fun concept for work groups to brainstorm about during an otherwise dull lunch hour. What kinds of policies could you suggest that would be for the greater good of all? Your ideas can be lofty, such as adopting a stretch of local highway to caretake as a group, or they can be as mundane as having a larger refrigerator in the break room so there's space for everybody's leftover Kung Pao chicken.
>
> **What would be on your list?**

_____

_____

_____

_____

_____

_____

_____

_____

_____

_____

_____

_____

Applause,
applause!

Roses all around—reward your team effort

Can you hear the roar of the crowd cheering for you? No? Okay, how about your team members jumping for joy because you've succeeded at creating some team cohesiveness? I talked a lot about communicating and repairing relationships in this chapter, so the first reward I'm going to suggest is one you can share with your co-workers. (Yes, at this juncture, you deserve two rewards.) The idea is to find or make some inexpensive but symbolic item that will be the prize you pass back and forth among your team to acknowledge good work. Sherrie skips lunch to meet a deadline, Jack picks up some slack when Dora is out sick, Lena pitches in to help you collate

500 reports even though she has her own deadline. When you celebrate the small victories over stressful situations, you reinforce your willingness to work together. Plus it becomes fun to see who can do something next that's worthy of moving the prize to their desk.

At a sportswear company, the marketing department uses an old Little League trophy, because to them the statue of the player at bat symbolizes hitting a home run. The office team at a wholesale nursery passes around a live venus flytrap plant because it (literally) catches bugs. A crafty office manager at a restaurant supply company created a trophy out of measuring spoons mounted on a block of wood and sprayed it gold. To the hard working folks in her department (who have to deal with a lot of yelling from restaurateurs), the trophy acknowledges the spoonfuls of sugar they have to dole out to placate frustrated customers.

Just think of something fun that would be meaningful to your team and surprise the first recipient. In addition, for implementing your dream job, of course you also deserve a giant reward.

This is a Big Deal!

Celebrate with friends. Have a party. Go on a weekend getaway. Take your boss out to lunch to thank her for approving your plan. Whatever will make you feel even more special than you already are.

I realize this has required a major dedication of time and thought on your part to go through this process, so again, I thank you for sticking with it and being part of the teeny percentage of people who are changing the world—one joy-filled day at a time. In the next—and final—chapter, you'll get to harvest all the bounty from your garden of realities. I'll also offer some ideas on how to sustain your newly won happiness. There'll be surprises, too. Maybe a marching band. (I guess you'll have to get the CDs for that.) Anyway, don't quit now. **Bring your bushel basket—I have lots of beautiful things to put in it.**

"If we could see the
miracle of a single flower
clearly, our whole life
would change."
~ Buddha

Chapter Eight
HARVESTING YOUR GARDEN

Chapter Eight At A Glance

- Work is personal
- TGIM
- Invest in yourself
- People, not gadgets
- Making hours golden
- Do you know where your boundaries are?
- Get lost
- Are you having fun yet?
- Bringing your spiritual self to work
- Your life is a work of art
- Pass it on
- May I have your card?
- Fall in love with the rest of your life

Just when you thought I was done with you, there's more! Even if you've successfully manifested your ideal job, **the honest truth is: it will only be your ideal job for awhile.** Companies change, teams expand or shrink, new expectations arise, but the tools in this book will help you adapt and keep pace with the changes. Perhaps you'll enjoy your dream job for years, but if you're growing and evolving as a person, in order to continue to stimulate you, **your ideal job has to grow right along with you**. Perhaps in time, you'll want to move into a different position in your company or even onto other pastures. My goals in this chapter are to teach you how to sustain your newfound joy in your job, expand your thinking even farther and to help you harvest the real bounty from the hard work you've been doing here.

Time out for a reality check

I've tried not to throw a lot of statistics at you, because as I said in my welcome, I wrote this book for you, and I want your experience of this process to be personal. It's not about how many other people hate or love their careers, it's about how much pleasure *you* can get from your work. Though now that you understand the path to finding more joy in your job, I want to give you a bit larger context to think about.

· **Work IS personal after all**. Organizations are organic systems made up of human beings with personalities, traits and problems that cannot simply be turned off or left at home. The company does not exist without its people. Without you, it's just a warehouse full of mufflers or a stack of requests that need filling.

· Because business is personal, **relationship building** is a skill you can't ignore. Communication is an art to master.

· Annual **turnover rates** vary from industry to industry, but they are ridiculously high—in part because most employees don't know how to find and develop a job that will bring them joy, and because many bosses and supervisors don't know how to attract and retain the best people.

· Today, business owners have more difficulty finding great employees than they do great customers. If you mold yourself into a prized team member, you become an **invaluable asset**.

· Being able to inspire your team—or even lead it—so that you function as a group of **accountable, inter-dependent individuals** is essential, since poor performance by co-workers is the number one reason that otherwise happy employees leave their jobs.

· The best people in any company continue to excel because they receive ongoing support and opportunities for growth. **Excellence is not a goal, it's a way of thinking and being.**

> "Find a job you like and you add five days to every week."
> ~H. Jackson Browne

TGIM

That look's wrong, doesn't it? TGIF, or Thank God It's Friday, is of course the refrain of all unhappy employees. What if at the beginning of each new work week, you could honestly say: TGIM: **Thank God It's Monday!** That's the level of joy I want for you. I want you to love your job so much that it's a pleasure to arrive at your place of work every day. I want you to walk into an environment that nurtures you, that reflects your values and is truly your home away from home. I want you to enjoy your team members so much that you miss them on weekends and are thrilled to see them again every Monday. I want you to tap into an endless fountain of enthusiasm for the opportunities you are given to grow. I want your creativity to find perfect expression. I want you to find such a deep level of personal fulfillment from your work that it has become your mission to excel at it. I want you to be well rewarded for your efforts—in both tangible and intangible ways. I want you to know you are an integral part of your company. Valued. Respected. Trusted.

I want you to flourish.

dream bigger

You may feel that's too high a target to aim for, and if so, I say

open your mind and heart and

I absolutely believe you can feel that much joy. In the rest of this chapter I'm going to stroll through the gardens we've planted and pluck some plum ideas from the orchard, a dozen advanced techniques for elevating your level of delight to the top of the mountain. You're going to like these, I promise.

What are you thinking…now what are you thinking?

I touched on this briefly in Chapter Five. If you master this technique, it will affect your life in more ways than you can imagine. It's the **ability to monitor your thoughts and words at all times, always on the alert for negativity creeping in**. I'm not talking about useful negative emotions like anger and fear. When that's an appropriate response to a situation, then those emotions should motivate you to take action. I'm talking about the useless negativity that infects us and spreads among companies like cancer. Monitoring

you can build new pathways in your brain

your thoughts is being aware of old impulses to blame and judge, of sour reactions that want to leap from your mouth unedited. It's choosing to avoid bash sessions and whine-a-thons. It's assuming the best about people instead of the worst. It's breaking up your old mindset—and *set* is the problem—your mind wants to revert to bad habits because they're familiar and require less exertion.

With some effort, **you can indeed, build new neural pathways in your brain for positive ideas to flow along, routes for optimism and joy. Here's how:**

- The first step is awareness of something negative you wish you hadn't said—and if possible, correcting it before it's too late.
- The next step is to catch yourself *before* you utter negative sentiments and rethink your position.
- The last step is becoming aware of useless ideas and reactions the moment they try to sneak into your brain, and booting them out before they can begin to discolor your perceptions, attitudes and actions.

It may sound too abstract to be possible, but it's really easier than it sounds. It's made much simpler if you practice this skill with a buddy—or even as a team. Ask a trusted colleague or friend to point out any time they notice you lapsing into a negative attitude—of course, without judgment on their part! Before long, you'll be able to spot it yourself. For some people, this is a revolutionary exercise, as they face their own level of negativity for the first time.

Just imagine—if your head is filled with even ten percent negative junk, how good would you feel if that ten percent was replaced with positive thoughts and feelings?

Thoughts create feelings and feelings lead to actions—and they're all within your control and a matter of your choice.

While you're at it, remember to share your joy for your new job with your associates, especially if you're among the first ones at your company to work through this process. Delight is contagious! Pass it on! Others on your team may be waiting to see how you do before they venture out to redesign their own jobs. Support them in their quest. The more happy campers the merrier.

Investing in your own stock

expand your own internal image of what's possible

Perhaps you're a veteran of the self-help movement and read books like this all the time—if so, you understand the value of what I have to say next. Expanding your own internal image of what's possible for you is one of the best ways I know to constantly infuse joy into all areas of your life.

My first job after college was as a sales representative for a major pharmaceutical company. I'll never forget my manager, Mike Mikkelson, from Seattle. For seven years I had the best mentor a young man could want. One thing he told me that really struck me was, "A year from now, you'll be the same person you are today—expect for the books you read and the people you meet." This was one of the defining moments in my life. I've continued to read, explore and grow from that day forward, and investing in myself has paid enormous dividends.

Money doesn't have to be a barrier.

· Chat with a librarian about books and DVDs that might enhance your skills or personal development.
· Ask your employer for additional training or see if you could attend a seminar or conference.
· Network and research online. The very latest trend on the Internet is what's being called **web 2.0**, which is a trendy name for more interactive, community-style websites where people go to collaborate, share resources and creations, as well as make connections (and this goes way beyond dating). Examples are YouTube, MySpace, Dogster, LinkedIn.
· Join a professional organization where you'll find endless opportunities for education. Check out the IAAP, The International Association of Administrative Professionals or other similar groups; the Soroptimists; the Business Women's Network and so on.
· Start a study group or a master mind group of like-minded people to further and support each other's personal and professional growth.

Keep it simple

The *Paradox of Choice* by Barry Schwartz, explains why too much of a good thing or a choice overload has proven detrimental to our psychological and emotional well-being. His book demonstrates that whether you're buying a pair of jeans, selecting your long distance carrier, or choosing a doctor, decisions from the mundane to the profound have become increasingly complex due to the overwhelming abundance of choice in our society. Those of you with a long memory (or an eye for detail in 1950s movies), will recall there used to be only one telephone. Everybody had a black desktop model with a round rotary dial. That was it. Just the other day, I wasted an hour picking out a phone for my house. When I got it home

"Don't be afraid your life will end; be afraid that it will never begin."
~Grace Hansen

and saw the instruction manual, I realized I'm doomed to never really understand how it works, because the instructions are just too darn complex to bother reading.

Do you ever feel that way? I figured you did.

Then there's the cereal aisle—what have they done to that? I need my reading glasses to decipher all the low-this and high-that options for my morning flakes. Having so many choices can do more than just waste your time or drive you nutty. It can make you doubt decisions you make before you even make them. It can set you up for unrealistically high expectations, and it can make you blame yourself for any and all failures.

Fine, Pat, but what's this got to do with my ideal job? As much as you let it. **Simplification is the solution.** Order all your office supplies from the same company. Can you place standing orders for things you use constantly? Learn your five favorite places to get lunch near your office and be done with it. Do you really need the fancier accounting software and the learning curve that goes with it? How many trade magazines can you read each month? Too much choice creates stress, and as you know, stress is your Number One Enemy.

In fact, many people have gathered around this idea and created the live simple movement, with the magazine *Real Simple* as one of the main purveyors of information about it. Learn more in the resource section at the back of this book.

"You don't get to choose how you're going to die, or when. You can only decide how you're going to live now."
~Joan Baez

People not gadgets

Do you remember how decades ago it was assumed that by now we'd all be using two-way video phones for all our calling needs? Sure, you can manage it with webcams and VOIP, but that hasn't turned out to be all that popular. I for one, am glad. While on the one hand, it would put a face with every voice, on the other hand, I fear it might distance us even farther from what we really crave as a species: **good old-fashioned, face-to-face, hand-on-the shoulder contact.** Babies deprived of people to interact with, fail to thrive. I doubt that adults fare much better.

Don't get me wrong. I love my computer as much as the next guy, and there's no denying how much technology has improved our

Are you on duty 24/7, are you wired to the max?

lives—up to a point—but **many of us are way over-wired**. We have so many gadgets and methods of staying "in touch" that we, ironically, are way out of real *human* touch—with our families as well as with our colleagues. Sometimes a lunch hour just needs to be a lunch hour, a full break in your day when you are *not* reachable. Cell phones are a very recent invention. Do you remember the carefree sensation of taking off on a lunch break and feeling your stress evaporate as you window shopped, or walked in the park or just sat in your car and read a novel? Questions can wait. News can travel a bit more slowly. Now more than ever, you really *do* deserve a break today!

If you carry a company beeper, cell phone or laptop, discuss the boundaries of usage with your supervisor. Set reasonable limitations. You deserve a genuine personal life not tethered to your office 24/7. As with all opposing forces, it comes down to finding the balance point between harnessing gadgets for your good and turning them off for your betterment. Comforting your son with one arm while checking email on your Blackberry with the other, rarely counts in anyone's book as quality time.

As technology continues to rush forward and drag us along, it will become increasingly more important to keep sight of your values and purpose.

Keep asking: what's really more important in this situation?

Your life.

Wouldn't you rather read your child a bedtime story than read another batch of stupid emails? Wouldn't you rather enjoy your morning run without taking a call and explaining for the sixth time where the peanut butter is? Have you ever noticed that even with 235 channels, there's often nothing worth watching on TV? Turn it off. Walk away from the chaos. Read a book. **Curl up by a fire and just dream.**

Create some golden hours

You'll need your supervisor to sign off on this one, as well as the support of you teammates—but it's something all of you can enjoy when it's your turn. The idea is simple. **How much could you get done if you had two solid hours with no interruptions?**

> **"Choose life!**
> Only that and always! At whatever risk. To let life leak out, to let it wear away by the mere passage of time, to withhold giving and spending it... is to choose nothing."
> ~Helen Kelley

When I ask that question of most people, they sigh and say that's sounds like heaven. Distractions and the lost time it takes to re-focus add up to a serious drain on your time. The amount of time you set aside for your golden hours can vary, but the lack of interruptions is what allows you to have a productive period of hyper-focus. If once a week, each person in your work group takes a turn while the rest cover for her, it's amazing what can get accomplished.

If you work in a busy open-plan office, perhaps there's another space where you could go to have your golden hours. Working in a

"To accomplish great things, we must not only act, but also dream; not only plan, but also believe."
~Anatole France

lively space has it challenges, but it's fair to set limits about how you work. **How you respond to interruptions is your choice.** Of course, many of us create our own interruptions by constantly checking email or reading every piece of paper as soon as it lands in our inboxes. If you allow yourself to work under those conditions, you set yourself up to be perpetually frazzled. As with all problems, awareness is the first step toward a solution. If your workplace is too noisy for you to concentrate, perhaps listening to instrumental music with earbuds would help. (Vocal music never works because the lyrics are too distracting.)

Do you know where your boundaries are?

Just as you can learn to monitor your thoughts for negativity, you can also **learn to be on the lookout for erosion to your self-esteem.** Becoming a stellar team member can have its downside. As you become a go-to gal who can solve all kinds of problems, people start to rely on you even more, which reinforces your capabilities as you evolve through ever greater challenges. So far, so good for your self-esteem. Where it suffers, is when you forget that "No" is an option, and you take on too many responsibilities. Then you start to feel taken advantage of, resentment creeps in, and your attitude deteriorates as you try to share some of your tasks with unreceptive teammates. Suddenly you're beating yourself up because you can't figure out how you got into such a mess.

It's all about **setting good boundaries** and recognizing the minute they are breached. Just because you become a strong team member doesn't mean your associates will become weaker—unless you let them. Share the fun. Make sure everyone in your work group gets a chance to prove herself. Know when it's *not* your turn and say so. **The best outcome for your mental health, the success of your team and the prosperity of the company, is for *everyone* to flourish.** If everybody relies only on you, then who will you lean on?

Did you end up where you thought you were going?

In order to guide you on this journey to your dream job, I had to write this book as though you were progressing right along with each chapter. In truth, you are probably very much in the middle of the process right now—or perhaps just getting started. That's fine— as long as you keep going until you bring your dream to life.

This feels like a good moment to look ahead a bit—say six months or so after you've implemented your dream job. **What if you get what you thought you wanted and then realize it's still not right?** That's what happened to Karin. Formerly a bookkeeper at a fairly large appliance manufacturer in Ohio, she was offered a promotion to a managerial position in the finance department. Though her gut instinct was to decline, Karin (and her husband) found the increased pay and benefits too tempting to refuse.

"What upsets me most is that I knew all along this wasn't a good match, but I succumbed to greed and convinced myself the new job would be an exciting challenge," she reveals. "It nearly killed me, and I don't know how I lasted the eight months that I did. I found myself doing nothing that I loved about my old job and everything I hated in my new job—mind-numbing meetings, endless paperwork, and enforcing policies that made no sense to me."

Karin was able to confide her unhappiness to people in her human resources department, and they were able to move her back to her former job. "The good thing about the experience is I have a new appreciation for my unique abilities, and I'm clear that I don't ever want to go into management."

If you discover that the job you thought you wanted isn't right for you after all, simply go back to the beginning of this process, adjust your dream and pursue a different one. Don't get stuck in a new job you dislike, either.

There is always a path that will lead you to fulfillment, even if you end up taking a few wrong turns along the way.

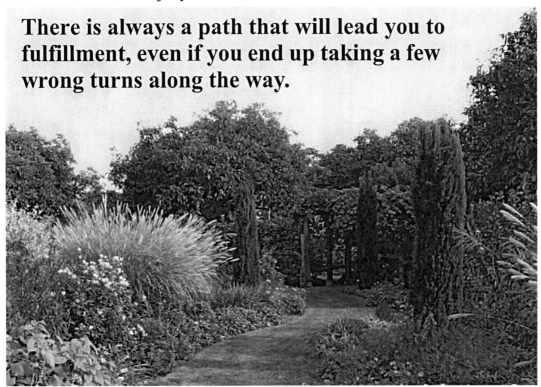

"Look at every path closely then ask yourself: Does this path have a heart? If it does, the path is good; if it doesn't, it is of no use."
~Carlos Castaneda

Of course, there may be another reason you aren't happy with your new job—it isn't your job that's making you unhappy. You may recall I warned you in the beginning about being sure you were ready to pursue this process. Sure, reducing stress at work can ease other tensions at home, and earning more money may do the same, but no matter how fabulous your ideal job is, it can't solve deeper issues in your personal life. If your perfect job isn't bringing you the level of joy you expected, then please take a long hard look at the underlying reasons. Address those problems, and I think you'll find your work becomes joyful again.

What really helps me, is to check in with myself at regular intervals to make sure I'm making progress toward my interim goals and my larger dream. What about you?

Are you doing everything possible to create and live the life of your dreams?

I can't overstate the value of keeping your dream always in view. If you let it slip from sight for a few days, then days turn into weeks and weeks turn into months. Before you know it, you've lost all the fire in your soul that first sparked when you thought about going after your ideal job. This is why I urge you to put a sign like this where you'll see it often:

> **Am I moving forward with my dream as anticipated?**
> **What am I doing right?**
> **What do I need to do more of to realize my dream?**
> **By what date will I take those steps?**

> "Nobody really cares if you're miserable, so you might as well be happy."
> ~ Cynthia Nelms

I learned a long time ago that **a dream without a plan is still just a dream**. The most contented people on earth understand that **happiness is a strategy**. They are much more fulfilled than people who just let life happen to them. They accomplish their goals, they get things done, they realize one dream and move on to the next. This book is overflowing with planning tools to help you manifest your perfect job—but guess what? They're worthless if they remain pages in this book. Unless you've already completed this process, I suggest you shut this book right now and do at least one action item toward your goal. (Then come back and finish the book—I've saved some of my best ideas for last.)

Write on . . . and on . . . and on

Throughout the book I've encouraged you to journal your thoughts as a tool for self-exploration. Now I'd like to suggest that you get yourself a nice blank book and continue the habit. If you're visually inclined, don't miss the books in the resource section on creating artistic journals. I believe journaling is one of the most essential tools for nurturing your spirit. In a journal you can record your actions and reactions to life, your ideas, your challenges and solutions, as well as your triumphs. I keep notebooks all over my house and sometimes a digital recorder in the car to record my thoughts. **It's a great way to discover the wisdom you already possess.** Journaling can be a safe place to express your fears and a wonderful way to play with and develop new ideas.

There are endless ways to use a journal, and there is no wrong way. Try writing at different times. Some women like to get up early and devote a few quiet moments to their own thoughts before the day overtakes them. Others prefer to write just before going to bed. I like to journal in the evening. After finishing my entry for the day, I often reread the entry, then write a summary for that day, pulling out important points or discovering the real message in key events of my day. For me, recording my thoughts helps me focus and clarify what's important. It can also reduce stress, as you wrestle with problems on paper before you have to deal with them for real. Best of all, you're creating a treasured keepsake, something you can use to document your journey through life.

Get away from it all

"Only I can change my life. No one can do it for me."
~ Carol Burnett

The best thing I do to nurture myself is go on a solo retreat. It doesn't need to be expensive, though I do love to go the Oregon coast and stay at a very nice place—my favorite hotel, the Stephanie Inn. The morning I leave home, I'm fully energized for this three-day experience. I leave my watch and even my cell phone behind. I especially enjoy going in late December, when I can look back over the year just ending and ahead to the new one.

These are the kinds of questions I ask myself on my retreat:

get out of town

> · How did my life work out this past year?
> · Who are the people I met?
> · What great books did I read?
> · What places did I explore?
> · What did I not do enough of?
> · What did I do too much of?
> · How is my spiritual life?
> · Am I taking care of my health?
> · With business goals, did I always think progress not perfection?
> · What do I want to have happen, and what am I willing to do about it next year?

give yourself the gift of time and space

I love to pursue this process at the Oregon coast, because even in stormy weather, being at the beach with its wide expanses drains my stress away and frees me to see the bigger picture of my life. Over the three days, I take long walks, I nap, I eat my favorite foods, and I write in my journal in front of a roaring fire. I plan my coming year, whether it's working on becoming a better employer or manifesting personal dreams. I write out my specific visions and the goals I believe I can realistically attain. At night, I leave the windows open enough so I can hear the ocean as it soothes me into deeply restful sleep. It's bliss.

On my last morning, as I take my walk on the beach, I look forward to the next twelve months of my life. My dreams include more interaction with my friends and relatives, more fun, but also a deeper commitment to my career. I absolutely love my life on such days. I drive home without a care in the world, knowing I've mapped out a marvelous year for myself, certain that many of my dreams are going to come true.

A retreat is really a state if mind, a gift of time and space you give yourself to be alone with your thoughts without any distractions. It's pure rejuvenation. Even if you just go stay at a friend's house while she's out of town, a change of scene can work wonders. However you can manage it, you deserve some quality time alone.

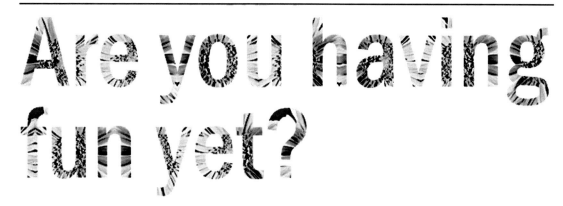

Are you having fun yet?

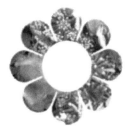

"The supreme
accomplishment
is to blur the line
between work
and play."
~Arnold Toynbee

I sure hope so! Does your work day include healthy doses of fun, or are you stuck in a mindset that believes *work is work and fun happens after work*? You've probably heard stories about what it's like to work at big, famous companies with deep pockets like Southwest Airlines, Google and Nike. Their employees are treated to all kinds of perks to keep them happy and loyal—everything from gyms to food service, from ping pong tables to having their cars washed in the parking lot. Well those grand gestures are usually beyond the means of most firms, but I contend there are endless things you can do on your own to make your workplace a much happier place to be. Then there are larger ideas that require management cooperation, which is why I suggest you discuss this with your team and present a mini-proposal as a group, citing the facts below as reason enough to mandate fun.

For a company with working moms, providing a **quiet place to power nap** during lunch breaks could be an easily instituted boon. Reorganize a storeroom, tuck a couch or single bed against one wall, add a soft lamp and a digital timer, and *voilà*! Imagine how refreshing it would be to lie down and close your eyes for 30 minutes in the middle of a hectic day. Maybe you'd rather have an exercise bike or treadmill in the back room. **Helping to keep employees fit is always a good investment.**

How about a **cheery employee lounge** with comfy furniture, a refrigerator, microwave and so on? Maybe you want a quiet spot to proofread a report, so you take it in there, kick your shoes off, put your feet up and savor a cup of tea while you work. Just sitting on

different furniture for a short time can relieve back and shoulder pain. Mini-basketball hoops can be fun for letting off steam, or try lawn darts or Pin the Tail on the Boss.

You could suggest that staff meetings during warm months be held outside on the grass and serve some lemonade, or bring sack lunches and meet in a nearby park. Perhaps the boss would reward teams at the end of big projects with a visit from a massage therapist, who could bring her portable chair and offer everyone back and shoulder massages. During the summer, maybe you have **Hyper Fridays**—you come in an hour early and work twice as hard so you can all leave at noon. You might challenge your supervisor to some kind of contest. If she loses, she has to do something silly and highly entertaining to the rest of you. Perhaps speak in French all day using an English to French dictionary, or wear a purple wig? Dress as an aardvark? (I'm not sure how an aardvark dresses, but I bet it's funny.) You get the comical drift.

> ## Some advantages of having fun at work include:
> - Reduced stress
> - Improved morale
> - Enhanced motivation
> - Increased focus and productivity
> - Improved health and fewer sick days
> - Stronger teams
> - Better employee retention

adopt some sort of Fun Policy

Being by nature a fun-loving guy myself, I'm practically rabid about this concept. Imagine spending half your waking hours working and NOT having some fun doing it! That's unacceptable. Life's way too short and precious to live in such drudgery. The coolest part about this attitude, is it absolutely pays off in so many ways, that any business owner would be nuts not to adopt some sort of Fun Policy. Whole books have been written on this topic (see the resource section) so I'll just list some of my favorites here, but I know they'll jazz you into thinking of dozens more ideas for your own situation.

As an overall concept, imagine if each person on your team or in your department rotated turns as the

POM-POM Person of the Week: the President Of Morale and Purveyor Of Merriment.

When it's your turn, for that week you're the cheerleader charged with boosting spirits, inciting laughter and instigating smiles. If someone in your work group is having a bad day, see what you can do to improve it. Could you send her home half an hour early and volunteer to finish up her task? Could you pick a deserving colleague to honor in a special way that week? As the POM-POM person, you could hand out your own awards in whatever categories you like. The whole point is, you get to decide. You have the pom-poms. You are entirely in control of what happens that week, and you get to unleash your creativity on your colleagues. Perhaps the boss donates $20 or so to each week's activities.

Maybe you'd only get a turn several times a year, but you could always be on the lookout for fun ideas and interesting things to collect and save up for your weeks as cheerleader. You might bring back treasures from your vacation and create a mini-beach on everyone's desk (a cigar box of sand, shells, stones and bits of driftwood). Maybe one of them has buried treasure in it…a fun prize of some sort. Just imagine how it would improve your mood to know that **every day there is someone assigned to boost the joy level at your office**… how much fun would that be? It makes me want to come and visit and see what great ideas you conjure.

That said, all of this needs to take into account the kind of work environment you have. Surprising the receptionist at the front desk of a staid law firm with Silly String would not be cool; having your 10-year-old daughter drop by after school in her fairy costume and grant wishes with her magic wand to people in back offices could be delightful. Before you do anything, be sure it won't inadvertently insult or offend someone. One woman's hilarity might be another's embarrassment. If in doubt, don't do it, or discuss it with your boss first. You also need to consider how disruptive your plans are and how much time they'll involve. A reasonable rule of thumb is to think of ideas that could take place during a 15-minute break or less. Just use common sense, and if you're a quart low in that department, then run your ideas by someone who isn't.

Okay, try on these fun ideas:

· Afternoon energy breaks to combat post-lunch dip: put on an up-tempo Motown tune and everybody **dance** now.

· Got Spring fever? Lead folks on a quick **jaunt** around the block or the complex and soak up some fresh air.

· Summer in the city? **Popsicles** or frozen yogurt for all.

· Is your son raising money for band uniforms? Get him and a few pals to stop by with a tuba, a trombone and a **glockenspiel** for a few minutes of marching music and then pass the hat with the fuzzy thing on top. (I told you there'd be a marching band!)

· Make a habit of **thanking** people with a pretty note and a chocolate kiss.

· Initiate a **Bring Your Dog To Work Day** (one dog per day!). Furry hugs are terrific stress relievers.

· Do you have a bumper crop of **tomatoes**, apples or lilacs? Bring enough for everybody.

· Get some gold **stars** and stick them on deserving memos or foreheads.

· Compose a team **song** or poem and perform it.

· Adopt a team **mascot** and bring in a *representation* of it—please, no live wolverines!

· Spoof a popular TV show—when you have a marathon project to finish, serve gummy worms and chocolate **turtles** and pretend you're on *Survivor*.

· You can't go wrong with **balloons** just because it's Tuesday.

- Bring in a bag of **fortune cookies**—or even better, insert your own company-centric fortunes.
- Promote **Funny Hat Day**, or pass out big nose glasses.
- You can fight over who gets to plan **April Fool's Day**.
- Afternoon microwave **popcorn** breaks
- Ask your boss to **subscribe** to the local newspaper or *O Magazine* to read during lunch.
- Fill everybody's desk drawer with gorgeous fall **leaves**.
- Hide nuts still in their shells, have a nut hunt, then sit around at lunchtime with nutcrackers and tell **squirrel stories**.
- Play musical chairs to win a restaurant **coupon**
- Have weekly drawings for other **prizes.**
- Have an Easter egg **hunt** or carve a jack 'o lantern in the image of your boss. Put green food coloring in the water cooler on March 17. Bring maracas on Cinco de Mayo. Plant a tree on Arbor Day.
- Celebrate lesser holidays too. Every day of the year honors something and someone, just look 'em up online. Did you know February 28 is Inconvenience Yourself Day or that March 1 is **National Pig Day**? I thought not. Celebrate Alexander Graham Bell's birthday with a game of telephone.
- If you're feeling altruistic, how about spending several lunch hours **crafting** valentines for an eldercare center? How about an old-fashioned quilting bee and make baby quilts for a children's hospital? There's no limit to what you, your teammates and some imagination can do.

> "Work is either fun or drudgery. It depends on your attitude. I like fun."
> ~Colleen C. Barrett

There are all kinds of books about team building exercises you could dip into for inspiration. One simple idea is to prepare a colorful piece of stiff tag board about 9"X12" for each person, punch two holes at the top, add enough yarn or ribbon to be able to hang the sign around each person's neck. Write one teammate's name across the top: (Janice is…) Hand out felt tip pens to all and have each person hang their sign down their <u>back</u>. Then go around writing positive statements and adjectives on each person's sign. It's totally anonymous, as you are all writing on each other simultaneously and are unaware of who is writing what on your own back. When each person has written something on every sign, take them off and read them aloud. They can make a nice keepsake to hang in your office.

That ought to be plenty of ideas to get you excited about instituting a **POM-POM** program at your workplace. Even if you can't get that going, there's nothing to keep you from doing some of these ideas on your own.

FUN!

It's an essential part of work. Work equals playing with life.

Journal exercise

Putting more spring in your step

Jot down some ideas for putting some zip and zoom into your days. What could you do personally to make your job more fun? What things could you suggest to management?

_____
_____
_____
_____
_____
_____
_____
_____
_____
_____

How to bring your spirit to work

Talking about religion often makes people uneasy, and I'm not going to do that. Instead, I'm going to talk about *spirituality* and how you might express some of your spiritual values at work. (I'm defining *religion* as an external organized set of doctrines you may adhere to and *spirituality* as your personal, internal beliefs and values about humanity and your place in the Universe.) **Feeling unable to express their spirituality is a common reason employees disconnect from their jobs.** I don't think you need to compartmentalize your life in that way. To be perfectly clear, it is utterly <u>inappropriate</u> to expound on religious beliefs in the workplace. What I am suggesting is that you **find ways to live your spirituality through your job.**

Isabella's journey expresses my point. A successful administrative professional at a large computer parts manufacturer in Portland, Oregon, Isabella earned an excellent living and enjoyed the material rewards of her career. However, on the inside, she was more miserable every year. "It took me a long time to figure it out," she confides. "None of my friends could understand my unhappiness. To them it looked like I had everything, the American dream, but inside I knew differently."

In her 40s Isabella came to realize she had a strong urge to express her spiritual beliefs about helping people in need, but she felt it was too late for her to go back to college to get a degree in social work. "I decided to explore jobs in the public sector and ended up in an administrative job—at quite a pay cut—in the county division dealing with domestic violence. Though I don't have a lot of substantive contact with the clients, I do feel my work contributes in small ways to helping them. After a time, I decided to take some

"I now see my life, not as the slow shaping of achievement to fit my preconceived purpose, but as the gradual discovery of a purpose which I did not know."
~Joanna Field

intensive training and volunteer for the crisis line, a 24-hour hotline for women and girls in need. That changed my life. My volunteer work enhances my job, and now I really feel I make a difference every week of my life. It can be emotionally distressing to handle some of the calls, but that's a really small price to pay for the ultimate fulfillment I feel."

Another way Isabella nourishes her spirit is by keeping a book where she records comments made to her by people she counsels on the crisis line. Since there is no ongoing contact and she rarely gets to know the outcome for a particular caller, writing down a few comments from each shift that have meaning for her, allows Isabella to preserve the experience. "When I have a down day, I take out my little book and remember the women I spoke to. Reading their words lifts me back up and re-energizes my passion for the work."

Journal exercise

What's your higher purpose?

What spiritual values could you share at your job? Integrity? Reverence for nature? Compassion? Caring? Humility? What aspect of your Higher Self can you express? How?

"The highest reward for a person's work is not what they get for it, but what they become by it."
~John Ruskin

_____

_____

_____

_____

_____

_____

_____

_____

_____

_____

_____

_____

_____

_____

Make your life a work of art

No, you don't have to be Picasso to do this one, but you do need to celebrate that you *are* an artist. Every single one of you is a creative person. You may have had much of it squelched by parents and teachers who made you feel inartistic or by a society that doesn't place much value on the artistic life. However, this isn't about drawing or painting. **It's about living your life as a work of art. It's about giving yourself permission to express your authentic self.**

Coming to work in any kind of disguise, whether physical or emotional, isn't good for your mental health. I'm not saying you don't need to dress appropriately for your job, but within those parameters there are always ways of letting the real you shine through. Maybe it's the vintage blouse you wear, the jewelry you designed yourself, your colorful shoes or your exotic nail polish—my point is, it's okay to make a statement about who you are as a person with definite tastes and interests.

How else could you creatively express yourself?

"When I stand before God at the end of my life, I would hope that I would not have a single bit of talent left, and could say, I used everything you gave me."
~Erma Bombeck

I've already shared my ideas about creating a working environment that reflects you (Page 227), but how about applying originality of thought to your actual work? Is there a way to make the intra-office website more dynamic, or your internal memos more scintillating? Can you add an inspirational quote or personal motto to your signature line on internal emails? Do you reveal yourself by trying extra hard to offer fresh ideas at staff meetings? At many companies there's an unspoken sense that conformity is somehow a good thing. Nonsense! Be real. Be the best you. Let your associates know you and be empowered by your authenticity.

"I choose to inhabit my days, to allow my living to open me, to make me less afraid, more accessible, to loosen my heart until it becomes a wing, a torch, a promise. I choose to risk my significance, to live so that which came to me as seed goes to the next as blossom, and that which came to me as blossom, goes on as fruit."
~Dawna Markova

I want to tell you about someone who exemplifies this idea so well, that it has infused her whole life with purpose. Right after finishing a two-year degree at a community college, Cassie took a job at a weekly newspaper in a small town in Montana—a job that few people wanted. Even the owner of the paper thought of it as a dead-end, low-paying job with little future and high turnover. Cassie, however, never saw it that way. Within a year she had turned it into a job that added so much value to the paper and the community that she was becoming a celebrity in town.

And she did it all by herself, applying her own creativity at virtually no cost to her boss.

The job was billed as a clerical position taking orders for classified ads in person and over the phone, then entering them in the computer. Doesn't sound like much, does it? Cassie looked at it as an opportunity to learn the newspaper business and develop some office skills. Right away, her outgoing personality charmed everyone who came in contact with her. Intuitively, she offered to help folks compose their ads. When someone called to place a notice for a found dog, she suggested to her boss that those kinds of ads ought to be a free community service and would earn them goodwill. Then she volunteered to take a photo of the found dog to run with the notice.

Week after week, as she saw the kinds of things people used the classified ads for, Cassie got more ideas for improvements. "Maybe it was because this was my first job, but I loved working at the paper from day one," she explains. "I just saw so many more ways we could be helping people in our town, and I kept asking my boss if I could do them. Since none of them really cost him anything, he was pretty willing. I think he was just shocked that anyone cared about that part of the paper."

Here's a partial list of improvements Cassie made:

· She created a buzz in town by using the filler space in a fun, new way. Instead of just filling the extra space in the classified columns with the paper's phone number, she found humorous quotes, funny sayings and even wished people happy birthday or happy anniversary. She asked the local librarian for old issues of *Reader's Digest, Farmers' Almanac,* etc., and culled fun snippets to use.

**"Your real boss is the one who walks around under your hat."
~Napoleon Hill**

- They were so popular that the publisher gave her more space.
- She recorded a new batch of snippets every week for her voicemail message and for the message people hear when they're put on hold.
- She redid the plain vanilla receipts by adding humorous quotes and a cute cartoon about newspapers.
- She started a policy that if you have something to give away, then the ad is free, which saved truckloads of stuff from going to the landfill.
- She also instituted free personal ads and got the paper to host mixers at a local restaurant. Many of the ads she wrote herself, and then each week she picked one to feature with special graphics.
- Whenever she saw a lost pet sign around town, she took down the number and called the person to let them know about the free notice she could place for them. Then she followed up and ran a short story about the reunion of pet and owner, along with a photo.
- She called every non-profit organization in the area and offered them free ads for volunteer positions. Then she highlighted one of those each week and ran a photo of a Volunteer of the Week.
- She featured help wanted ads, and contacted the state employment office to solicit ads from them.
- She arranged for seniors to get free ads and ran profiles honoring town elders.
- Cassie redesigned the classification titles to be more entertaining, and before long, ad sales were way up. Her boss took note and moved the ads to their own separate section, which Cassie renamed The Connection Section, since by then **she understood that she wasn't typing up ads—she was connecting everyone in her community to one another.**
- The new section showcased ever-changing photos of Cassie with a short weekly column, which eventually grew into a prominent feature of the paper. Soon she was recognized wherever she went.
- In time she was able to feature stories about couples who met via her personal ads.
- She taught herself to make a simple website and put the ads online so people could see them faster.

> **"Do not follow where the path may lead. Go instead where there is no path and leave a trail."**
> **~Muriel Strode**

After a few years, The Connection Section was honored with awards for community service and was voted the best classified section in the state by the newspaper publishers association. That in turn led to Cassie being named editor of her section with full leeway to improve it however she saw fit. She also received offers to work for a lot more money at bigger newspapers. "I turned them all down," she says happily. "I absolutely love my job, and I would never want to leave it. Not a day goes by without somebody thanking me for helping them find their dog or meet a new friend. It's very rewarding, and I never run out of ideas to make my section more exciting. Everywhere I go in town, I see ways to help people with the paper. I think I have the greatest job ever."

(A low-end job that no one else wanted.)

What can you do with your job?

Journal exercise

Will the real you please stand up?

List some ways you could be more expressive at work, both personally and professionally.

_____

_____

_____

_____

_____

_____

_____

_____

_____

_____

_____

I have one last secret for you: **Doing your job well isn't the point of going to work.** Learning new things, meeting new people, hearing new ideas, **evolving as a person through the process of your job is the real value of work**. Your job is an arena for your personal growth.

Lend a helping hand and heart

Few things in your professional life will be as gratifying as becoming a mentor. If you benefited from the wise counsel of a more seasoned individual in your own life, then you know first hand how valuable unbiased, neutral advice can be. Often, when we ask friends and family for advice at junctures in our working lives, the feedback we get is tinged by their limiting beliefs about our potential. Parents are full of ideas about what we *should* be doing. Even your spouse can't be neutral. A mentor can look at your life objectively and offer insight into your field of endeavor as well as other challenges, such as the classic conundrum of work/life balance.

You may be enjoying the input of your own mentor right now, and that's great, You may not feel ready to help out someone else, and that's fine, too. Yet at some point in your career, I do hope you'll volunteer your services if asked, or even seek out opportunities to mentor someone through business organizations. Men have been doing this for generations (often referred to as the old boys' club) so I encourage you to do your part on behalf of women.

I don't have space in this book to go into much depth about mentoring, but there are some wonderful books on the subject in the resource section. In addition, many women are now finding—and volunteering as—mentors online, with specific sites dedicated to some of the fields most resistant to women, such as science and technology. Another trend is peer mentoring, where women in similar jobs at other companies gather to share solutions to common problems. Local business organizations are good places to look for that kind of program.

As anyone who has ever volunteered her time knows,

what you receive in nourishment of your soul from the act of giving, far exceeds the price of what you gave.

"The fragrance always stays in the hand that gives the rose."
~ Hada Bejar

"To get more out of life, give more of yourself."
~Amy Liao

Sharing closer to home

In a similar vein, also consider sharing what you've learned through this process with teens and young adults in your life. People just starting their working lives can really benefit from getting off to a great start by choosing jobs that satisfy them. Imagine sparing someone from ever having a job they hate or a job that doesn't suit them. Imagine helping your daughter figure out ahead of time what her real gifts are and how best to express them. Imagine showing your son how to avoid some of the most debilitating forms of job stress. **Then after you imagine it, do it!**

Look what you just learned!

I really hope you'll hang onto this book and refer to it often as you progress through your working life. The techniques you've learned for evaluating yourself and your job situations will be useful to you over and over as you grow and modify your dreams. Guess what else? **You can apply most of this process to other areas of your life as well.** Use the **G.R.O.W. Chart** to measure your happiness level with your personal relationships or your satisfaction with how well your daughter takes care of Lucky the Labrador. Construct AWEsome Charts with your teens to help them get in touch with their strengths, or show them how to use the **APTitude Checklist** to evaluate the subjects they're studying in school. Most of all, teach your friends and family the power of dreaming and consciously mapping out plans to achieve their dreams.

"If you have knowledge, let others light their candles in it."
~Margaret Fuller

One of the joys of living a successful life is sharing yourself with others, both professionally and personally. Successful people share themselves without effort, through quiet confidence.

What's your purpose? Pass it on.

You didn't think I'd end without one last bouquet, did you? Not me! Since I made you work for your last several rewards, I have something much simpler in mind to celebrate your settling into your dream job. When people receive a promotion or a new job, they often receive business cards. You may even be the one who orders them. How would you like your own cards (at almost no cost) that say something about you as a person and your purpose, your values and interests? Would it be fun to have colorful cards to hand out to people you meet? Something that might make them think about the interaction you just had? You could reference your actual job or not, include your MySpace address, your email address, whatever you like. **The idea is to celebrate you.** Here are some examples.

Remember Anna, the florist in Chapter One? Here's her card:

> **Anna Rennick**
> floral designer
> What milestone can I help you mark?

Here's what I might do, if I wanted to focus on this book.

> Pat Healey
> Ask me how I can help you find more joy in your job.
> www.findingjoybook.com

Here's one for a dental assistant.

> **Tara Shaw**
> Let me give you something to smile about.
> Tompkins & Tompkins, DDS

Molly the poodle person has this one.

"Life is no brief candle for me. It's a sort of splendid torch which I've got to hold up for the moment and I want to make it burn as brightly as possible before handing on to future generations."
~George Bernard Shaw

> **Molly McMahon**, (Smidgen's Mom)
> Show me your dog photo and I'll show you mine.
> www.myspace.com/perfectpoodle

Doesn't that sound like fun? Let your creativity go wild. After all, you're the President of You! I know an online company that will print you 250 full-color cards *free* for the low cost of shipping. There are lots of designs to choose from, or you can pay extra and upload your own design. You'll find a link to it on my website, at: **www.findingjoybook.com/cards**

your job
should
not be the
sum of
your life

If your job is what you do for a living, what do you do for your life?

You are not your job. Your job should not be the sum of your life. For single women this is sometimes an issue. It can be easy to immerse yourself in an exciting position and use working long hours as a handy excuse for not having a personal life. No matter how rewarding your work is, you need a larger life as well.

I learned that the hard way back in 1992 when we became the number two (CAC Points) producer in the country out of 17,000 State Farm Insurance agencies—but there was precious little joy in it for me or my hard-working team. By the following year, when our ranking dropped to 39 out of 17,000 (still great by almost anyone's standards) colleagues kept asking me "What happened? What went wrong?"

What happened was I was absolutely burned out in my quest to reach the top rung. Shortly after my success experience, my best friend died of cancer within six months of being diagnosed. It wasn't long after his death that I heard my long-time office manager tell her sister she enjoyed working for me but felt we had a love-hate relationship. Love-hate relationship? In my quest to be the best—as measured by others' standards—I had become the archetypal alpha boss. Linda, my office manager, reminded me of the number of team members who had left over the previous three years. It was staggering and had made her life miserable.

Talk about the perfect storm. It was these three experiences that ignited my quest to create a more balanced and fulfilling life.

My personal goal is to think progress not perfection in all things I do.

Today, I'm still a top agent in my region, for the largest casualty company in the country. I'm certainly not saying you can't reach the top of the corporate mountain and still lead a balanced life. Some of my best friends have been top producers for years, enjoying balance between their careers, family and hobbies. As you've seen from the many stories in this book, there are as many ways to create fulfillment in life as there are people in the world.

We all bring to the table of life our own set of aspirations and dreams. My personal goal is to think *progress not perfection* in all things I do. I want to continue creating the life of my dreams, sharing it with my loving family and cherished friends. I'd also like to be an inspiration to those who meet and work with me, as well as show appreciation for the hard work and dedication of my business team members. My ideal life also includes never forgetting to enjoy my own luscious garden on the banks of the Willamette river. **I want to embrace *all* the things that matter to me in life—and my work is just one of them.**

What about you? Are you singing your song? Are you creating and enjoying the best life you can for yourself? Are you an inspiration to those you love? Does everyone who meets you feel better for it? This is the magic of the process in this book—it sets you free to create any kind of life you want. Although he certainly doesn't need to work, at 65, Paul McCartney is still touring and giving his all in three-hour concerts. When asked by Larry King what he plans to do with the rest of his life, Sir Paul replied: "Well Larry, I'm going to enjoy it!"

Joy is an infinitely abundant resource.

How are you going to enjoy the rest of your one precious life?

"I haven't a clue as to how my story will end. But that's all right. When you set out on a journey and night covers the road, that's when you discover the stars."
~Nancy Willard

Let's stay in touch

I'd love to hear from you about your reaction to this process, about the fun you're having on the job, about the creative ways you've reinvented your work life. Please zip me an email at:

Pat@findingjoybook.com

For downloadable versions of many of the forms in this book, please visit **www.findingjoybook.com**

For more information about me or my workshops, please check out Page 296 or stop by **wowteams.com**

Dream big, start small, but start today

Thanks so much for doing all this gardening with me. I hope you harvested fun and inspiration, but most of all I hope you take action. It's a big accomplishment to work through all these exercises. (If you didn't, then what are you waiting for?) Still, it's just a book of ideas until you put them in motion.

I know we haven't met, but I do feel like I know you—after all, I wrote this book for you! I know you may not think you have enough extra time to implement all these ideas, but you found time to read the book, didn't you? Life intervenes in the best of plans, and you may need to revise your vision more than once. There's nothing wrong with that. Don't get overwhelmed by the process—we all learn to walk by taking baby steps. Just work through the process step by step, and you'll be able to create your perfect job where you already work.

That's what I want for you— that ideal job that relieves your stress, brings you joy and fills you with deep satisfaction. A job that adds to your life, rather than subtracts from it. I believe all the way down to the tips of my toes, that it's possible for you to flourish doing work you love.

Go plant a
bountiful garden!

QUICK GUIDE TO
PAGES OF SPECIAL INTEREST

RESOURCES

BOOKS

The Science of Happiness
Stefan Klein, Ph. D.

The 100 Simple Secrets of Happy People
David Niven, Ph.D.

Toxic Emotions at Work
Peter J. Frost

Coaching and Mentoring for Dummies
Marty Brounstein

Creating A Mentoring Culture
Lois J. Zachary

Wake Up and Live The Life You Love
Steven and Lee Beard

Making Your Dreams Come True
Marcia Wieder

Beyond Boredom and Anxiety
Mihaly Csikszentmihalyi

Younger Next Year For Women
Chris Crowley and Henry S. Lodge, M. D.

Walking, Weight and Wellness
Dr. Martin Collis

WEBSITE
I highly recommend that you take the Kolbe
index at www.kolbe.com .

ACKNOWLEDGMENTS

First and foremost I'd like to thank my parents, whose life lessons taught me independence, perseverance, compassion and most importantly acceptance of differences.

To the many gifted, talented and caring employees who I've had the privilege to work with and learn from, over the years. Their lives have provided me volumes of life lessons I shall carry with me forever. A special note of thanks and appreciation to my trusted Office Manager par excellence, Linda Nelson. Her kind and gentle spirit has helped to make me a better boss. I'm deeply grateful.

I also wish to express my deep appreciation to my biggest fan, confidante and life partner Debbie Davis. Her love of life, cheerful disposition and never ending support of my next "special" project always inspires and moves me beyond my wildest dreams.

An extra special note of thanks and appreciation to Oriana Green, the "Book Goddess," who through many late nights and early mornings, patiently and skillfully transformed my manuscript and life experiences into a magnificent work of art. We laughed hard, worked harder and in the process became great friends. Oriana has my deepest respect and admiration.

Thank you to the many mentors and coaches I've had in my life, especially Ann McIndoo, who first convinced me I could write a book. Her Boot Camp for Writers helped me create a dynamic manuscript that will make a difference in people's lives. The following mentors and coaches have helped me take on this project as well: Glenn Plaskin, editor and author, who inspired me to make this business book fun; Dan Sullivan, founder of The Strategic Coach Program, who taught me about the importance of creating unique talent teams and instilled in me the concept that enjoying your life shouldn't be a "top of the mountain" experience; Kathy Kolbe, founder of Kolbe Corp., changed my life, my children's lives and my team members' lives, by helping all of us understand the importance of being who we already are and following our instincts;

Tim O'Brien, CEO of the Personal Branding Group, who was instrumental in helping me define myself professionally; Marsha Wieder, America's Dream Coach, who taught me that no dream is too big as long as it aligns with my purpose; Barbara Stanny, for helping me define my market and sharing her inside secrets to becoming a successful author; and Judson Vaughn who expanded my world by helping me discover the magic in the everyday lives of extraordinary people.

A special debt of gratitude to my friends and colleagues in the Hunt'n Club Study Group. The "best of the best" celebrating differences, knowledge and life lessons annually for the betterment of all: Scott Foster, Dan Combs, Joe Dorris, Terry Cropp, Gerry Moody, E.G. Warren, Garnett West Jr., Ray Poole, Ricky Price, Dave Andes, Harold Dishner, Brad Campbell, Warren Hodges and Chris Dorris.

Last, but certainly not least, thank you to my many friends who have helped with the editing process of my book. These include: my Oregon City connection, Dale and Donna Davis; Cindy Olsen, who shed the first tear for the book; and Brent Ward, a friend for 30 years, whose wisdom and gracious manner have been a constant inspiration to me.

PAT HEALEY

Pat Healey is a native of the Pacific Northwest where he continues to enjoy living and writing in his country cottage on the meandering banks of the Willamette River.

As one of five children, Pat worked his way through college at Western Washington University. He is the proud father of three adult children, has one grandchild and twin grandbabies on the way. Thirty years ago, he started his own business, owning and operating a State Farm Insurance and Financial Services agency. Pat continues to love his business and in particular the great people who make up his business team. Since 2001, Pat has also been conducting Team

Dreamers Workshops™ around the country, helping business teams find more joy in their work.

Pat enjoys many outdoor activities, including skiing, biking, gardening, hiking, scuba diving, rowing, golf and sipping Oregon pinot noir on his deck overlooking the river.

TESTIMONIALS

"I know it was written primarily for women, but much of it applies to both genders. When can you write one for the executive/business owner that needs to find his/her work more enjoyable and fun?" **~John Gregory, CEO ProTech**

"This is an incredible book that clearly demonstrates the value of implementing fun and joy in the workplace and its resulting success. Pat Healey has identified the steps and actions necessary to provide a lifetime of personal and professional fulfillment." **~Brian Schmidt, General Manager, Olsen Homes, Inc.**

"When I first received the book I didn't read it but gave it to my office manager. After she was done she MADE me read it. I've read the entire book two times this week…this book will change lives." **~Joe Dorris, State Farm Insurance and Financial Services**

"I am the Executive Director of a nonprofit organization that provides cancer patients with experiences of the creative arts that inspire hope and joy. I continually seek out resources that will help me do a better job in supporting the families the foundation serves. In this sometimes awkward role of "joyologist" I find myself all over the spectrum of joy - life, relationships, parenting, careers, religion, etc. I seek out others who are helping people bring joy into their lives. Having worked in career services, I understand how work can be a wonderful life affirming and joyous experience, or completely joyless and draining day-to-day burden. So, I'm a HUGE advocate of helping people create occupational joy. As you can imagine, most people who survive cancer expect more from their life once it's flashed before them—no more putting up with cruddy jobs! We would love to purchase a number of your books to help not only the survivors of cancer but their families too! Your message is so perfect for them."
~Kathryn Feldt, The Joy Foundation

TESTIMONIALS

"As a human resource manager, I heartily recommend Pat Healey's book, *Finding Joy in Your Job*. It addresses many of the problems we face today in retaining good employees--becoming bored or burned out, ending up in the wrong job, struggles with teammates and management--and much more. Besides, it's fun to read and full of great tips for supervisors, too." ~**Mary Ellen O'Brien, National VP Human Resources, Lucent Technologies**

During my 30 year career in the grocery industry, I have been an employer to thousands of hard working people. I only wish that I would have had access to Pat's book along the way. This is the best resource that I have come across that helps its readers better understand ways to improve their attitude about their choice of employment and to focus more on the present than the future. While this book is written with women in mind, I believe that its insights have value for anyone wishing to improve their life." ~**Ron Brake, Chairman, Associated Grocers, Inc., Seattle, WA & Owner, Food 4 Less stores, Portland, OR**

"Pat, I want to compliment you on your new book. Based on what I have read, it will be a great success. As an employer I am delighted that someone out there is helping people understand that it is a career opportunity and not just a job. I intend to have my entire team read your book when it is available."
~**Terry Cropp, State Farm Insurance and Financial Services**

"As a woman who owns her own company, I rather arrogantly thought I knew how to take good care of my staff. Reading this book showed me I still had lots to learn about creating an employee-centric workplace, one where my people can blossom to their highest potential. My team and I especially appreciated the section on infusing meaning and a higher purpose to our work."
~ **Winette Jacobs, Heron House**

Printed in the United States
119384LV00004B/99-998/P